A True and Historical

NARRA...

OF THE

Colony of GEORGIA

IN

AMERICA,

From the First SETTLEMENT thereof, until this present PERIOD;

CONTAINING,

The most authentick FACTS, MATTERS, and TRANSACTIONS therein.

TOGETHER WITH

His MAJESTY's CHARTER, REPRESENTATIONS of the PEOPLE, LETTERS, &c. and a DEDICATION to his Excellency General OGLETHORPE.

By PAT. TAILFER, *M. D.* HUGH ANDERSON, *M. A.* DA. DOUGLAS, and others, Landholders in *Georgia*, at present at *Charles-Town* in *South-Carolina.*

—— *Qui Deorum*
Muneribus sapienter uti,
Duramque callet Pauperiem pati,
Pejusque Letho Flagitium timet,
Non ille pro caris Amicis
Aut Patria timidus perire. HOR. 4. O.

Printed for P. TIMOTHY, in *Charles-Town, South-Carolina;* and sold by J. CROKATT, in *Fleet-street, London.*

A True and Historical Narrative
of the Colony of Georgia

With Comments by
THE EARL OF EGMONT

THE EARL OF EGMONT

A

True and Historical Narrative
of the Colony of Georgia

By PAT. TAILFER and Others

With Comments by
THE EARL OF EGMONT

Edited with an Introduction by

CLARENCE L. VER STEEG

WORMSLOE FOUNDATION PUBLICATIONS
NUMBER FOUR

UNIVERSITY OF GEORGIA PRESS

ATHENS

Contents

 *Foreword*

THE Wormsloe Foundation is a non-profit organization chartered on December 18, 1951 by the Superior Court of Chatham County, Georgia. In the words of its charter, "The objects and purposes of this Foundation are the promotion of historical research and the publication of the results thereof; the restoration, preservation and maintenance of historical sites and documents and the conduct of an educational program in the study of history of the State of Georgia, and in states adjacent thereto."

As the first important activity of the Foundation, it has begun the publication of a series of historical works under the title of "Wormsloe Foundation Publications." They will consist of important manuscripts, reprints of rare publications, and historical narratives relating to Georgia and the South. The first volume appeared in 1955, written by E. Merton Coulter and entitled *Wormsloe: Two Centuries of a Georgia Family*. This volume gave the historical background of the Wormsloe estate and a history of the family which has owned it for more than two hundred years.

The second publication of the Foundation was *The Journal of William Stephens, 1741–1743*. The third volume in the series was *The Journal of William Stephens, 1743–1745*, which is a continuation of the journal so far as any known copy of it is still extant. The present volume is a republication of the unique copy of Pat. Tailfer et al., *A True and Historical Narrative of the Colony of Georgia in America, . . .* with comments by the First Earl of Egmont, in the John Carter Brown Library at Brown University and published by its permission.

E. Merton Coulter
General Editor

Introduction

THE founding of Georgia is a complex story, representative in many ways of the tug of opposing forces in the English world of the eighteenth century. In one capacity, Georgia served as a battleground for imperial rivalries, an English spear poised to prick the lordly domain of the Spanish sovereign and to warn the Bourbon monarchy of France that the English penetration into the Mississippi Valley, long a matter of dispute between the Carolina traders and French outposts, was but a premonition of what was to come. As a result, interested observers were entertained with the rare spectacle of a restricted settlement in Georgia challenging the skill of some of Europe's most accomplished diplomatists.

Like a jewel, however, the story of early Georgia can only be appreciated when turned and examined, to be illuminated from a variety of vantage points rather than one. From a slightly different perspective, for example, its story can be described as a link in the American frontier; but even in this capacity, as well as in many others, Georgia's experience was distinctive. First of all, the colony acted as a dual frontier, for Europe and England on the one hand, and for the established colonies, especially Carolina, on the other. Even more important in setting Georgia apart, however, was one of the creative impulses that had produced the settlement —philanthropic enterprise. The colony was not only to act as a haven for debtors, an emphasis commonly accepted, but it was also to serve as a model community, a more sweeping objective that has not always commanded the attention it merits.[1]

Indeed, it cannot be stated too strongly that the widely separated aims and purposes that Georgia was to serve were, in most instances, at the root of the disputes that characterize its early history—an observation, so far as it can be determined, nowhere

1. Verner W. Crane, *The Southern Frontier, 1670–1732* (Durham, North Carolina, 1928), 303–25. Also Crane, "The Philanthropists and The Genesis of Georgia" in *American Historical Review*, XXVII (October, 1921), 63–69. In addition to the work of Professor Crane, John Tate Lanning has emphasized the international theme in *The Diplomatic History of Georgia: A Study of the Epoch of Jenkins' Ear* (Chapel Hill, North Carolina, 1936).

made in the historical literature of the colony. Within this framework of divided aims, the episodes, the personal differences, the issues that disturbed the settlers, and the successes and failures of the colony readily fall into place.

To be more specific, if the single objective had been to found a flourishing colony, the question of policy would be simplified by an obvious test: what measures would contribute to the prosperity of the settlement? With a divided purpose and sometimes contradictory objectives, however, profound problems inevitably manifested themselves. A policy fashioned in Britain with an eye to fulfilling Georgia's role as a military outpost was not necessarily congenial to the aim of making Georgia into a model community. Or again, those who wished to establish a model community, often by selective migration, were actually working at cross-purposes with those who envisioned Georgia as a frontier outpost of the settled colonies where men of every station and background, each with his own aim and purpose, could migrate. With such fundamental differences as to what Georgia should be and should become, it is scarcely surprising that the early history of the colony is such a fascinating study, not merely because it is another English settlement in the New World but because it comprises in miniature so much that is important for the eighteenth century Atlantic community.

Although much has been accomplished to delineate and interpret these eventful proceedings—the founding of Georgia has a secure place in our texts—careful students of colonial history agree that the full story has yet to be told. New materials are now becoming available—the significant collection of Egmont papers at the University of Georgia, for example—which greatly enrich our understanding of early Georgia and, as a result, illuminate many phases of the eighteenth century history on both sides of the Atlantic. The time is rapidly approaching when a more definitive study of the first decades of settlement can be attempted.[2]

To contribute to this understanding is the aim of making available the Earl of Egmont's copy of *A True and Historical Narrative*,

2. A relatively complete modern bibliography of secondary works is available in Milton S. Heath, *The Role of the State in Economic Development in Georgia to 1860* (Cambridge, Massachusetts, 1954), 400–11. A new study on early Georgia, not yet available to scholars, has been undertaken by Professor Paul S. Taylor, the first documentary material of which appears in "Johann Martin Bolzius Answers a Questionnaire on Carolina and Georgia" translated and edited by Klaus G. Leowald, Beverly Starika, and Paul S. Taylor in *The William and Mary Quarterly*, XIV (April, 1957), 218–61.

written by Patrick Tailfer, Hugh Anderson, and David Douglas, a booklet more generally known as the "Tailfer Book." The Tailfer book by itself holds a distinctive place in the literature of early Georgia; but published with a running commentary by the Earl of Egmont, the articulate member of the Trustees, it is a unique document, for it contains the essentials of the Georgia story from both points of view, those who saw the struggling settlement for its virtues and its successes, as represented by Egmont, and those who saw its weaknesses and failures, as represented by Tailfer and his associates. Even if all the other pertinent material on early Georgia should somehow be destroyed, this document, by giving sides, would provide enough information to allow an historian to come to a reasonable evaluation of the earliest history of Georgia.[3]

Consideration as an historical document is reason enough for the publication of Egmont's copy of the Tailfer book, but what gives the document added significance is its literary quality. It is interesting to notice that two leading historians of early American culture and thought, although widely separated in time, pay their respects to the literary excellence of the Tailfer book. Writing in the 1870's, Moses Coit Tyler, whose splendid work is greatly respected but too seldom read, summarizes and appraises the Tailfer book in his *History of American Literature, 1677–1765* by concluding: "Whatever may be the truth or the justice of this book, it is abundantly interesting. . . . Certainly, as a polemic it is one of the most expert pieces of writing to be met with in our early literature." Louis B. Wright, writing for the *Literary History of the United States*, describes the book as a "brilliant satire." His evaluation goes on to say that "Jonathan Swift himself need not have been ashamed of the satirical skill demonstrated in the dedication." [4]

Because of new material which has recently become available, we have better information on the authors of this remarkable booklet and the circumstances and background surrounding its publication in 1741. We also have a precise knowledge of Egmont's reaction to the pamphlet and some of the reasons that prompted him to take the trouble to write such an elaborate, page by page, and, at times, phrase by phrase critique.

3. It was first identified as Egmont's copy by Professor Verner Crane. See his "The Promotion Literature of Georgia" in *Bibliographical Essays: A Tribute to Wilberforce Eames* (Cambridge, Massachusetts, 1924), 297n.
4. Robert E. Spiller *et al., Literary History of the United States* (New York, 1948), II. 48. Moses Coit Tyler, *A History of American Literature, 1607–1765* (New York, 1878), II, 293.

First, let us give a succinct sketch of the authors, starting with the leader Dr. Patrick Tailfer. Tailfer arrived in Georgia in August, 1734, with a group of gentlemen from Scotland, or, as the Trustees noted it, from "North Britain." This group financed its own undertaking, paying the cost of transportation and provisions not only for themselves but for their servants. In October, 1733, Tailfer had received a grant of 500 acres of land, the maximum that could be obtained under the regulations established by the Trustees. When he arrived in Georgia the following year, he discovered that his land was some seventy miles from Savannah, a prospect he found so forbidding he never seriously attempted to cultivate his holdings. Some members of Patrick Tailfer's group planted a settlement in this inhospitable, remote area, building a fort and investing time, funds, and equipment; but it never prospered.

Many reasons can readily be assigned for the failure, but Tailfer and some of his associates complained soon after their arrival that they had not received the help they had expected from the Trustees. They "expected to have the same encouragement as other settlers; such as provisions for our selves and servants for one year, tools for building our houses and for clearing and cultivating the ground, nails and other necessary iron work, arms and ammunition, etc.," wrote Tailfer five months after his arrival. "But when we arrived here," he continued, "contrary to our expectation, we could receive none of them." More than likely, Tailfer and his companions had misunderstood the terms of settlement, for it was not the practice of the Trustees to assist those who financed their own migration. On the other hand, there is no reason to question, at this early date, Tailfer's good faith, for it is apparent that he sincerely believed that the arrangements with the Trustees included initial support and assistance.[5]

Tailfer spoke of other discouragements as well, the loss of servants being the most vital. Shortly before the ship on which the Scottish group was sailing had embarked, a large number of bound servants had apparently run away and another group of servants disappeared when the ship was forced to put into Portsmouth, England, for repairs. Tailfer himself said that he had lost nine servants before embarkation and four at Portsmouth, leaving him

5. Patrick Tailfer to the Trustees, 15 March 1734/35, Savannah, in Egmont Papers, University of Georgia, Vol. 14200. Patrick Tailfer and others to Peter Gordon, 21 January 1734/35, Savannah, *ibid.*

but five servants for his Georgia experiment: three men, a boy, and one woman.

Tailfer's servant problem, his disappointment in not receiving the help he expected from the Trustees, and his distaste for cultivating land so far removed from Savannah prompted him to abandon the idea of becoming a planter. Although there is every reason to believe that he intended his decision to be temporary, it proved to be permanent. Tailfer rented a house in Savannah and began to practice his profession as a physician and surgeon, eighteenth century style. To judge from the contemporary comments, Tailfer hired out his servants to supplement his income; but it is questionable whether he was so dependent on this extra income that he was left unprovided for when their indentures expired, an accusation that his severest and indiscriminate critics voiced rather freely.

Indeed, as a physician, the only one in Savannah for a time, Tailfer prospered. William Stephens, the secretary of the colony, spokesman in a sense for the Trustees and a vigorous opponent of Tailfer, commented in January, 1737/8 that Tailfer "has made money at an easier rate, and few have done it so fast." A year later, Stephens found Tailfer's fortune enhanced, if anything, rather than diminished. His practice and his letting of servants "soon put a pretty deal of money in his pockett; by which means he has lived, and dressed in a superiour manner to any of this place; and has vanity enough to set up for a Dictator among those he converses with who generally give way to his overbearing Discourse." [6]

Tailfer added to his prestige when he married the sister of Robert Williams, a merchant of means and reputation who was respected in Georgia, the West Indies, and England. Of course, some observers who were inclined to regard every action of Tailfer as a reflection of base motives viewed this union as an attempt to cement an alliance whose objective was to obtain a monopoly of the slave trade in Georgia, once the Trustees were persuaded to alter their ban on the use of slaves; but there is no evidence to sustain this observation. To be sure, both Williams and Tailfer strongly advocated the limited introduction of slaves, but it is difficult to see how this objective could have been furthered through a matrimonial tie.

Dr. Tailfer's success and prestige in the midst of so much failure

6. Allen D. Candler, ed., *The Colonial Records of the State of Georgia* (Atlanta, 1911), XXII, 73 (first quote), 369 (second quote).

unquestionably explains why he was acknowledged as a leader among the so-called "malcontents," but it does not really explain why he should be a malcontent at all. After all, was he not doing remarkably well, despite his complaints? What prompted him to take the lead against the representatives of the Trustees, and to confront the Trustees with representations and letters urging modified land policies, limited slavery, and self-government? Was he motivated by the sincere wish to see Georgia prosper? Did he expect to play a larger role in policy making if these changes were made? Did he hope for greater rewards as a planter? Was he moved by the condition of his friends and associates who had not done well? Did he act from basic prejudices, against Oglethorpe or against the Trustees?

Unfortunately, Dr. Tailfer did not take us into his confidence in the small legacy of correspondence that remains, but using what evidence there is, some tentative observations seem warranted. It would not appear, for example, that Tailfer was motivated by a basic animosity toward the Trustees or Oglethorpe. In 1736 he was a member of a Grand Jury that strongly defended principles laid down by the Trustees, and the letters that exist do not reflect strong personal antagonism. It is true that Oglethorpe bore the brunt of the attack in *A True and Historical Narrative* and the Trustees came in for their share of criticism, but this orientation is, in large part, the result of circumstances, as will be shown when the events surrounding the publication of the booklet are discussed. There is every reason to believe that Tailfer was sincere, though not necessarily accurate, in his conviction that the colony could only flourish if the measures he advocated were adopted. Of course, he was thinking of success in terms of those such as himself, men of position who wished to engage in plantation agriculture, but it would somehow seem out of character if Tailfer were advocating such changes just out of consideration of his associates and friends.

On the other hand, it seems very much in character to believe that Dr. Tailfer hoped to gain a more influential role in conducting the affairs of the colony, especially if a greater degree of self-government should be allowed the Georgia settlers. Whatever his motivations, Tailfer seriously misjudged the reaction of the Trustees to the movement he led; Tailfer's actions and letters caused the Trustees to stiffen rather than relax their position.

During 1740, Tailfer let it be known that he was thinking of leaving Georgia with some of his followers. If he expected this

threat to cause the Trustees and their servants in the colony mis-
givings—that such an important, solid citizen with a devoted following was abandoning the colony, a sign for all to see that the
entire endeavor would soon come crashing down—then again
Tailfer misjudged. William Stephens, secretary to the colony,
greeted Tailfer's departure with relief, believing that when Tailfer
left the "poison" was being drained from the settlement and that
all would be well. Such a belief on Stephens' part was naive, for
it tended to attribute all the grief in the colony to a single group
whereas the problems were infinitely more basic. In addition,
Stephens failed to foresee that Tailfer's departure would, if anything, give this articulate colonist even greater freedom to criti-
cize the colony than he had previously enjoyed. By leaving Savannah and going to Charlestown, Dr. Tailfer set the stage for the
eventual publication of *A True and Historical Narrative*.[7]

It is not clear how soon Tailfer began to practice medicine in
Charlestown. In 1741 he was renting a house "next the land opposite to the pond in Church street," owned by Capt. Cooper. He
repeatedly advertised his remedy, "a decoction" for "bloody fluxes"
and dysentery, for which he claimed positive results if used in
time and "if the patient was able to take a sufficient number of
doses." Later that year Dr. Tailfer moved to King Street, to a
house owned by Capt. Beale, where he continued to practice and
to advertise his remedies, especially, in this case, a method to convey medicines to the lungs by a process too involved to place in
the advertisement but described as "by fumigation and vapour."
It was during this period, from January, 1741, onward, that preparations were being made for the publication of the *Narrative*.[8]

What kind of person was Dr. Tailfer? The best glimpses are those
provided by his critics. The Earl of Egmont, apparently never
having met Tailfer but relying on letters he had read and material
supplied by his informants, labelled Tailfer "a proud sawcy fellow,
and a ring leader for negroes, and change of tenures." William
Stephens in Georgia described Tailfer as vain, overbearing, a
troublemaker. Thomas Jones, another severe critic of Tailfer,
quoted a supporter of the good Doctor as saying that Tailfer was
a "proud, obstinate, silly coxcomb." Jones himself accused Tailfer
and his group of keeping concubines, presumably congenial Indian
maidens, and producing numerous "spurious" children. This last

---

7. *Stephens' Journal* in Candler, ed., *Colonial Records*, IV, 465, 645–46.
8. *South Carolina Gazette*, June and July, *passim*. See also October 24 and November 28.

accusation seems exaggerated because no other critic reinforces the observation, which Tailfer's opponents would be quick to do, in view of the controversy surrounding Tailfer, if the charge were true. On the other hand, Tailfer was recognized as a leader by everyone, and his intelligence and self-assurance are clearly reflected in his correspondence. It would not be surprising, in fact, if his confidence proved overbearing, especially to people who disagreed with him. Certainly it is doubtful whether Tailfer could be described as a warm-hearted, cordial person, held in affection by his associates, for his letters and actions do not convey the impression of a man particularly sensitive to the feelings or thoughts of others.[9]

The second of the three authors, David Douglas, is a much more shadowy figure, so obscure in fact that the outline of his career remains indistinct. He came to Georgia, as the phrase had it, "on his own account," probably with the same group as Dr. Tailfer. Whether or not Douglas ever received a large grant of land is not clear. He is mentioned as a merchant in 1735, along with Andrew Grant, another important figure among the Scotch group. These two drew a 100-pound sterling bill of exchange, a large sum of money for that time and place, using the offices of Thomas Causton, who held a key position in Georgia as the Trustees' Storekeeper; and in 1736 Douglas was granted a town lot. Later, Douglas' name is invariably found among the signers of the memorials sent to the Trustees requesting a change of policy. In 1740, in conjunction with some associates, Douglas petitioned the Trustees for a grant on Wilmington Island. Their original request was denied, but the decision was later revised.[10]

It is not certain how successful Douglas was in the Georgia settlement, but it is obvious that he did not share the gains reported of Tailfer. William Stephens does mention Douglas' "great House," but this description is so vague as to be meaningless. Whatever success Douglas might have enjoyed, it did not deter him from leaving the colony the same time as Tailfer, although rumors had circulated freely on earlier occasions that Douglas and others planned to leave. Hearing these rumors Stephens remarked: "This

9. This comment is made by Egmont on a document that attempts to analyze the individuals who signed the Memorial of December 9, 1738. Egmont Papers, Vol. 14203. Stephens' appraisal of Tailfer is sprinkled throughout his correspondence and his Journal, but see particularly, William Stephens to Trustees, 2 January 1738/39, in Candler, ed., *Colonial Records*, XX, 368–69.

10. Thomas Causton to Trustees, 15 October 1735, Savannah, in Egmont Papers, Vol. 14201.

[the prospective move] by some few, very few, was looked on and talked of as a considerable loss to the Colony; but people of more discernment could not think so; for what loss can it be to any place, if such leave it, who will put their helping hands to no good in it?" Again, Stephens tended to minimize the consequences.[11]

The career of the third author, Hugh Anderson, is an illuminating introduction to the struggle in early Georgia. To employ a much overworked but, in this case, suitably descriptive phrase, Anderson was "a man of parts"—well educated, of "good" family ties, a person of some station and affluence. He had come to Egmont in May, 1736, to ask for permission to migrate to Georgia, there to seek his fortune and future, having recently experienced financial losses that made it impossible for him to support himself and his family in acceptable circumstances. He told Egmont that because of varied losses, part of which were brought on by "dancing after the promises of a principal nobleman concerned in the administration of Scotland," only two hundred pounds sterling remained of his legacy. Egmont warned Anderson that this sum would scarcely permit him to transport his family, his wife and five children and his servants, a maid and four men servants, much less to maintain them after their arrival, but Anderson was not dissuaded and he asked for encouragement and assistance from the Trustees.[12]

Within a few days, the Trustees approved Anderson's application to go to Georgia. They granted him land in the country "in proportion to the servants he shall be able to employ in cultivating it," and a town lot in Savannah. Anderson had made a special request for the town lot, stating that his wife was the granddaughter of an Earl, that she had been "tenderly brought up, and would require some society." In addition, Anderson was appointed "Inspector of the Public Garden and Mulberry plantation," albeit without salary, or so Egmont's *Diary* records it at the time, although later, in his refutation to the *Narrative*, Egmont maintains that Anderson received compensation. What is obvious is that Anderson, when he migrated to Georgia, was an uncommon settler, not typical in any way of the rank and file.[13]

Hugh Anderson arrived in Georgia in June, 1737, a year after he first visited Egmont and three years later than the "old-timers" such as Dr. Tailfer. There is every indication that Anderson ap-

11. Candler, ed., *Colonial Records*, IV, 453, 655, 465 (for the quote).
12. *Diary of the First Earl of Egmont* (Historical Manuscripts Commission, London, 1920–23), II, 276. To be cited hereafter as Egmont's *Diary*.
13. *Ibid.*, 276, 278.

plied himself faithfully, trying to create a profitable working plantation, or what he called more appropriately, "my little farm." Within
a year he had completed modest living accommodations, cleared
and fenced ten acres of land and planted it with corn, peas, and potatoes; he also had planted four acres of rice, in addition to garden crops, a nursery, and cotton and tobacco "in small quantities
for experiments." Few colonials, regardless of the time and place
of settlement, accomplished as much in so short a time as did
Anderson. His industry assuredly is persuasive evidence of his intentions.[14]

Obstacles soon drove Anderson to the conclusion, however, that
"I do sincerely and positively affirm, that it is not practicable to
defray the necessary charges, or supply the most scanty necessaries
of life." Although he believed that the long range possibilities of
obtaining a productive crop, particularly the manufacture of silk,
were exceedingly good, settlers would in the interim need help for
the essentials of life. This was due, in part, to special hardships:
"the land here, Sir, is not so fruitful by far as represented at home,"
its loose, sandy character together with the blazing sun quickly
exhausting the fertility even when helped with "the strongest mix-
tures and manures"; the attrition on livestock and crops caused
by insects and wild animals; and the losses resulting from drought.
As the colony developed, asserted Anderson, conditions would be
improved. He suggested livestock enclosures, rotation of crops, the
use of ploughs and European grains, and other adjustments, to
"suit" the climate and soil. "The inference from the whole is," he
continued, "that the overcoming those many difficulties, must be
the consequence of the Publick's supporting the diligent and industrious of the colony, and of such I only speak, until some staple
manufacture takes place: But without such support, the feeble
endeavours of infant planters can never support them, till that
period arrives." [15]

In his capacity as Inspector of the Public Gardens, Anderson
was praised and criticized, praised for improving it with the help
of Fitzwalter, a gardener in the employ of the Trustees, and criticized for spending most of his time on his own lot rather than the
public garden. That he should favor his own work over that of the
Public Gardens when it appears he received no compensation for
his public task seems quite understandable to an outside observer,

14. Extract of letter, Hugh Anderson to Adam Anderson, 15 June 1738, Savannah,
in Egmont Papers, Vol. 14203.
15. *Ibid.*

although it seemed to be a point overlooked by his critics. Anderson did make an extensive report to the Trustees, however, soon after he arrived. His observations reflect a keen intelligence, but they also reveal his inexperience with the realities of a newly planted colony. He suggested a number of far-reaching improvements—a greenhouse, a library containing books that would be helpful for planting and for agricultural experimentation—all wonderfully useful but demanding a capital investment and maturity of settlement yet unknown in the struggling settlement.[16]

During these years, Anderson was a respected member of the community, but he does not seem to have been active politically. Indeed, at one time, he wrote: "To write of any unlucky divisions or party's among us, is a point too ticklish for a private person: . . . the properest channel is what they have to our universal satisfaction appointed, I mean Col. Stephens, who no doubt will acquit himself of his commission, with honour and integrity." Even after Anderson left Georgia for Charlestown he informed the Earl of Egmont, "My genius inclines me to the naturall and retired scenes of life. Politicks surmounts my capacity; so are they without [outside] the aim of my ambition." In this light, it is ironical that Hugh Anderson's name should become identified with the most explosive political document in early Georgia history, as if in some way, after acting in good faith, he found himself caught in a situation brought about by factors beyond his control.[17]

Several facts about Anderson are ironical. Though the last of the prospective authors to arrive in Georgia he was the first to leave. Though he devoted the most energy and time to cultivating his holding he appears to have been the most impoverished when he left. Though he was the most judicious in his behavior and the most understanding of Oglethorpe and the Trustees he received as much condemnation from them as did Tailfer and Douglas, and possibly received more. Anderson left Savannah in March, 1739, as he stated it, "upon finding my little stock exhausted[,] my family decreased, my servants useless and burthensome[,] and all the attempts of industry and frugality unavailing." He had been invited to give weekly lectures in Charlestown on natural philosophy, natural history, agriculture, and gardening. His compensation was

16. Egmont's *Diary*, II, 476. Also III, 54. Hugh Anderson to Trustees Concerning the State of the Public Garden at Savannah, 10 August 1737, in Egmont Papers, Vol. 14203.

17. Extract, Hugh Anderson to Adam Anderson, 15 June 1738, Savannah, in Egmont Papers, Vol. 14203; Hugh Anderson to The Earl of Egmont, 13 June 1739, *ibid.*, Vol. 14204.

assured by a subscription of three guineas annually from forty Charlestown gentlemen, supplemented by the purchase of tickets, worth two shillings each, by non-subscribers for individual lectures. A few years later, in 1741, Anderson was identified as the head of a school in Charlestown. A highly prejudiced witness later informed Egmont that Anderson's school was dwindling, but the evidence is inconclusive.[18]

It is interesting to trace the change in attitude toward Anderson over half a decade. If the Earl of Egmont had been asked for his opinion in 1736, he probably would have repeated what he inscribed in his diary: "I found him [Anderson] a decent, considerate, and very intelligent gentleman." By 1741, when circumstances had warped his judgment, Egmont was less generous, condemning Anderson as an indolent person whose word was not to be trusted and whose integrity was to be questioned.[19]

To an outside observer, however, Egmont's original judgment seems essentially sound. Anderson's letters and actions convey a sense of balance and reasonableness that almost appears out of place in the extravagant display of charges and countercharges that characterize the opposing forces in the struggle over policy. Anderson did not leave Georgia, for example, without going to Oglethorpe to obtain permission. His explanation is calm, marked by good taste and free of animosity, with none of the toughness, almost truculence, that can be detected in the letters of Tailfer. Moreover, when William Stephens and others who supported the position of the Trustees report to the home authorities on the "malcontents," Anderson's name is not mentioned. Only when *A True and Historical Narrative* appears does Anderson become identified with the "malcontents."

In common with most documents, the background of *A True and Historical Narrative* is fully as illuminating as its authorship. In this particular case, the document grew out of a series of complaints,

18. *Stephens' Journal* in Candler, ed., *Colonial Records*, IV, 307. Hugh Anderson to Earl of Egmont, 13 June 1739, Charlestown, Egmont Papers, Vol. 14204. When Anderson's letter was received by Egmont, the latter remarked: "It appeared to us that it was only calculated to persuade us to agree to a change of tenure and admission of negroes." Egmont's *Diary*, III, 82. Egmont's observation reveals how quickly any suggestion or idea was channelled, perhaps distorted would be a better word, into the familiar preconceived notions of what the controversy was about. There was really no thought given to the possibility that Anderson might be reporting accurately, without any thought to special pleading. Hennig Cohen, *The South Carolina Gazette, 1732–1775* (Columbia, South Carolina, 1953), 31, 69, 77, 124; Egmont's *Diary*, III, 230.
19. Egmont's *Diary*, II, 276.

beginning in 1735, that the policies established by the Trustees required modification if the settlement was to flourish. At the outset the emphasis was definitely placed upon two requests, that a limited number of slaves be allowed and that there be some alterations in land tenure, but, by late 1740, when the dissatisfaction was reaching a crescendo, the emphasis was greatly broadened to include limited self-government, release from excessive quitrents, and the right to take up land where it was convenient rather than by Trustee assignment, as well as the issue of slaves and a more drastic change in land tenure. This transition from 1735 to 1741 in the objectives of the discontented settlers has not always been observed and its significance has seldom been appreciated.

In addition to the expanded demands during this period, the proportion of settlers involved in the dissatisfaction greatly increased. This can be explained, in part, by the agitation of the leaders within the movement, but the Trustees and their representatives in the colony assigned these men a more influential role than they deserved. By late 1740, the discontent was widespread through the colony, although its focal point continued to be Savannah.

It is true that the ill feeling was often local in character, as the Trustees' spokesmen in the colony so often noted. William Stephens, Thomas Jones, and later Egmont, called the leaders a "Scotch Club," centered at Savannah, given, so they said, to plotting against the Trustees' representatives, living wastefully and wantonly, with "an imperious manner of behaviour." Thomas Causton, first Bailiff of Savannah and employed as Storekeeper by the Trustees, reported that the bad feeling was so intense that a millwright, having taken more than his share of spirits, threatened two stalwarts of the Scotch Club "and swore if he could have his will, he would knock them Scotch Sons of Bitches brains out." A delegation from the Club visited Causton after this incident and complained heatedly, but received little satisfaction. Others, especially Thomas Jones, laid out a more general indictment against the Scotch group: dressing gaily; setting up a Freemasons club, a St. Andrews club, and "other tipling societies"; keeping concubines; and holding horse races for pleasure at a time when the colony was in danger of an invasion from the Spanish. Although the bad feeling created by such incidents probably contributed to the problems of the infant settlement, the base of the discontent was much more deep-seated. Not only did many more settlers than the so-called "Scotch Club" sign the Memorials to the Trustees, but the evidences of dissatisfaction persisted long after many of the Club's leaders had left the colony.[20]

The truth is that the colony was in serious trouble. The hardships and the signs of failure were apparent to everyone, even to the officials who represented the Trustees. Drouth, illness, and fear of invasion coupled with crop failures and inability to develop a staple for export caused distress throughout the colony. Even the Salzburgers, whose method of settlement and desire to achieve a homogeneous community made them an efficient economic unit as well as a close social-religious community and thus the most successful settlers in Georgia, found the situation depressing. The Reverend Bolzius, their leader, wrote in 1737, when the despair and discontent were beginning to make themselves felt, that half of his group had died and the remaining half were hard pressed. They could live, he said, only through the goods supplied by the Trustees' store. Three years later, George Whitefield, the noted preacher, thought it his "duty" to inform the Trustees of the "declining state" of the colony, noting particularly the sad condition of Frederica, Darien, and Savannah.[21]

Although the "Scotch Club" and other dissatisfied elements obviously were not responsible for Georgia's troubles, as some contemporaries erroneously believed, it is certainly apparent that the problems which arose in the colony presented these leaders with an opportunity to seek their own ends: they were able to force concessions from the Trustees that would, first of all, enable the planter who wished to carry on commercial agriculture to use greater discretion in exploiting his holding, and second, that would assure the planter and his associates extensive policy-making power over the affairs of the province. It is entirely possible and, in fact, highly probable that the leaders did not have these goals clearly in mind at the outset, but there can be no question about their intentions by 1741. They wished to alter the character of the colony, to refashion it in the image of other English settlements with control firmly retained by themselves.

It is important, once again, to note that a distinction must be maintained between the fundamental "causes" of the problems that arose in Georgia and the goals sought by the leaders of the

20. Journal of Thomas Causton, 31 May 1737, Egmont Papers, Vol. 14203; Thomas Jones to Jo. Lydes, 18 September 1740, Savannah, *ibid.*, Vol. 14205.
21. Bolzius to Captain Coram, 28 July 1737, Ebenezer, in Egmont Papers, Vol. 14203; Whitefield to (Trustees), 7 April 1740, On Board Ship from Savannah to Philadelphia, *ibid.*, Vol. 14204.

discontented group, something that contemporaries often failed to do. Although the goals of the leaders tended to complicate basic problems and confuse the issues, they were, primarily, the *result*, not the cause of Georgia's troubles. This, then, constitutes the general outline. Its detail, however, can be traced through the various memorials drawn up and presented by the dissatisfied Georgia settlers, documents that also provide needed background to understand the publication of the *Narrative*. Individual grievances had been presented to the Trustees ever since the founding of the colony, but formal evidences of deep-rooted discontent did not appear until December 9, 1738, when approximately 130 prominent settlers, mostly from Savannah, signed a Memorial protesting against the management of the colony. William Stephens asserted that Robert Williams and Patrick Tailfer were the "chief fabricators," but it would be a mistake to think that the Memorial was the product of a minority, for a large group was persuaded to sign despite warnings from the representatives of the Trustees.[22]

The Memorial itself was not an impassioned document but a remarkably able, logical disquisition—from a distinct point of view. It included a discriminating account of the progress of the Georgia settlement and its problems, stressing the limitations of the soil and the absence of a staple for export. Without a staple for export, the Memorial argued, there could be no market, no trade, and no prosperity. Using lumber products as an example, the Memorialists complained that it was difficult to compete with the cheaper slave labor of South Carolina, adding that their inability to obtain credit seriously hampered the colony's economy. As for the money provided by Parliament and dispensed by the Trustees, it had been used primarily for defense. And what would bring about a solution? A change should be made in land tenures, giving the landowners titles in fee simple, and permission should be given to import a limited number of Negroes.

Many of the problems described in the Memorial were genuine enough, and much of the analysis was sound; but the same rigorous evaluation that had been directed toward the problems was not applied to the recommended solutions. It is difficult to see how the changes suggested would have disposed of Georgia's urgent problems. As later generations were to learn, what could be grown in Virginia or the Carolinas could not necessarily be produced profitably in Georgia. Perhaps the best explanation as to why the Memorialists advocated limited slavery and a change of land tenure

22. Memorial to Trustees, 9 December 1738, in Egmont Papers, Vol. 14203.

is that, when they surveyed differences between Georgia and the other colonies, they jumped to the conclusion that the relative prosperity of the remaining southern colonies as opposed to their own distress must be due to the most obvious dissimilarities, a distinctive labor force and land system. To attribute their difficulties to these dissimilarities did not, of course, touch the essential problem.

When the Trustees learned of the Memorial in April, 1739, their response was relatively apathetic. Specifically, they remained unmoved by the request for limited slavery, and they hesitated on the question of land tenure; but more important, they tended to minimize the distressing conditions prevalent within the colony, to dismiss the discontent as inspired by men of limited vision guided only by self interest, and to magnify the accomplishments of the colony and its immediate prospects.[23]

Despite the obvious sincerity and good intentions on the part of the Trustees, no attitude could, in fact, be better calculated to provoke animosity among those who signed the Memorial than apathy. Active hostility would have placed the signers on the defensive, but apathy could only result in more strenuous efforts to break through the ring of complacency and to oppose the acceptance of things as they were, efforts that by their very nature would be less moderate in tone, less concerned with good faith and reasonableness.

The mood created by growing tension was accented by two developments made by the supporters and representatives of the Trustees in the colony. In October, 1739, Colonel Oglethorpe himself sent a long message to the Trustees under the general title of the "State of Georgia," defending the policies that had operated in the colony since its founding. And on November 10, 1740, William Stephens, Secretary to the Colony, called a meeting of the inhabitants of Savannah, placed a memorial before them entitled "A State of the Province of Georgia," which noted the colony's accomplishments and flourishing condition, and asked the people to sign it. The similarity between many parts of "A State of the Province of Georgia" and Oglethorpe's original "State of Georgia" suggests rather strongly that the Savannah inhabitants were being asked to sign a statement, prepared in large part by Oglethorpe, giving Oglethorpe's and the Trustees' view of the state of the colony, yet it was to be circulated as representing the views and

23. Egmont's *Diary*, III, 38, 51; *Journal of the Earl of Egmont* in Candler, ed., *Colonial Records*, V, 154–57. Hereafter this will be cited as *Journal of Egmont*.

opinions of the settlers. Despite the obvious pressure from the local authorities, only twenty-odd inhabitants signed the document.[24]

The reaction to the document was swift and certain. Not only did the settlers forward a strong remonstrance to the Trustees, enlarging upon their earlier complaints, but they also took steps to carry their case directly to the Crown and Parliament. In addition to the old standbys, modification of land titles and the limited importation of slaves, the Remonstrance advocated (1) that land be taken up where it was convenient, (2) that the excessive quitrent be relaxed, (3) that constables and tything men be under the order of the Trustees and magistrates only, and (4) that a greater voice be given the settlers in choosing the colonial magistrates. The Petition to authorities beyond the Trustees complained that the Trustees regarded their requests as coming from "a set of clamorous people, influenced by designing men and negroe merchants." This, asserted the petitioners, was absolutely false. Their sole concern was to alleviate the conditions within the colony, and they asked the civil government to rally to their side, appealing, interestingly enough, to "ye [the] famous Declaration of Rights made by our Fore Fathers at ye Glorious Revolution." [25]

The hands of the leaders can be detected in the new surge of events. Patrick Tailfer, now living in Charlestown, forwarded the documents to England, together with a Memorial from those Georgia settlers who had left the colony for Carolina. There is no evidence, however, to indicate that Tailfer and his associates initiated the new Georgia Memorials; indeed, it appears that the inhabitants wrote and sent the Memorial without advice or suggestion from Tailfer or others in South Carolina.[26]

24. Oglethorpe, "State of Georgia," 11 October 1739, received 13 March 1739/40, in Egmont Papers, Vol. 14204. "A State of the Province of Georgia Attested under Oath in the Court of Savannah, November 10, 1740" is published in *Collections* of the Georgia Historical Society, II, 67–85. It was originally published in pamphlet form in 1742.

25. Remonstrance of the Inhabitants of the Town and County of Savannah, and the Rest of the Inhabitants of the Province of Georgia in America. To the Honourable Trustees. 22 November 1740, (Copied 2 December 1740), Received 22 May 1741, in Egmont Papers, Vol. 14205; Humble Petition of the Poor Distressed Inhabitants of the Province of Georgia to (Parliament? or King?), 29 December 1740, in Egmont Papers, Vol. 14205.

26. Memorial to the Trustees from Anderson, Tailfer, Mackintosh, *et al.*, 2 December 1740, Received 22 May 1741, in Egmont Papers, Vol. 14205. The sequence presented in Amos E. Ettinger's *James E. Oglethorpe: Imperial Idealist* (Oxford, 1936), 212–13, does not present a balanced version, for it makes assumptions that new evidence tends to contradict.

By late 1740 and early 1741 the arguments on both sides, that of the Trustees and that of the discontented colonists, had been fully formed, each side reflecting its confusion as to what was the basic cause of Georgia's distress and each side blending truth and illusion, misunderstanding and presumption, opinion and prejudice to bolster its position. But the views at first had been expressed, for the most part, in private correspondence or in unpublished memorials and remonstrances. With the appeal of Parliament, the controversy entered a new stage, the area of public communication. It was now merely a question of time as to which side would be the first to publish its version of the story.

Although the stage was set, one final element probably encouraged the publication of *A True and Historical Narrative:* the bitterness created in South Carolina by Oglethorpe's disappointing and now famous siege of St. Augustine in 1740. This story has recently been re-evaluated by Professor John Tate Lanning in his introduction to *The St. Augustine Campaign of 1740.* The emphasis has been changed from the traditional story that South Carolina delayed in furnishing men and material and that her militia lacked courage, a version given wide contemporary circulation by Oglethorpe. Professor Lanning suggests that Oglethorpe's judgment in conducting the siege was responsible for what was regarded as a tragic failure; his view is reinforced by a contemporary investigation conducted by the South Carolina legislature following the disaster. So far as the *Narrative* is concerned, it makes little difference whether or not Oglethorpe's version of the siege was correct, but it is enlightening to recognize that strong public and private criticism against Oglethorpe assured a more favorable reception locally for *A True and Historical Narrative* than it might otherwise have had.[27]

The first indication that a serious publication was being contemplated was a statement that appeared in *The South Carolina Gazette,* on January 15, 1741, to be repeated in succeeding weeks, stating that *A True and Historical Narrative* was being prepared for the press "and speedily to be published by subscription." The notice also indicated that the document would be ready the following week and that it could be seen in the hands of either Hugh Anderson or David Douglas, the latter apparently being in the employ of Steel and Hume, merchants in Charlestown.

27. *The St. Augustine Expedition of 1740* (Columbia, South Carolina, 1954). Reprinted from *The Colonial Records of South Carolina* with an introduction by John Tate Lanning.

In April a new statement appeared, indicating that the *Narrative* was "now in press and will speedily be published." It warned, moreover, that "no more copies will be given out in this province than its numbers agreed for according to the proposals," confirming that the original plan to publish on a subscription basis was being carried out. This advertisement appeared repeatedly through April and early May. Finally, in the *South Carolina Gazette* of May 28, the subscribers were informed that they could have their copies delivered to them the following Wednesday by either Hugh Anderson or David Douglas. *A True and Historical Narrative* now moved into the area of controversy, and, at the same time, into the stream of eighteenth century colonial literature.

It is difficult to judge how much each author finally contributed to the *Narrative*. There is good evidence, for example, to believe that the letter from the "Plain Dealer," incorporated into the *Narrative*, is from Anderson's pen, though historians have generally credited it to Tailfer; and, in his critique, Egmont singles out Anderson as the "principal" author. On the other hand, the style and approach of Tailfer manifests itself throughout the *Narrative*, particularly in the introduction and those parts of the text which describe a specific endeavor carried out in the colony by order of the Trustees. Because of the absence of material on Douglas, his contribution is the most difficult to assess. What is obvious is that the three authors were gifted, well-educated men who were thoroughly aware of what constituted effective prose.

To describe the literary quality of the *Narrative* is insufficient, for, like any literary effort, it needs to be read to be appreciated. It is doubtful, however, whether the authors thought, even for a moment, that they were composing a piece of literature. Rather, they were consumed with a passion to express themselves on a series of problems that dramatically affected their lives. They were deeply and personally involved, and they were searching for a form that would be most effective in presenting their case. As the *Narrative* demonstrates, they followed the best traditions of English satirical writing. The elaborate preface with its mock dedication to Oglethorpe, the use of Samuel Wesley's eulogistic poems on Georgia as a backdrop against which the "true" story would be told, and the comparison between what was said to have been accomplished and a seemingly detached version of what was actually accomplished, contribute the distinctive flavor that has given the *Narrative* a special place in colonial literature.

Although the immediate response to the *Narrative* may have

proved disappointing to the authors, the document certainly affected the Trustees of Georgia, especially the Earl of Egmont. Egmont had enjoyed a distinguished career. His was a full eighteenth century life of political influence and activity, graced with social festivities and favorite projects—in his case the colony of Georgia. At the time Georgia was first settled, Egmont had reached the mid-century mark. A product of genteel training and good schools, he served in the Irish House of Commons, first in 1703; and, having been created Baron Percival, in 1715 he entered the Irish House of Lords. In 1723 he was made Viscount Percival. Four years later he entered the British House of Commons, in time to serve on the Committee that inquired into the State of the Gaols, an inquiry that had a direct relation to the founding of Georgia; in 1732 he was made a Trustee of the Georgia undertaking, and a year later he was made Earl of Egmont in the peerage of Ireland. It is probably for his service as Trustee of Georgia that the Earl of Egmont is best and most justly remembered.

Egmont, who usually kept a close check on the activities of the colony, received word in May from William Stephens that the publication of the *Narrative* was impending, but he did not see a copy until July. At that time Dr. Tailfer's father, Captain Tailfer, appeared at Egmont's home to show him a copy of the *Narrative* and to ask Egmont's advice as to whether he should reprint it in England as he had been asked to do by David Douglas. What strange motive prompted Captain Tailfer to come to Egmont is not clear. Whether he came out of good will, or out of ignorance, or out of curiosity to see and be the guest of a man of great importance will never be known. According to Egmont, Captain Tailfer and he "had much discourse" about the pamphlet with the result that Egmont, treating Captain Tailfer "very civilly," suggested that the pamphlet would not sell, that it would cost Captain Tailfer money to publish it, and that, because the *Narrative* was so full of satire and personal scandal, he knew Captain Tailfer would not care to have a hand in an enterprise that would injure the characters of gentlemen. The two agreed, therefore, that Captain Tailfer's copy of the *Narrative* would remain with Egmont for a short period, and that Egmont might show the *Narrative* to a few selected Trustees and, of course, use it for additional study.[28]

Egmont's initial reaction to the *Narrative* is contained in a letter to Harman Verelst, the Trustees' Accountant in England. "As to the book itself," Egmont wrote, "I believe some facts are true,

28. Egmont's *Diary*, III, 225–26.

but there are others disguised, and it is manifestly wrote partially and maliciously." He continued: "However, dirt will stick to the whitest hand till wash'd away, and I think it would not be amiss that some remarks were made on certain passages in it which may make us prepared the better and readyer to answer to the complaints, and justyfy our conduct if call'd on; . . . ." Here Egmont advocated a course of action that eventually led to his incisive critique of the *Narrative,* as it is printed for the first time in the pages that follow the present introduction.[29]

At this critical juncture the *Narrative* became involved with still another development, a design on the part of the Trustees to publish extensive promotional literature on the colony similar to that issued at the time of the founding. Someone had come up with the idea that such an adventure in eighteenth century public relations would win a more definite commitment from the Parliament for a long-term subsidy and thus make unnecessary the annual plea for funds that was subject to all the whims and fancies of that august body and its political leaders. The first effort of the Trustees, *An Impartial Inquiry into the State and Utility of the Province of Georgia,* was published early in 1741, although it had been prepared late in 1740; but with the appearance of *A True and Historical Narrative* the Trustees were forced to deviate, at least in part, from their original purpose in order to answer the criticism that had been raised.[30]

The result was a war of pamphlets between those who supported the existing policies of the Trustees and those who condemned them. The most direct published reply to the *Narrative* was given in *An Account Showing the Progress of the Colony of Georgia in America from its first Establishment* (London, 1741) supposedly drawn up by Benjamin Martyn, Secretary of the Trustees in England, and published by the Trustees. Its tone and intent are clearly indicated by its preface where the *Narrative* is severely censured as "being a mean, low-witted sneer, a malicious ill-natured invective . . . ;" and the authors are treated with condescension, for they "without any regard to good manners or common civility treat his Excellency [Oglethorpe] . . . with such rudeness as ill becomes any person to use even to an inferior." Moreover, the *Narrative* was "inconsistent, spiteful, false . . . founded in lies and misrepresentations, projected and published by a few persons of no estate," persons who because of their "seditious and rebellious

29. Egmont to Verelst, 25 July 1741, in Egmont Papers.
30. Crane, "The Promotion Literature of Georgia," 294–98.

practices" were daily stirring up trouble "as incendiaries against the peace of the government." Here was venom to match *A True and Historical Narrative,* although it was inserted into the stream of the text somewhat less adroitly. If proof were needed, here is ample evidence to show that neither side could be accused of objectivity and detachment.

The publications of the Trustees were answered by Thomas Stephens, the son of William Stephens, who had been selected as the "Agent for the people of Georgia," in *The Hard Case of the Distressed People of Georgia,* a strong and able indictment of the Trustees' management and policies. Moreover, when the Trustees issued *A State of the Province of Georgia* as an "antidote" to the *Narrative*—this document, it will be recalled, was signed by a few colonists on November 10, 1740, after strong pressure had been applied by the Trustees' representatives in the colony—Thomas Stephens countered with *A Brief Account of the Causes that have Retarded the Progress of Georgia in America* (London, 1743). This, in turn, was answered by the Earl of Egmont in *Remarks upon a Scandalous Piece entitled 'A Brief Account of the Causes that have retarded the Progress of the Colony of Georgia.'* This exchange of pamphlets clearly reflects the bitterness of the controversy afer 1741. Genuine compromise was unthinkable, for each side considered its position as absolute.

The impasse that resulted had some immediate repercussions, and some that filtered down for a decade or more. The Earl of Egmont, for example, whose communications became increasingly bitter, resigned from the Georgia Trustees, an action that he makes clear was taken because the motives of that administrative governing body, so he thought, had been impugned. Another repercussion was felt in Parliament where the Georgia situation was debated and where in 1742, for the first time in the history of the colony, a decision was made not to grant the annual subsidy to the colony. Parliament quickly reversed itself, however, not only by renewing the subsidy but by making Thomas Stephens, the agent of the dissatisfied settlers, kneel before Parliament to confess his wrongs— or so the story goes; but the truth is that the Trustees never fully recovered from the storm aroused by the petitioners from Georgia, as it manifested itself in *A True and Historical Narrative.*[31]

31. Oglethorpe to Egmont, 18 June 1742, Frederica, in Egmont Papers, Vol. 14206. See also, Egmont to Oglethorpe, 18 February, 1742/43, in Egmont Papers, Vol. 14213. For the incident on Thomas Stephens, Egmont (written by his servant, George Lewis) to Jo. Dobel, 11 March 1742/43, London, see Egmont Papers, Vol. 14213. Egmont's *Diary,* III, 266.

The cause, of course, was much deeper than the *Narrative* or Egmont's critical commentary of it. Georgia was still an economic experiment. It had not yet discovered a commodity either for subsistence or for market that could vitalize its economy in the way that tobacco gave Virginia its lease on life, or that fisheries supported Massachusetts, or that grain supplied Pennsylvania. This is wonderfully illustrated by the illusion, shared by the critics of Trustee management as well as its supporters, that silk-making promised to be the ultimate answer. Even the Salzburgers, that industrious, zealous, godly group, whose closely knit social-religious-economic community ideally suited them to achieve the most effective results from their industry, required outside support. How much more did economic factors operate on the commercial farmer or planter whose investment not only failed to provide a return but whose capital was swallowed up by the costs of settlement and maintenance!

More basic still was the question: what type of colony was Georgia to be? It could serve its function as a military outpost without necessarily affording a hospitable reception to commercial planters. If modifications were made to encourage the commercial planter, its character as a model community and as a philanthropic endeavor, as envisioned by the Trustees, would be impaired if not destroyed. Or again, Georgia could fail as an experiment and still serve as an effective frontier buffer for South Carolina against the Spanish and the French. No two groups answered the question as to what Georgia should be in quite the same way; and as long as each clung tenaciously to its objective, controversy was inevitable. Only when a single voice rather than a series of contradictory voices gained supremacy would the controversy be finally resolved.

Something should be said briefly about the publication history of *A True and Historical Narrative* and about procedures followed by the editor in preparing for publication the text and Egmont's comments.

In the original *Narrative*, Egmont underlined the passages on each page of the pamphlet upon which he wished to comment, numbering each passage consecutively but beginning each page with number one. In the original, there is a blank page opposite each page of text, made possible, it is quite apparent, by having the pamphlet rebound with the blank pages appropriately inserted. Egmont used the blank pages for his comments, numbering these comments to correspond with the underlined passage of the text to which his remarks refer. To avoid the confusion that would inevitably arise in the printed text because its pages do not always coincide with the pages of the original pamphlet, it was decided that the Egmont comments, along with the passages to which they refer, be numbered consecutively throughout the pamphlet, rather than beginning each page with number one. It also seemed wise to eliminate the underlining—it would entail underlining the major share of the text—for it is always clear, because of the numbering, to what passage Egmont refers. Moreover, because so much of the text is already in italics, it would be misleading, if not improper, to underline as well. In addition, the few footnotes that appear in the original pamphlet have been brought up into the text, set off with brackets.

An overabundance of italics in the original has been modified slightly in the modern version in the interest of clarity. In the original, for instance, numbers, proper names, and the like were automatically italicized. At the same time, the authors used italics for emphasis. To a modern reader this could prove misleading. The italics have been retained, therefore, only when it is apparent that the authors intended to give a passage, word, or phrase special stress.

With the minor exceptions stated above, each designed to produce clarity, the text follows the original. The punctuation of the original has been retained, except where the meaning is obscured because of it; and, although abbreviations and contractions have been spelled out, the spelling has been retained. Whenever there is a possibility that a modern reader will misunderstand a word— for example, the use of "past" meaning "passed"—then the modern usage is placed in brackets immediately after the original. The problem of capitalization is difficult to resolve, but the lower case rule has been applied whenever possible.

The facts of publication are important in themselves. The first printing of *A True and Historical Narrative* was undertaken in 1741 by Peter Timothy in Charlestown, South Carolina. It was unquestionably a limited edition for it was published by subscription. There is some indication that Thomas Stephens in England had a manuscript copy of the text of the Tailfer booklet in March, 1741, a date in advance of its actual publication in Charlestown; but a London edition, differing slightly in format from the Charlestown edition, was not made until December, 1741.[32]

32. There are three editions of *A True and Historical Narrative*. The first edition has 176 pages and an imprint reading "Charlestown, South Carolina: Printed by

The Earl of Egmont possessed at least two copies of the London edition of the *Narrative*, "printed for P. Timothy in Charles-Town, South-Carolina; and sold by J. Crokatt, in Fleet-street, London." Both of Egmont's copies are now owned by the John Carter Brown Library of Brown University. Egmont scribbled some observations on each copy of the London edition, but he apparently discovered that the close printing of the first copy prevented him from elaborating as fulsomely as he wished. It is Egmont's second copy of the London edition, therefore, where blank pages were bound into the *Narrative* to provide writing room, that contains his extensive commentary; and it is that copy which has been followed in this modern publication. It should be said that Egmont's restricted comments in the first copy of the London edition have been compared with the elaborate comments in the second, without revealing any observations in the former that are not displayed to better advantage when elaborated upon by Egmont in the latter.

A number of people have contributed to make the publication of this volume possible. The editor is deeply indebted to Lawrence Wroth for calling this valuable material to his attention and to the John Carter Brown Library at Brown University not only for permission to publish it but for their generous cooperation in its use. The editor also wishes to acknowledge, with particular pleasure, the pioneer work of Professor Verner Crane who originally was responsible for the identification of Egmont's handwriting on the pamphlets. To John Nelson, a graduate student at Northwestern University, who, in his own right, promises to contribute much to our understanding of early America, I am most grateful for the performance of numerous tasks in the preparation of the documentary materials for the press; and without the effort of E. Merton Coulter the illuminating historical evidence that follows might have remained unavailable to scholars. It gives me special pleasure to express my appreciation to the Howard Foundation, for the ma-

P. Timothy for the Authors, 1741." It was printed in Charlestown. The second has 118 pages and the same imprint except that the date is in Roman numerals. There is some question as to whether this edition was printed in Charlestown or London. The third edition has 112 pages with the imprint reading "Printed for P. Timothy, in Charles-Town, South-Carolina; and sold by J. Crokatt, in Fleet-street, London." Evidence of Egmont would place the publication date as December, 1741, and the place as London. The John Carter Brown Library of Brown University owns one copy of each of the first two editions, and Egmont's unique two copies of the third edition. It should be stated that, although the editions are traditionally listed in the order given above, the proper chronology of the "second" and "third" editions has not been absolutely established.

terials incorporated into this publication were originally examined when I was engaged in research made possible by one of their generous Fellowships. I also wish to acknowledge with appreciation the funds provided by the Northwestern University Graduate School for typing the manuscript, and to Professor Gray C. Boyce of the Department of History and Dean Moody E. Prior for making available additional research money when it was needed. It is also a delight to acknowledge the help of the Huntington Library where I carried on research in colonial American history, part of which related to the founding and growth of early Georgia.

Clarence L. Ver Steeg

Northwestern University
Evanston, Illinois

A True and Historical
NARRATIVE
OF THE
Colony of *GEORGIA*
IN
AMERICA,

From the First SETTLEMENT thereof, until
this present PERIOD;

CONTAINING,

The most authentick FACTS, MATTERS, and
TRANSACTIONS therein.

TOGETHER WITH

His MAJESTY's CHARTER, REPRESENTATIONS of
the PEOPLE, LETTERS, &c. and a DEDICATION to
his Excellency General OGLETHORPE.

By PAT. TAILFER, *M. D.* HUGH ANDERSON, *M. A.*
DA. DOUGLAS, and others, Landholders in *Georgia,* at
present at *Charles-Town* in *South-Carolina.*

——— *Qui Deorum*
Muneribus sapienter uti,
Duramque callet Pauperiem pati,
Pejusque Letho Flagitium timet,
Non ille pro caris Amicis
Aut Patria timidus perire.   HOR. 4. O.

Printed for P. TIMOTHY, in *Charles-Town, South-Carolina;*
and sold by J. CROKATT, in *Fleet-street, London.*

[This first observation of Egmont, found opposite the title page of the *Narrative*, is actually an extract from the Journal of William Stephens who, as the Trustee-appointed Secretary for the colony, submitted lengthy reports to his superiors in England. Egmont undoubtedly introduced his comments with this extract because it suited the temper of his own feelings and opinions about the *Narrative*.—Editor's note.]

1. Extract of Col. Stephens Journal 24 June 1741. Among other things sent me from Mr. Hopton by Penrose, I received the famous (or rather I should say infamous) Narrative of the State of Georgia, that had been so long expected, and advertised to be ready for publication, written by some of our acquaintance the Remnant of the Scotch Club; and which I had bespoke Mr. Hopton to get for me, as soon as it came abroad: and I hope he will also take care to send the same for the perusal of the Honble. Trustees. Such a heap of malicious calumny and vile falshoods, perhaps no instance can be found of, put together in the like compass. Twould be vain and silly in me to pretend here taking it to pieces, or to offer at answering any particulars, when I find almost as many lies as pages—possibly I may foul a little paper, in making some attempt to expose a few of those falshoods in a true light, which with such unparalel'd impudence they have dared to assert as Facts, without any foundation.

If the Honble. Trustees are contented to sit tame under such audacious Ribaldry as they will find in this Libel void of all shame and truth, then it may become me to be passive too, whom the World owes little or no regard to in comparison of those I serve: but I neither think they'l acquiesce patiently under such insults, nor leave me unprotected to the mercy of a wicked Crew, employ'd to worry my good name, which I must set at a very low value, if I did not esteem it a little more durable than the little remains of life yet left me.

Some passages will be found now in this journal which I concieve will appear sufficient to draw conclusions what farther may be expected from a Band, whose rage and madness plainly means bringing all into confusion: my son may now consider, whether or not the base treatment his father finds here from his precious correspondents, be the wages due for all the pains he has been at in promoting their work.

To His EXCELLENCY
JAMES OGLETHORPE, Esq;

General and Commander in Chief of His Majesty's Forces in South Carolina and Georgia; and one of the Honourable Trustees for Establishing the Colony of GEORGIA in AMERICA, &c.

May it please Your Excellency,

As the few surviving Remains of the Colony of *Georgia* find it necessary to present the World (and in particular *Great-Britain*) with a true State of that Province, from its first Rise, to its present Period; Your Excellency (of all Mankind) is best entitled to the Dedication, as the principal Author of its present Strength and Affluence, Freedom and Prosperity: And tho' incontestable Truths will recommend the following *NARRATIVE* to the patient and attentive Reader; yet your Name, *SIR,* will be no little Ornament to the Frontispiece, and may possibly engage some courteous Perusers a little beyond it.

THAT Dedication and Flattery are synonimous, is the Complaint of every Dedicator, who concludes himself ingenuous and fortunate, if he can discover a less trite and direct Method of flattering than is usually practised; but we are happily prevented from the least Intention of this kind, by the repeated Offerings of the *Muses* and *News-Writers* to Your Excellency, in the publick Papers: 'Twere presumptuous even to dream of equalling or encreasing them: We therefore flatter ourselves, that Nothing we can advance will in the least shock Your Excellency's Modesty; not doubting but your Goodness will pardon any Deficiency of Elegance and Politeness, on account of our Sincerity, and the serious Truths we have the Honour to approach you with.

WE have seen the ancient Custom of sending forth Colonies, for the Improvement of any distant Territory, or new Acquisition, continued down to ourselves: but to Your Excellency alone it is owing, that the World is made acquainted with a Plan, highly refined from those of all former Projectors. They fondly imagin'd it necessary to communicate to such young Settlements the fullest

3

Rights and Properties, all the Immunities of their Mother Countries, and Privileges rather more extensive: By such Means, in deed, these Colonies flourish'd with early Trade and Affluence; but Your Excellency's Concern for our perpetual Welfare could never permit you to propose such transitory Advantages for us: You considered Riches like a Divine and Philosopher, as the *Irritamenta Malorum,* and knew that they were disposed to inflate weak Minds with Pride; to pamper the Body with Luxury, and introduce a long Variety of Evils. Thus have you *Protected us from ourselves,* as Mr. *Waller* says, by keeping all Earthly Comforts from us: You have afforded us the Opportunity of arriving at the Integrity of the *Primitive Times,* by intailing a more than *Primitive Poverty* on us: The Toil, that is necessary to our bare Subsistence, must effectually defend us from the Anxieties of any further Ambition: As we have no Properties, to feed Vain-Glory and beget Contention; so we are not puzzled with any System of Laws, to ascertain and establish them: The valuable Virtue of Humility is secured to us, by your Care to prevent our procuring, or so much as seeing any *Negroes* (the only human Creatures proper to improve our Soil) lest our Simplicity might mistake the poor *Africans* for greater Slaves than ourselves: And that we might fully receive the Spiritual Benefit of those wholesome Austerities; you have wisely denied us the Use of such Spiritous Liquors, as might in the least divert our Minds from the Contemplation of our Happy Circumstances.

OUR Subject swells upon us; and did we allow ourselves to indulge our Inclination, without considering our weak Abilities, we should be tempted to launch out into many of Your Excellency's extraordinary Endowments, which do not so much regard the Affair in Hand: But as this would lead us beyond the Bounds of a Dedication; so would it engross a Subject too extensive for us, to the Prejudice of other Authors and Panegyrists; We shall therefore confine ourselves to that remarkable Scene of Your Conduct, whereby *Great-Britain* in general, and the Settlers of *Georgia,* in particular, are laid under such inexpressible Obligations.

BE pleased then, *Great SIR,* to accompany our heated Imaginations, in taking a View of this Colony of *Georgia!* this Child of your auspicious Politicks! arrived at the utmost Vigor of its Constitition, at a Term when most former States have been struggling through the Convulsions of their Infancy. This early Maturity, however, lessens our Admiration, that Your Excellency lives to see (what few Founders ever aspired after) the great Decline and almost final Termination of it. So many have finish'd their Course during the Progress of the Experiment, and such Numbers have retreated from the Fantoms of Poverty and Slavery which their cowardly Imaginations pictur'd to them; that you may justly vaunt with the boldest Hero of them all,

> ———— *Like Death you reign*
> *O'er silent Subjects and a desart Plain.*
>   Busiris.

YET must your Enemies (if you have any) be reduced to confess, that no ordinary Statesman could have digested, in the like Manner, so capacious a Scheme, such a copious Jumble of Power and Politicks. We shall content ourselves with observing, that all those beauteous Models of Government which the little States of *Germany* exercise, and those extensive Liberties which the Boors of *Poland* enjoy, were design'd to concenter in your System; and were we to regard the Modes of Government, we must have been strangely unlucky to have miss'd of the best, where there was an Appearance of so great a Variety; for, under the Influence of our *Perpetual Dictator,* we have seen something like *Aristocracy, Oligarchy,* as well as the *Triumvirate, Decemvirate,* and *Consular Authority* of famous Republicks, which have expired many Ages before us: What Wonder then we share the same Fate? Do their Towns and Villages exist but in Story and Rubbish? We are all over Ruins; our Publick-Works, Forts, Wells, High-Ways, Light-House, Store and Water-Mills, &c. are dignified like theirs, with the same venerable Desolation. The Logg-House, indeed, is like to be the last forsaken Spot of Your Empire; yet even this, through the Death, or Desertion of those who should continue to inhabit it, must suddenly decay; the Bankrupt Jailor himself shall be soon denied the Privilege of human Conversation; and when this last Moment of the Spell expires, the whole shall vanish like the Illusion of some *Eastern Magician.*

BUT let not this solitary Prospect impress Your Excellency with any Fears of having your Services to Mankind, and to the Settlers of *Georgia* in particular, buried in Oblivion; for if we diminutive Authors are allow'd to prophesy (as you know Poets in those Cases formerly did) we may confidently presage, That while the Memoirs of *America* continue to be read in *English, Spanish,* or the Language of the *Scots* High-Landers, Your Excellency's Exploits and Epocha will be transmitted to Posterity.

SHOULD Your Excellency apprehend the least Tincture of

Flattery in any Thing already hinted, we may sincerely assure you, we intended nothing that our Sentiments did not very strictly attribute to your Merit; and, in such Sentiments, we have the Satisfaction of being fortified by all Persons of Impartiality and Discernment.

BUT to trespass no longer on those Minutes, which Your Excellency may suppose more significantly employ'd on the Sequel; let it suffice at present, to assure you, that we are deeply affected with your Favours; and tho' unable of ourselves properly to acknowledge them, we shall embrace every Opportunity of Recommending you to higher Powers, who (we are hopeful) will reward Your Excellency according to your MERIT.

> *May it please Your Excellency,*
> *Your Excellency's*
> *Most devoted Servants,*
> The Land-Holders of GEORGIA,
> Authors of the following *Narrative.*

Preface

THE colony of Georgia has afforded so much subject of conversation to the world, that it is not to be questioned, but a true and impartial account of it, from its first settlement, to its present period, will be generally agreeable; and the more so, that the subject has hitherto been so much disguised and misrepresented in pamphlets, poems, gazettes, and journals.

If it is asked, Why this NARRATIVE has not been published to the world sooner? we assign two reasons, which (we doubt not) will be satisfactory.

First, a number of honourable gentlemen accepted the charge of Trustees for executing the purposes in His Majesty's most gracious Charter; gentlemen, whose honour and integrity we never did, or yet do, call in question: But, to our great misfortune, none of that honourable body (excepting Mr. Oglethorpe) ever had opportunity of viewing the situation and circumstances of the colony, and judging for themselves as to the necessities thereof. How far Mr. Oglethorpe's schemes were consistent with the welfare or prosperity of it, will best appear from the following NARRATIVE.

When experience gradually unfolded to us the alterations we found absolutely requisite to our subsisting, we made all dutiful and submissive applications to these our patrons, in whom we placed so much confidence: This course we judged the most proper and direct, and therefore repeated these our dutiful applications, both to the body of the Trustees and to Mr. Oglethorpe; but alas! our miseries could not alter his views of things, and therefore we could obtain no redress from him; and the honourable board we found were prejudiced against our petitions (no doubt) through misinformations and misrepresentations; and this (we are confident) a further enquiry and time will convince them of.

The inviolable regard we paid to the honourable board, kept us from applying to any other power for redress, whilst the least hopes could be entertained of any from them: And we make no doubt, but that our moderation, in this respect, will recommend us to all persons of humanity.

A *second* reason is, that as we had daily occasion of seeing our supreme magistrates, who ruled over us with unlimited power, exercising illegal acts of authority, by threatenings, imprisonments, and other oppressions; therefore we had just reason to apprehend, that any further steps, to obtain relief, might subject us to the like effects of arbitrary power; so, until now, that a handful of us have made our escape to a LAND OF LIBERTY (after having made shipwreck of our time and substance in that unhappy colony) we had it not in our power to represent the state of that settlement to the world, or to make our application to higher powers for redress.

We are hopeful, that the perusal of the following sheets will rectify two sorts of readers in their surprize in relation to the colony of Georgia, viz. those of Great Britain, who have never known this part of the world but by description; and those of America: The first are no doubt surprized, to think it possible, that so pleasant and temperate a clime; so fruitful a soil; such extensive privileges; all which were publickly given out; and such considerable sums of publick and private benefactions, have not satisfied and enriched us: Them we refer to the following Narrative for satisfaction. The American reader, on the other hand, must be equally surprized to find that such numbers should have been so fooled and blind-folded, as to expect to live in this part of America by cultivation of lands without Negroes, and much more without titles to their lands, and laid under a load of grievances and restrictions: And though these were redressed, how could persons in their senses ever imagine, that fifty acres of pine-barren, not value fifty six pences in property (and whereof many thousands may be purchased at half that rate in the [2] neighbouring province) could maintain a family

---

2. Capt. Horton a landholder now here, says there ought to be a considerable proportion of pine barren to every plantation for fodder to cattle.

He also says that whoever is industrious may live, and instances Henry Myeres a freeholder at Frederica, who from his 50 acre lot maintains a wife and 6 children.

There lately came a letter from this man to Mr. Beasent[?] in London, (who communicated it to the Trustees) dated 7 May 1741, wherein he writes, "It is here as in all parts of the world, labour and great industry must be used, and when peace is made, this will be a happy place. As to me and my family we have been ailing, but all in a mending condition. I have 5 acres of land cleared and planted these several years: what is usual to plant in this Country in new land is Indian corn, pease, potatoes and Several Sorts of viney plants, such as pumpkins, watermelons, melons, and cowcumbers. We have choice Sorts of pulse and roots. All the European garden seeds thrive well here. Now that the roots of the trees are rotten I intend to plant next year, when I'll sow wheat, barley, oates and other grain. Several of our people who have gone home to England, have given a vile character of the place and government, without any reason, but because they were idle and seditious: finding it hard to get bread at that rate, they went off, tho such people will find it hard to live anywhere."

of white people, and pay such duties and quit-rents in a few years,[3]

3. *Such duties & quit-Rents* etc. Here a deceit is cast on the Reader, for no person possessing a 50 acre lot, pays a higher Quitrent than any in Carolina or other parts, neither do any in the Colony pay a farthing duty. The term before payment of Quit-Rents is 10 years compleat, which is not too few years for any industrious Man to commence payment and for 50 acres but 2 Shillings proclamation money.

as the richest grounds in Carolina,[4] or other provinces in America

4. *The richest grounds* etc. They would have it thought that the land of Georgia is not so good as that of Carolina: to answer this, I shall give the following passage in Col. Stephens journal 12 feb. 1738–9.

"The gentlemen of Carolina shewing a desire of seeing the nature of the adjacent parts of the Country, we got horses, and they passed away a few hours, diverting themselves that way, and at their return, confessed that they little expected to see such a Tract of Land as they found on each side, after leaving the pine barren, and discending into the flat Country, which exceeded any thing about Charlestown."

To the same purpose the Reverend Mr. Bolzius, Minister of the Saltsburgers in Georgia, wrote in his printed journal sent to Germany, as follows:

"9 Sept. 1741. Some time ago, I wrote to an honoured friend in Europe, that the land in this Country if well managed, and laboured, brings forth, by the blessing of God, not only hundred fould but thousand fould, and I this day was confirmed therein. A Woman having picked out of Indian corn, bought at Purysburg no more than three grains of Rye (called here German corn) and planting them here at Ebenezar, one of these grains produced an hundred and seventy stalks and ears: and the 3 grains yeilded to her a bag of corn as big as a coat pocket, the grains whereof were good and full grown. One of our Saltsburgers brought to me also a like bag of beans, all grown out of One bean. The land is able to provide every good thing, and more particularly is pasturage very plenteous."

And in his letter to the Reverend Dr. Frank of Hall, dated 23 July 1741 he writes: "The land is really very fruitfull, if the sins of the Inhabitants, and the curse of God for such sins doth not eat it up, which was formerly the case of the blessed land of Canaan. And I am heartily sorry to acquaint you, that I dont find in some of the Inhabitants of the Colony, due thankfullness for, and contentment with the many benefits bestowed on them for several years to-gether; altho those who are industrious and will labour for their maintenance may as we do, live contentedly, and subsist under the blessing of God, which blessing the idle and unthankful are not entitled to."

To the same purpose:

Mr. John West who voluntarily quitted the magistracy, and came to England to obtain a grant of 500 acres, and engage servants to cultivate the same, acquainted the Trustees 14 Sept. 1735, that there was no body in the Colony but might comfortably subsist if diligent and laborious.

Again: Peter Thickness wrote to his mother 3 Nov. 1736, "If a man had there but 20£ and laid it out in cattel, he might clear that 20£ the first year, and have the cattel too. That there were a parcel of good for nothing Chaps who gave the place an ill name to all Strangers, and had like to have frighted him away when he first came, that there was no man but might live upon his own Improvements if industrious."

Again: Capt. Jenkins acquainted the Trustees 23 feb. 1735–6 "that the people were in a happy way."

Mr. Augustin a Land-holder of 500 acres assured that in one place alone there was a thousand acres of choice land some miles from Savannah.

On the 12 Feb. 1735–6 Mr. Nathl. Pothill a Landholder wrote—"I like my land very well, and as soon as so bad a road which leads to it can be mended I shall settle entirely upon it. So good a Country as I am now in obliges me to a desire of Settling my posterity in it, for which reason I humbly beg of my honble. Patrons a Town lot for my younger Son, Nathaniel, and I would duly see to the performance of all conditions required from holding such a lot."

It seems he had no objections to the being debard Negroes, or those restrictions in grants, of which these clamourers make such heavy complaints.

On 5 March 1735–6 Mr. Eveleigh of Carolina wrote from Charlestown to Mr. Verelts as follows: "Capt. Barnes a native of New York, is very much surprised at the goodness of the Land at St. Simons, and says he never saw such in his days, and that Rhode Island is Looked upon to be a very fine Island, but that that is much superiour. He is a man (as I take him) of judgment and truth."

In Jany. 1738–9 Mr. Coolesey [?] a Freeholder of Savannah acquainted the Trustees, that he had been 4 years in the Colony: that half the land is good, the rest—pine barren, but this last bore 3 good crops of corn, after which it is fit for pasture, and he had seen Cinque foil and Trefoil grow thereon.

In April 1739 Lt. Col. Cochran returned from Georgia to England, and acquainted Sr. Robert Walpole, that the report of the land being bad was false, there being none better in America than round Savannah, tho there was also some bad, call'd pine barren.

In June 1739 Robt. Howes a freeholder of Savannah came to England, and acquainted the Trustees that there was good land enough if the people would cultivate it, and a truly laborious Man might subsist himself by his own cultivation.

In Dec. 1736 Mr. Mcbane told the Trustees that the land at Frederica bore good barley, Indian wheat, hemp, and flax.

In April 1741 Mr. Carteret a landholder returned to England, and acquainted the Trustees, that the Colony would flourish were the people more industrious, for there were none but might find subsistence if they would labour, provisions being cheap.

---

will never bear? To these last we shall only beg leave to observe, that such fatal artifice was used (we shall not say by whom) such specious pretences were made use of, and such real falsities advanced, and the smallest foundations of truth magnified to hyperbole; that we, who had no opportunity of knowing other ways, or means of learning the real truth, and being void of all suspicion of artifice or design, easily believed all these, and fell into the decoy.

The mind of man is naturally curious and enterprizing; we easily feed our wishes into realities, and affect and look upon every novelty in the most favourable light; how easy then is it, for cunning and artifice to lay hold on the weak sides of our fellow-creatures, as we catch fish with a hook baited to their particular gout?

To prove this charge, we shall only transcribe some passages from a piece of prose, and some from a piece of poesy; by which specimens, the reader may judge of some considerable number which were dispersed and vended of the same stamp.

The first are from a pamphlet printed at London, 1733, entitled *A New and Accurate Account of the Provinces of South Carolina and Georgia*. The author has not thought fit to favour us with his name; but it is easy to conceive, that we, who suspected no artifice or design, must conclude, that it came from the best authority, from the circumstances of its being dispersed publickly, and not being contradicted, and from the author's intimate acquaintance (at least so pretended) with all the Trustees' measures and designs. After a high encomium upon the Trustees, page 7, he says, "The air of Georgia is healthy, being always serene and pleasant, never subject to excessive heat or cold, or sudden changes of weather; the winter is regular and short, and the summer cooled with refreshing breezes; it neither feels the cutting north-west wind that the Virginians complain of, nor the intense heats of Spain, Barbary, Italy, and Egypt. The soil will produce anything with very little culture." Page 19, "All sorts of corn yield an amazing increase; one hundred fold is the common estimate; though their husbandry is so slight that they can only be said to scratch the earth, and meerely

to cover the seed: ALL the best sort of cattle and fowls are multi-
plied without number, and therefore without a price: Vines are
natives here." Page 21, "The woods near Savannah are not hard
to be cleared; many of them have no under-wood, and the trees do
not stand generally thick on the ground, but at considerable distances asunder; when you fall the timber for the use, or to make
tar, the root will rot in four or five years; and in the mean time
you may pasture the ground; but, if you would only destroy the
timber, it is done by half a dozen strokes of an ax surrounding
each tree alittle above the root; in a year or two the water getting
into the wound rots in the timber, and a brisk gust of wind fells
many acres for you in an hour, of which you may make one bright
bonfire. Such will be frequently here the fate of the pine, the
wallnut, the cypress, the oak, and the cedar. Such an air and soil
can only be described by a poetical pen, because there is no danger
of exceeding the truth; therefore take Waller's description of an
island in the neighbourhood of Carolina, to give you an idea of
this happy climate:

> "The Spring, which but salutes us here,
> Inhabits there, and courts them all the Year;
> Ripe Fruits and Blossoms on the same Tree live;
> At once they promise what at once they give.
> So sweet the Air, so moderate the Clime,
> None sickly lives, or dies before his Time.
> Heav'n sure has kept this Spot of Earth uncurst,
> To shew how all Things were created first."

Page 27, "The Indians bring many a mile the whole deer's flesh,
which they sell to the people who live in the country, for the value
of sixpence sterling; and a wild turkey of forty pounds weight, for
the value of two pence." In page 32, the author when recommending the Georgia adventure to gentlemen of decayed circumstances,
who must labour at home or do worse, states the following objection, viz. "If such people can't get bread here for their labour,
how will their condition be mended in Georgia?" Which he solves
in the following manner, "The answer is easy; part of it is well
attested, and part self-evident; they have land there for nothing,
and that land so fertile, that, as is said before, they receive a hun-
dredfold increase, for taking a very little pains: Give here in England ten acres of good land to one of those helpless persons, and I
doubt not his ability to make it sustain him, and by his own cul-

ture, without letting it to another; but the difference between no
rent, and rack'd rent, is the difference between eating and starving." Page 32, "These Trustees not only give land to the unhappy
who go thither, but are also impowered to receive the voluntary
contributions of charitable persons, to enable to furnish the poor
adventurers with all necessaries for the expense of their voyage,
occupying the land, and supporting them, till they find themselves
comfortably settled; so that now the unfortunate will not be obliged
to bind themselves to a long servitude to pay for their passage; for
they may be carried *gratis* into a land of liberty and plenty, where
they immediately find themselves in the possession of a competent
estate, in an happier climate than they knew before, and they are
unfortunate indeed, if here they cannot forget their sorrows."
Nay, as if such assertions as these were not powerful enough to
influence poor people, calculations are subjoined, to demonstrate,
that a family consisting of one poor man, his wife, and child of
seven years old, may in Georgia earn sixty pounds sterling per
annum, and this abstracted from silk, wine, &c. Page 41, "Now this
very family in Georgia, by raising rice and corn sufficient for its
occasions, and by attending the care of their cattle and land (which
almost every one is able to do in some tolerable degree for himself)
will easily produce in gross value the sum of sixty pounds sterling
per annum,[5] nor is this to be wondered at, because of the valuable

---

5. I am not concerned to justify this calculation, but thus much Mr. Beaufain
Collector of Charlestown in Carolina informed me, that Patrick Graham a
freeholder of Savannah made 59£ last year (1741) only by selling his mulberry plants to the Inhabitants. Moreover, if the annual maintenance of a
hired white Servant be 12· 3· 4, the labour of an industrious Man who works
for himself is worth as much to him. Some of these Servants have before their
contract expired, attained the property of 7 or 9 cows, hogs, poultry etc.

---

assistance it has from a fertile soil and a stock given gratis; which
must always be remembered in this calculation."

"The calculation of one hundred such families when formally
extended, stands thus,"—Page 43,

	l.	s.	d.
"In London one hundred poor men earn,	500	00	0
One hundred women, and one hundred children,	500	00	0
	1000	00	0

In Georgia an hundred families earn,

One hundred men for labour,	. .	1200 00 0
Ditto for care of their stock at leisure hours,	. . .	1200 00 0
One hundred women and one hundred children,	. .	2400 00 0
Land and stock in themselves,	. . .	1200 00 0

Total, . . 6000 00 0

Q. E. D."

But we must conclude this head, lest we tire the reader. We shall now beg leave to quote a few poetical accounts of this paradise of the world, and of the fatherly care and protection we might depend on from Mr. Oglethorpe. An hundred hackney Muses might be instanced; but we shall confine ourselves to the celebrated performance of the Rev. Mr. Samuel Wesly [Wesley], where we might well expect a sufficient stock of truth and religion, to counterbalance a poetical licence. *Vide* a poem entitled *Georgia, and Verses upon Mr. Oglethorpe's Second Voyage to Georgia.* Printed London, 1736.

> "See where beyond the spacious Ocean lies
> A wide waste Land beneath the Southern Skies; [6]

---

6. One would expect the Hyperboles of Poetry Should not have influenced so wise an Author as Mr. Anderson to quit his native Country. The meanest School boy makes due allowance for such flights.

> Where kindly Suns for Ages roll'd in vain,
> Nor e'er the Vintage saw, or rip'ning Grain,
> Where all Things into wild Luxuriance ran,
> And burthen'd Nature ask'd the Aid of Man.
> In this sweet Climate and prolifick Soil,
> He bids the eager Swain indulge his Toil;
> In free Possession to the Planter's Hand,
> Consigns the rich uncultivated Land.
> Go you, the Monarch cries, go settle there,
> Whom *Britain* from her Plenitude can spare:
> Go, your old wonted Industry pursue;
> Nor envy *Spain* the Treasures of *Peru.*"

> "But not content in Council here to join,
> A further Labour, OGLETHORPE, is thine:

In each great Deed thou claim'st the foremost Part,
And Toil and Danger charm thy gen'rous Heart:
But chief for this thy warm Affections rise;
For oh! thou view'st it with a Parent's Eyes:
For this thou tempt'st the vast tremendous Main,
And Floods and Storms oppose their Threats in vain."

"He comes, whose Life, while absent from your View,
Was one continued Ministry for you;
For you were laid out all his Pains and Art,
Won ev'ry Will and soften'd ev'ry Heart.
With what paternal Joy shall he relate,
How views its Mother Isle your little State:
Think while he strove your distant Coast to gain,
How oft he sigh'd and chid the tedious Main,
Impatient to survey, by Culture grac'd,
Your dreary Wood-Land and your rugged Waste.
Fair were the Scenes he feign'd, the Prospects fair;
and sure, ye *Georgians,* all he feign'd was there,
A Thousand Pleasures crowd into his Breast;
But one, one mighty Thought absorbs the rest,
And gives me Heav'n to see, the Patriot cries,
Another BRITAIN in the Desert rise."

Again,
"With nobler Products see thy GEORGIA teems,
Chear'd with the genial Sun's director Beams;
There the wild Vine to Culture learns to yield,
And purple Clusters ripen through the Field.
Now bid thy Merchants bring thy Wine no more
Or from the *Iberian* or the *Tuscan* Shore;
No more they need th' *Hungarian* Vineyards drain,
And *France* herself may drink her best *Champain.*
Behold! at last, and in a subject Land,
Nectar sufficient for thy large Demand:
Delicious Nectar, powerful to improve
Our hospitable Mirth and social Love:
This for thy jovial Sons.—Nor less the Care
Of thy young Province, to oblige the FAIR;
Here tend the Silk Worm in the verdant Shade,
The frugal Matron and the blooming Maid."

From the whole, we doubt not, the reader will look upon us as sufficiently punished for our credulity: [7] And indeed, who would

---

7. *Sufficiently punished* etc. Had Mr. Anderson been more credulous he had not gone over, for I discouraged him from it all I could, believing a man of sedentary life, bred only to books and Philosophical lectures, which he afterwards Set-up in Carolina, would succeed but ill at the plough, and soon distast the labour and accidents attending such as settle in an infant Colony.

---

not have been catched with such promises, such prospects? What might not the poor man flatter himself with, from such an alteration in his situation? And how much more might a gentleman expect from a plentiful stock of his own, and numbers of servants to set up with? Could a person, with the least faith, have questioned the committing his interests to such guardians, and such a tender father as Mr. Oglethorpe was believed to be? Whether he has acted that generous, that human[e], that fatherly part, the following NARRATIVE must determine.

As for those poetical licences touching the wine and silk; we do not transcribe them as a reflection upon the author; but as a satyr upon the mismanagement of those manufactures; since no measures were taken that seemed really intended for their advancement.[8]

---

8. *No measures were taken* etc. Surely he forgets that on the 10 [20?] Aug. 1737 he wrote to me "that in general he was satisfied the prudent measures of the Trustees and supplies of the publick, would soon bring the Colony in great measure to answer the expectations of the Nation."

And that on the 15 June 1738 he wrote to Mr. Adam Anderson, that "the Trustees had with indefatigable labour, to their great honour chalked out the ways and means of making the designs of the Nation effectual: nay, such means as he doubted not would repay the present national advances with great advantage. I shall readily own, that the silk manufacture will in all probability in some time answer that End."

The confidence of this writer is astonishing; was there no seeming real intention in the Trustees to advance the silk, when they made himself Inspector and Overseer of the Mulberry Plantations at a sallary? did they not send with the first embarkation, an experienced silk man from Piedmont, and after him his brother? have they not from that time to this maintained a family of the same nation in the Province to instruct the people? is he ignorant that since numbers[?] of the white mulberry trees have been planted and have come to bear leaves for food to the worm, the quantity of silk made, annually encreases? and that the planting Mulberry trees is a condition in every Inhabitants Grant? That there is a premium given of 4 shillings p pound on Cocons or silk balls? That in every years Estimate, there is a sufficient sum appropriated for encouraging the silk, and that the number who propose to follow it encreases every day well satisfied with the Encouragement given? Does he not acknowledge in the above mention'd letters the prudence of the Trustees in general? or did he commence to complain till 4 months after he was turned out of his Employment for neglecting his duty?

As to neglect of encouragement for producing wine, see p. 38.

We no wise question the possibility of advancing such improvements in Georgia, with far less sums of money, properly applied, than the publick has bestowed. But not even the flourishing of wine and silk can make a colony of British subjects happy, if they are deprived of the liberties and properties of their birthright.[9]

---

9. This is an infamous suggestion: they have the liberties and properties of their birth right. What he clamours for is the use of negroes, the liberty to sell and take up land at will when and where he pleases, the choice of Magistrates independent of the Trustees etc. in a word to be on the foot of the other American Colonies, All of them inconsistent with the Peace and welfare of this infant and frontier Province, inhabited by Natives of different Countries, and where all sects of Religion, but Papists, are allowed. The exclusion of Negroes is by an Act past [passed] by his majesty on the most solid and necessary grounds, and the choice of Magistrates is in the Trustees by charter The Restrictions in their Grants were voluntarily submitted to by the Grantees. and have gradually been removed from time [them] as the circumstances of the Colony would admit of, in so much that by the confession of the Inhabitants themselves, several of whom were consulted therein, all reasonable men among them are, and ought to be satisfyed, for females may inherit, Possessors may bequeath to whom they please, and by gift, succession, marriage etc. enjoy 2000 acres of land. They may likewise lease during their life time for 21 years, which by taking a large fyne [tyne?] answers the End of selling, and all forfeitures have been remitted. After this, the Reader will judge whether the people are deprived of their liberties and properties of their birth-right.

After the Act against Negroes past [passed] 3. April 1735 and when the Restrictions were at the highest, the Grand Jury of Savannah in a presentment made 14 June 1736 declared as follows: "We are proud of being governed by laws made at London, the seat of the Legislature of Great Britain, and we are truly sensible of the happiness we enjoy, by having the Trustees our Representatives and Guardians, who under the immediate influence of his Majesties presence, are capable of providing laws for our good, without sacrificing us to factious schemes and corrupt gain of particular members, who too frequently sway the Assembly of small Colonies. We the Grand jury being sensible of the many advantages and benefits we enjoy under so happy a constitution and government think it our duty to request the Honble. Ja. Oglethorpe Esq, that he would be pleased to continue strenuously to put in execution those laws which have already been, or those which shall be for the future legally enacted by the kings most excellent Majesty in Council with the advice of the Trustees."

We have endeavoured to the utmost to be tender of characters; but as we undertake to write an account of facts and truths; there is no help for it, when those facts and truths press home.

It is a common satisfaction to sufferers, to expose to the publick the rocks upon which they split, and the misfortunes by which they suffered; and it may well be allowed us, to publish the causes to which we attribute the ruin of that settlement and ourselves; and more especially as we are prosecutors for justice from higher powers; which we doubt not receiving as the case deserves.

We hope the truth of the following NARRATIVE will recommend itself to the perusal of the candid reader. The fatal truth of this tragedy hath already been sealed with the death of multitudes of our fellow-creatures; but still (thanks to the providence of the Almighty) some survive to attest and confirm the truth of what is herein contained, against any persons or names, however great, however powerful. Our circumstances and sincerity will excuse our want of that politeness and accuracy of stile, which might have represented our case to greater advantage, to the courteous reader, whom we shall no longer detain from the subject in hand.

A True and

Historical Narrative, &c.

Nothing is more difficult for authors, than to divest themselves of byass and partiality, especially when they themselves are parties or sufferers in the affair treated of.

It is possible, this may be supposed the case with us the publishers of this *Narrative;* it may be imagined, that the hardships, losses, and disappointments we have met with in the colony of Georgia, will naturally sour our humours, and engage us to represent every thing in the worst light.

As the probability of those surmises is very obvious to us, we have, to the utmost of our power, guarded against the weak side of ourselves; and, to convince the world of our sincerity, shall no further descend into the grievances of particular persons, than is absolutely requisite for making our *General Narrative* intelligible; and to a faithful detail of publick vouchers, records, extracts, missives, memorials and representations,[10] shall only adjoin

---

10. Not faithfull

---

so much of history, as may be necessary to recount the most material events, and complete the connexion.

We are hopeful, that an information, founded upon the strictest truth,[11] will effectually introduce any further steps that Providence

---

11. Not founded on the strictest Truth, but on disguisement of the Truth, as will appear in many instances.

---

shall enable us to take towards procuring the redress of our grievances. While we had the least hopes of redress from our immediate superiors and patrons, we would not; and when we began to despair of relief by that channel, we durst not, make application to any other tribunal, unless we would expose ourselves to the dreadful effects of the resentment of those who had before reduced us to poverty by oppression: [12] And indeed, in all the applications

---

12. This very pamphlet shews they dare do anything, and as they say in the preface (p. 16) attest the truth of what is herein contained against any persons, or names, however great, however powerfull, which seems to aim higher than at the Trustees.

---

we made for redress, we were brow-beat, obstructed, threatened, and branded with opprobrious names, such as proud, idle, lazy, discontented and mutinous people,[13] and several other appellations of that kind; and were always afterwards harrassed by all means whatsoever; [14] several instances of which will appear to the

---

13. That they deserve this appelation of proud etc. is true: but who browbeat them etc. we do not know:
14. Neither do we know they were harrassed: but we know that they harrassed the Magistrates by defaming them, and personally abusing them: by despising their authority, assuming to themselves illegal powers, fomenting faction, petitioning against them, and encouraging a mutinous behaviour even in open court. The Trustees journals and letters from Georgia are full of this.

---

reader in the sequel.

Our late retreat from that confinement, to a *Land of Liberty,* puts it in our power to speak the truth; [15] and though our en-

---

15. They never were confined, tho they richly deserved it but did what they pleased, and went to Carolina without hindrance; they boast they may speak the Truth there, but had they spoke and acted in that land of liberty, as they did in Georgia, justice could have layn them by the heels.

---

deavours are too late to relieve the dead, the dying, and those many now dispersed in all the corners of His Majesty's dominions; yet they may be the means of ushering in sympathy and assistance to the survivors, and to multitudes of widows and orphans of the deceased, from the human[e] and generous.

As our sole design is to give a *plain narrative of the establishment and progress of the colony of Georgia, from its rise to its present period;* [16] we shall court no other ornaments than those of

---

16. Their design is more than this: it is to defame General Oglethorpe, the Magistrates, and the Trustees, to overturn the Plan of Goverment prudently laid down, pursuant to the Ends of his Majesties Charter, and confirmed by his laws, and by representing the Colony as already deserted, to persuade the Parliament and Nation that tis money thrown away to support it longer. To

this end, whilst in the Colony, they discouraged as many as they could from labour as fruitless, and while out of it, by speech and letters endeavour to prevail on whom ever they can, not to joyn the Colony, or to abandon it, as a Region of slavery and only to starve in, though they know the contrary to be true by the number of Inhabitants who express themselves contented with their condition, and the Government they live under. Thus Capt. William Thompson, a Freeholder of Savannah, who came lately from the Darien, declares that the Scotch Inhabitants assured him, they at no time were better contented with their condition: The Bailif also of Frederica, in his last letter to Capt. Horton, a Landholder on Jekyl Island, now here, acquaints him that since the departure of some turbulent spirits, the town is at perfect peace, and Col. Oglethorpe writes that they are falling earnestly upon planting vines, and Mulberry trees.

As to Augusta, these libellers acknowledge the town is in a flourishing way:

And the letters from Ebenezar continually repeat their Thanks to God for the blessings they enjoy and great success of their feild labours.

The German Trust servants who are out of their time or near it, have wrote, unknown to the Trustees, for more of their countrymen, assuring them they will live happy: They have agreed to form a vilage and labour in common. Some of them have 8 or 9 cows, hogs, poultry, etc. gained by parsimony during their servitude. The Town of Savannah only, inhabited by an idle profligate Race, produces a clamour for Negroes, and for absolute liberty to sell their lands, or morgage them, without which the Negroe merchant will not advance them slaves. Their vicinity to Carolina, where they hope to make a timely escape should their own Negroes rise upon them, and the being eased of labour themselves, together with an intention to follow the raising of Rice (which would much prejudice Carolina and divert the Georgians from raising silk and wine) and which yeilds a more immediate profit, have for some time been thought the real motives of these peoples complaint; but there is reason to fear they had a further view, namely to put an end to the Charter, and re-anex Georgia to Carolina, of which it formerly was part. For as divers Gentlemen of Carolina pretend a Title to lands in Georgia, as being run out by them before this last was erected into a separate Province, but which were forfeited for non-performance of Articles, those original owners might well hope to have their lost Titles confirm'd to them, if Instruments could be procured to sink the Credit of the Trustees, and make the World believe the Colony cannot subsist under their management, or the constitution by them layed down, and therefore that it would be necessary to make it part of Carolina again: What Instruments then so proper as those whose notions of life, and manners are the same with the Carolinians, and whose pride and poverty might be worked on with the expectation of offices or other rewards to serve that scheme, they esteeming themselves no longer Georgians but Carolinians. The Carolinians may also have some jealousie, that if Georgia should flourish she would in some years out do them in trade, as being more conveniently situated, and possest of better harbours: wherefore *delenda est Carthago.*

These are no vain surmises, as appears from the following extract, out of Col. Stephens journal.

June 24, 1740

"I accidentally met Mr. Williamson, who soon found something to say to me; and so we fell into discourse from one thing to another, wherein he took pains (as I thought) to make me believe, how much better opinion he had of Georgia, where he once lived, than he had of Carolina, where the business he was in (Provost Marshal) obliged him at present to reside: then he inveighed against the vanity of the Inhabitants, and the inveterate ill will they almost in general bore the Colony, which they would talk of with great contempt, tho at the same time, they were under strong apprehensions that in a few years it would out do them in trade and Manufactures too, who in such length of time had attained to nothing but Rice. I told him in my turn, that we were under no pain at several of our people deserting this place, last year particularly, most part of whom have experienced to their cost, some with the loss of their lives, what an unhappy change they made: some are escaped out of their misery there, and return'd to poor Georgia, glad to be admitted again to work for their bread among us, and one family or two more, as I am advised from them, are purposing the like, just now. I could not refrain from adding, that if we can be so happy, to get possession of Augustine, I did not doubt but we should quickly see some of the fine folks at Charlestown, looking out for a place to sit down in, more in the way of a Spanish and West India trade, than where they are, and might be glad to submit to the Constitution of Georgia, which so much pains had been taken to explode. He replyed, that he was firmly of that opinion, and what ever some might think of *him,* he would not quit what interest he had in land here for 200£ Sterl. Then he told me, that I guest [guessed] right in what I said; for that to his knowledge, several were hunting about for Titles of Grants of lands, run out here formerly, and among others, he said the Attorney General had sent his service to me by him, and advised me as a friend, not to be at any expence in making improvements as I was going on at my Plantation; for that he had a good Title to a large Tract of Land (I think he said a Barony) wherein mine which I held from the Trust was included."

But what puts it past doubt that Carolina purposes to reduce the two Provinces again into one, is a passage in the latest journal of Col. Stephens ending 28 Oct. 1741, received the 4th Feb 1741/2, wherein he informs the Trustees, that the Lt. Governor and Council of Carolina were projecting a petition to the King to send them some aid for their defence, for they did not look on Georgia, under the Regulations they now are, to be a defence, and intimating to him that it would be a benefit to both Provinces, if he would take Georgia into his own hands, and appoint a Governor and Council to direct all affairs.

Our Malecontents may flatter themselves that if this advice be followed, they shall be made Counsellors and obtain Employments, but Carolina must with better reason think, that if his Majesty should take Georgia into his own hands, he would sooner put it into their hands, than continue it a separate Government at considerable expence.

The manner Col. Stephens relates this affair, gives suspicion that this application from the Governor and Council of Carolina to his Majesty was concerted in England. His words are these:

Oct. 1. "In a little confabulation with my son, I learnt that the Lt. Governor and Council of Carolina were projecting a Petition to his Majesty, that he would please to send them some aid for their defence; for the[y] did not look upon Georgia under the Regulations that it now was, to be a Barrier against the Enemy; intimating farther their opinion, that it would conduce to the benefit of both these Provinces, if his Majesty would take the care of this Colony into his own hands, and appoint a Governour and Council to direct all Affairs, as in others of his Majesties Plantations. This indeed was so daring a piece of impudence to approach the Throne with, that I could not help thinking they durst not attempt it, unless it had been first concerted in England, in conjunction with some of the principal Fomenters of all our discord: Wherefore demanding peremptorily of my son, whether or not he came over to America charged by his Employers (among other things) with the promoting such a petition: He neither affirmed or denied it; from whence I concluded that it was so. I therefore purposed with my self, in my next letter to the Trust, to offer humbly some thoughts of mine upon it, hoping, without much difficulty, to shew from whence the danger arises which they are apprehensive of in Carolina (if they are really so affrighted) and the falsity of the grounds they go upon, with relation to the Want of a better Barrier etc."

Again, Oct. 6.

"I asked him only two or three questions, about some few steps he had lately taken, which apparently discovered a bad intent, and could produce nothing but mischief to Georgia: One more particularly I named, viz. his abetting that design which was a foot at Charlestown when he came thence (as before noted on Thursday last) whereupon I farther asked him, if he was so ignorant as not to know, that the principal view of that Province was to annihilate this, and reduce the Government of the whole under one, as it formerly had been; which if it would be effected, great part of the Lands near the Sea Coast, which had been formerly run out, would soon find Claimants to eject the present Possessors; among which lands, Ockstead [Oshstead?], Thunderbolt, all the Isle of Sheedeway, and the Isle of Hope, with the several settlements, together with Bethesda, Bewly[?], and divers others must all into their hands; to all which he could say little; and perceiving he had stirred me up to such a resentment as was due, he left me to recover as well as I could, the sedateness of mind I stood in need of, to prossecute what I had to do."

truth and perspicuity; and shall endeavour to carry the reader's attention regularly, from the first to the last motions we make mention of.

In the year 1732, His Majesty was pleased to erect, by his ROYAL CHARTER, into a separate province, distinct from South Carolina, that space of land lying between the rivers Savannah and Alatamaha, under the name of Georgia.

As this gracious Charter is the basis and foundation of all the transactions relating to this province, which have so much amused and perplexed the world, and which our endeavour is to set in a true light; we cannot dispense with inserting the Charter at large, which we are confident, for many reasons, will be acceptable to the reader.

"GEORGE THE SECOND, by the grace of God, of Great Britain, France, and Ireland, King, Defender of the Faith, &c. To all whom these presents shall come, greeting. *Whereas* we are credibly informed, that many of our poor subjects are, through misfortunes and want of employment, reduced to great necessity, insomuch as by their labour they are not able to provide a maintenance for themselves and families; and if they had means to defray their charges of passage, and other expenses incident to new settlements, they would be glad to settle in any of our provinces in America; where, by cultivating the lands at present waste and desolate, they might not only gain a comfortable subsistence for themselves and families; but also strengthen our colonies, and increase the trade, navigation and wealth of these our realms. And *whereas* our provinces in North America have been frequently ravaged by Indian enemies; more especially that of South Carolina; which in the late war, by the neighbouring savages, was laid waste by fire and sword, and great numbers of the English inhabitants miserably massacred; and our loving subjects who now inhabit there, by reason of the smallness of their numbers, will, in case of a new war, be exposed to the late calamities; inasmuch as their whole southern frontier continueth unsettled, and lieth open to the said savages. And *whereas* we think it highly becoming our Crown and Royal Dignity, to protect all our loving subjects, be they never so distant from us; to extend our fatherly compassion even to the meanest and most infatuate of our people, and to relieve the wants of our above mentioned poor subjects; and that it will be highly conducive for accomplishing those ends, that a regular colony of the said poor people be settled and established in the southern territories of Carolina. And *whereas* we have been well assured, that if we would be graciously pleased to erect and settle a corporation, for the receiving, managing and disposing of the contributions of our loving subjects; divers persons would be induced to contribute to the purposes aforesaid. *Know ye therefore,* that we have, for the consideration aforesaid, and for the better and more orderly carrying on the said good purposes, of our special grace, certain knowledge, and mere motion, willed, ordained, constituted and appointed, and by these presents, for us, our heirs and successors, do will, ordain, constitute, declare and grant, that our right trusty and well beloved John Lord Viscount Purcival, of our Kingdom of Ireland, our trusty and well beloved Edward Digby, George Carpenter, James Oglethorpe, George Heathcote, Thomas Tower, Robert Moor, Robert Hucks, Roger Holland, William Sloper, Francis Eyles, John Laroche, James Vernon, William Beletha, Esqrs., A. M. John Burton, B. D. Richard Bundy, A. M. Arthur Bedford, A. M. Samuel Smith, A. M. Adam Anderson and Thomas Coram, gentlemen, and such other persons as shall be elected in the manner herein after mentioned, and their successors to be elected in the manner herein after directed, be, and shall be one body politick and corporate, in deed and in name, by the name of *The Trustees for establishing the Colony of Georgia in America;* and them and their successors by the same name, we do, by these presents, for us, our heirs and successors, really and fully make, ordain, constitute and declare, to be one body politick in deed and in name forever; and that by the same name, they and their successors shall and may have perpetual succession; and that they and their successors, by that name, shall and may, forever hereafter, be persons able and capable in the law, to purchase, have, take, receive and enjoy, to them and their successors, any manors, messuages, lands, tenements, rents, advowsons, liberties, privileges, jurisdictions, franchises, and other hereditaments whatsoever, lying and being in Great Britain, or any part thereof, of whatsoever nature, kind or quality, or value they be, in fee and in perpetuity; not exceeding the yearly value of one thousand pounds, beyond reprises; also estates for lives, and for years; and all other manner of goods, chattels and things whatsoever they be; for the better settling and supporting, and maintaining the said colony, and other uses aforesaid; and to give, grant, let and demise the said manors, messuages, lands, tenements, hereditaments, goods, chattels and things whatsoever aforesaid, by lease or leases, for term of years, in possession at the time of granting thereof, and not in reversion, not exceeding the term of thirty-one years, from the time of granting thereof; on which, in case no fine be taken, shall be reserved the full; and, in case a fine be taken, shall be reserved at least a moiety of the value that the same shall, reasonably and bona fide, be worth at the time of such demise; and that they and their successors, by the name aforesaid, shall and may forever hereafter, be persons able, capable in the law, to purchase, have, take, receive and enjoy, to them and their successors, any lands, territories, possessions, tenements, jurisdictions, franchises and hereditaments whatsoever, lying and being in America, of what quantity, quality or value whatsoever they be, for the better settling and supporting, and maintaining the said colony; and that by the name aforesaid they shall and may be able to sue and be sued, plead and be impleaded, answer and be answered unto, defend and be defended in all courts and places whatsoever, and before whatsoever judges, justices and other officers, of us, our heirs and successors, in all and singular actions, plaints, pleas, matters, suits and demands, of what kind, nature or quality soever they be; and to act and do all other matters and things in as ample manner and form as any other our liege subjects of this realm of Great Britain; and that they and their successors, forever hereafter, shall and may have a common seal, to serve, for the causes and businesses of them and their successors; and that it shall and may be lawful for them and their successors, to change, break, alter and make new the said seal, from time to time and at their pleasure, as they shall think best. And we do further grant, for us, our heirs and successors, that the said corporation, and the Common Council of the said corporation hereinafter by us appointed, may from time to time, and at all times, meet about their affairs when and where they please, and transact and carry on the business of the said corporation. And for the better execution of the purposes aforesaid, we do, by these presents, for us, our heirs and successors, give and grant to the said corporation, and their successors, that they and their successors forever may, upon the third Thursday in the month of March yearly, meet at some convenient place to be appointed by the said corporation, or major part of them who shall be present at any meeting of the said corporation, to be had for the appointing of the said place; and that they, or two thirds of such of them that shall be present at such yearly meeting, and at no other meeting of the said corporation, between the hours of ten in the morning and four in the afternoon of the same day, choose and elect such person or persons to be members of the said corporation, as they shall think beneficial to the good designs of the said corporation. And our further will and pleasure is, that if it shall happen that any persons hereinafter by us appointed as the Common Council of the said corporation, or any other persons to be elected or admitted members of the said Common Council in the manner hereafter directed, shall die, or shall by writing under his and their hands respectively resign his or their office or offices of Common Council man or Common Council men; the said corporation, or the major part of such of them as shall be present, shall and may at such meeting, on the said third Thursday in March yearly, in manner as aforesaid, next after such death or resignation, and at no other meeting of the said corporation, into the room or place of such person or persons so dead or so resigning, elect and choose one or more such person or persons, being members of the said corporation, as to them shall seem meet: and our will is, that all and every the person or persons which shall from time to time hereafter be elected Common Council men of the said corporation as aforesaid, do and shall, before he or they act as Common Council men of the said corporation, take an oath for the faithful and due execution of their office; which oath the president of the said corporation for the time being, is hereby authorized and required to administer to such person or persons elected as aforesaid. And our will and pleasure is, that the first president of the said corporation is and shall be our trusty and well-beloved the said John Lord Viscount Purcival; and that the said president shall, within thirty days after the passing this Charter, cause a summons to be issued to the several members of the said corporation herein particularly named, to meet at such time and place as he shall appoint, to consult about and transact the businesses of the said corporation. And our will and pleasure is, and we, by these presents, for us, our heirs and successors, grant, ordain, and direct, that the Common Council of this corporation shall consist of fifteen in number; and we do, by these presents, nominate, constitute and appoint our right trusty and well-beloved John Lord Viscount Purcival, our trusty and beloved Edward Digby, George Carpenter, James Oglethorpe, George Heathcote, Thomas Laroche, James Vernon, William Beletha, Esqrs. and Stephen Hales Master of Arts, to be the Common Council of the said corporation, to continue in the said office during their good behaviour. And *whereas* it is our royal intention, that the members of the said corporation should be increased by election, as soon as conveniently may be, to a greater number than is hereby nominated; Our further will and pleasure is, and we do hereby, for us, our heirs and successors, ordain and direct, that from the time of such increase of the members of the said corporation, the number of the Common Council shall be increased to twenty-four; and

that, the same assembly at which such additional members of the
said corporation shall be chosen, there shall likewise be elected,
in the manner herein before directed for the election of Common
Council men, nine persons to be the said Common Council men,
and to make up the number, twenty-four. And our further will and
pleasure is, that our trusty and well-beloved Edward Digby, Esq:
shall be the first chairman of the Common Council of the said
corporation; and that the said Lord Viscount Purcival shall be
and continue president of the said corporation; and that the said
Edward Digby shall be and continue chairman of the Common
Council of the said corporation respectively, until the meeting
which shall be had next and immediately after the first meeting
of the said corporation, or of the Common Council of the said corporation respectively, and no longer: at which said second meeting, and every other subsequent and future meeting of the said
corporation, or of the Common Council of the said corporation
respectively, in order to preserve an indifferent rotation of the
several offices of president of the corporation, and of chairman of
the Common Council of the said corporation; we do direct and
ordain, that all and every the person and persons members of the
said Common Council for the time being, and no other, being
present at such meetings, shall severally and respectively, in their
turns, preside at the meetings which shall from time to time be held
of the said corporation, or of the Common Council of the said corporation respectively: And in case any doubt or questiton shall at
any time arise touching or concerning the right of any member of
the said Common Council to preside, at any meeting of the said corporation, or at the Common Council of the said corporation, the
same shall respectively be determined by the major part of the said
corporation, or of the Common Council of the said corporation
respectively, who shall be present at such meeting. Provided always, that no member of the said Common Council having served
in the offices of president of the said corporation, or of chairman
of the Common Council of the said corporation, shall be capable
of being or of serving as president or chairman at any meeting of
the said corporation or Common Council of the said corporation,
next and immediately ensuing that in which he so served as president of the said corporation, or chairman of the said Common
Council of the said corporation respectively; unless it shall so happen, that at any such meeting of the said corporation there shall not
be any other member of the said Common Council present. And
our will and pleasure is, that at all and every of the meetings of

the said corporation, or of the Common Council of the said corporation, the president or chairman for the time being, shall have a
voice and shall vote and shall act as a member of the corporation,
or of the Common Council of the said corporation, at such meeting;
and in case of any equality of votes, the said president or chairman
for the time being, shall have a casting vote. And our further will
and pleasure is, that no president of the said corporation, or chairman of the Common Council of the said corporation, or member
of the said Common Council or corporation, by us by these presents
appointed, or hereafter from time to time to be elected and appointed in manner aforesaid, shall have, take or receive, directly
or indirectly, any salary, fee, perquisite, benefit or profit whatsoever, for or by reason of his or their serving the said corporation,
or Common Council of the said corporation, or president, chairman or Common Council man, or as being a member of the said
corporation. And our will and pleasure is, that the said herein
before appointed president, chairman or Common Council men,
before he and they act respectively as such, shall severally take an
oath for the faithful and due execution of their trust, to be administered to the president by the Chief Baron of our Court of Exchequer, for the time being, and by the president of the said
corporation to the rest of the Common Council, who are hereby
authorized severally and respectively to administer the same. And
our will and pleasure is, that all and every person and persons who
shall have, in his or their own name or names, or in the name or
names of any person or persons in trust for him or them, or for his
or their benefit, any office, place or employment of profit, under
the said corporation, shall be incapable of being elected a member
of the said corporation; and if any member of the said corporation,
during such time as he shall continue a member thereof, shall in
his own name, or in the name of any person or persons in trust
for him, or for his benefit, have, hold, exercise, accept, possess or
enjoy any office, place or employment of profit under the said corporation, or under the Common Council of the said corporation;
such member shall from the time of his having, holding, exercising, accepting, possessing and enjoying such office, place and employment of profit, cease to be a member of the said corporation.
And we do, for us, our heirs and successors, grant unto the said
corporation and their successors, that they and their successors, or
the major part of such of them as shall be present at any meeting
of the said corporation, convened and assembled for that purpose
by a convenient notice thereof, shall have power from time to time

and at all times hereafter, to authorize and appoint such persons as they shall think fit, to take subscriptions, and to gather and collect such moneys as shall be by any person or persons contributed for the purposes aforesaid, and shall and may revoke and make void such authorities and appointments as often as they shall see cause so to do. And we do hereby, for us, our heirs and successors, ordain and direct, that the said corporation every year lay an account in writing before the chancellor or speaker or commissioners for the custody of the great seal of Great Britain, of us, our heirs and successors, the Chief Justice of the Court of King's Bench, the Master of the Rolls, the Chief Justice of the Court of Common Pleas, and the Chief Baron of the Exchequer, of us, our heirs and successors, for the time being, or any two of them, of all moneys and effects by them received or expended for the carrying on the good purposes aforesaid. And we do hereby, for us, our heirs and successors, give and grant, unto the said corporation and their successors, full power and authority to constitute, ordain and make such and so many by-laws, constitutions, orders and ordinances, as to them or the greater part of them, at their general meeting for that purpose, shall seem necessary and convenient for the well ordering and governing of the said corporation, and the said by-laws, constitutions, orders and ordinances, or any of them, to alter and annul as they or the major part of them then present shall see requisite; and in and by such by-laws, rules, orders and ordinances, to set, impose and inflict reasonable pains and penalties upon any offender or offenders who shall transgress, break or violate the said by-laws, constitutions, orders and ordinances, so made as aforesaid, and to mitigate the same as they or the major part of them then present shall think convenient; which said pains and penalties shall and may be levied, sued for, taken, retained and recovered by the said corporation and their successors, by their officers and servants from time to time to be appointed for that purpose, by action of debt, or by any other lawful ways or means, to the use and behoof of the said corporation and their successors; all and singular which by-laws, constitutions, orders and ordinances so as aforesaid to be made, we will, shall be duly observed and kept, under the pains and penalties therein to be contained; so always, as the said by-laws, constitutions, orders and ordinances, pains and penalties, from time to time to be made and imposed, be reasonable, and not contrary or repugnant to the laws or statutes of this our realm; and that such by-laws, constitutions and ordinances, pains and penalties, from time to time to be made and imposed;

and any repeal or alteration thereof, or any of them, be likewise agreed to, be established and confirmed by the said general meeting of the said corporation, to be held and kept next after the same shall be respectively made. And *whereas* the said corporation intend to settle a colony, and to make an habitation and plantation in that part of our province of South Carolina in America, herein after described; know ye, that, we, greatly desiring the happy success of the said corporation, for their further encouragement in accomplishing so excellent a work, have, of our 'foresaid grace, certain knowledge, and mere motion, given and granted, and by these presents, for us, our heirs and successors, do give and grant to the said corporation and their successors, under the reservation, limitation and declaration hereafter expressed, seven undivided parts, the whole in eight equal parts to be divided, of all those lands, countries, and territories, situate, lying and being, in that part of South Carolina, in America, which lies from the most northern part of a stream or river there, commonly called the Savannah, all along the sea coast to the southward, unto the most southern stream of a certain other great water or river, called the Alatamaha, and westerly from the heads of the said rivers respectively in direct lines to the South Seas; and all that share, circuit, and precinct of land within the said boundaries, with the islands on the sea lying opposite to the eastern coast of the said lands, within twenty leagues of the same, which are not inhabited already, or settled by any authority derived from the crown of Great Britain, together with all the soils, grounds, havens, ports, gulfs and bays, mines, as well royal mines of gold and silver, as other minerals, precious stones, quarries, woods, rivers, waters, fishings, as well royal fishings of whale and sturgeon, as other fishings, pearls, commodities, jurisdictions, royalties, franchises, privileges and preëminences, within the said frontiers and precincts thereof, and thereunto in any sort belonging or appertaining, and which we by our letters patents may or can grant; and in as ample manner and sort as we may, or any our royal progenitors have hitherto granted to any company, body politick or corporate, or to any adventurer or adventurers, undertaker or undertakers of any discoveries, plantations or traffick of, in, or unto any foreign parts whatsoever, and in as legal and ample manner, as if the same were herein particularly mentioned and expressed: To have, hold, possess and enjoy, the said seven undivided parts, the whole into eight equal parts, to be divided as aforesaid, of all and singular the lands, countries and territories, with all and singular other the premises herein before by these presents granted, or mentioned or intended to be granted to them the said corporation and their successors, for ever, for the better support of the said colony; to be holden of us, our heirs and successors, as of our honour of Hampton Court, in our county of Middlesex, in free and common soccage, and not in capite; yielding and paying thereenfor, to us, our heirs and successors, yearly for ever, the sum of four shillings for every hundred acres of the said lands which the said corporation shall grant, demise, plant or settle; the said payment not to commence, or to be made until ten years after such grant, demise, planting or settling, and to be answered and paid to us, our heirs and successors, in such manner, and in such species of money or notes, as shall be current in payment by proclamation, from time to time, in our said province of South Carolina; all which lands, countries, territories and premises hereby granted, or mentioned and intended to be granted, we do, by these presents, make, erect and create, one independent and separate province by the name of Georgia, by which name, we will, the same henceforth be called; and that all and every person or persons who shall at any time hereafter inhabit or reside within our said province, shall be and are hereby declared to be free, and shall not be subject to or be bound to obey any laws, orders, statutes or constitutions which have been heretofore made, ordered and enacted, or which hereafter shall be made, ordered or enacted by, for, or as the laws, orders, statutes or constitutions of our said province of South Carolina (save and except only the command in chief of the militia of our said province of Georgia, to our governor for the time being of South Carolina, in manner hereafter declared) but shall be subject to and bound to obey such laws, orders, statutes and constitutions as shall from time to time be made, ordered and enacted, for the better government of the said province of Georgia, in the manner hereafter declared. And we do hereby, for us, our heirs and successors, ordain, will and establish, that for and during the term of twenty-one years, to commence from the date of these our letters patents, the said corporation assembled for that purpose, shall and may form and prepare laws, statutes and ordinances, fit and necessary for and concerning the government of the said colony, and not repugnant to the laws and statutes of England, and the same shall and may present, under their common seal, to us, our heirs and successors, in our or their privy council, for our or their approbation or disallowance; and the said laws, statutes and ordinances being approved of by us, our heirs and successors, in our or their privy council, shall from thenceforth be in full force and virtue within our said province of Georgia. And forasmuch as the good and prosperous success of the said colony cannot but chiefly depend, next under the blessing of God and the support of our royal authority, upon the provident and good direction of the whole enterprize; and that it will be too great a burthen upon all the members of the said corporation, to be convened so often as may be requisite to hold meetings for the settling, supporting, ordering and maintaining the said colony: Therefore we do will, ordain and establish, that the said Common Council for the time being, of the said corporation, being assembled for that purpose, or the major part of them, shall from time to time, and at all times hereafter, have full power and authority to dispose of, extend and apply all the moneys and effects belonging to the said corporation, in such manner and ways, and by such expenses as they shall think best to conduce to the carrying on and effecting the good purposes herein mentioned and intended: and also, shall have full power, in the name and on the account of the said corporation, and with and under their common seal, to enter under any covenants or contracts for carrying on and effecting the purposes aforesaid. And our further will and pleasure is, that the said Common Council for the time being, or the major part of such Common Council, which shall be present and assembled for that purpose, from time to time, and at all times hereafter, shall and may nominate, constitute and appoint, a treasurer or treasurers, secretary or secretaries, and such other officers, ministers and servants of the said corporation, as to them, or the major part of them as shall be present, shall seem proper or requisite, for the good management of their affairs; and at their will and pleasure to displace, remove, and put out, such treasurer or treasurers, secretary or secretaries, and all such other officers, ministers and servants, as often as they shall think fit so to do, and others in the room, office, place, or station of him or them so displaced, removed or put out, to nominate, constitute and appoint; and shall and may determine and appoint such reasonable salaries, perquisites, and other rewards for their labour, or service of such officers, servants and persons, as to the said Common Council shall seem meet; and all such officers, servants and persons shall, before the acting their respective offices, take an oath, to be to them administered by the chairman for the time being of the said Common Council of the said corporation, who is hereby authorized to administer the same, for the faithful and due execution of their respective offices and places. And our will and pleasure is, that all such person and persons, who shall from time to time be chosen or appointed treasurer or treasurers, secretary or secretaries of the said corporation, in manner herein after directed, shall, during such times as they shall serve in the said offices respectively, be incapable of being a member of the said corporation. And we do further, of our special grace, certain knowledge and mere motion, for us, our heirs and successors, grant, by these presents, to the said corporation and their successors, that it shall be lawful for them and their officers or agents, at all times hereafter, to transport and convey out of our realm of Great Britain, or any other our dominions, into the said province of Georgia, to be there settled, and so many of our loving subjects, or any foreigners that are willing to become our subjects, and live under our allegiance in the said colony, as shall be willing to go to inhabit or reside there, with sufficient shipping, armour, weapons, power, shot, ordnance, munition, victuals, merchandise and wares, as are esteemed by the wild people, cloathing, implements, furniture, cattle, horses, mares, and all other things necessary for the said colony, and for the use and defence, and trade with the people there, and in passing and returning to and from the same. Also we do, for ourselves and successors, declare, by these presents, that all and every the persons which shall happen to be born within the said province, and every of their children and posterity, shall have and enjoy all liberties, franchises and immunities of free denizons and natural born subjects, within any of our dominions, to all intents and purposes, as if abiding and born within this our kingdom of Great Britain, or any other dominion. And for the greater ease and encouragement of our loving subjects, and such others as shall come to inhabit in our said colony, we do, by these presents, for us, our heirs and successors, grant, establish and ordain, that for ever hereafter, there shall be a LIBERTY OF CONSCIENCE allowed in the worship of God, to all persons inhabiting, or which shall inhabit, or be resident, within our said province, and that all such persons, except papists, shall have a free exercise of religion; so they be contented with the quiet and peaceable enjoyment of the same, not giving offence or scandal to the government. And our further will and pleasure is, and we do hereby, for us, our heirs and successors, declare and grant, that it shall and may be lawful for the said Common Council, or the major part of them assembled for that purpose, in the name of the corporation, and under the common seal, to distribute, convey, assign, and set over such particular portions of lands, tenements and hereditaments, by these presents granted to the said corporation, unto such of our loving subjects naturally born, or denizons, or others, that shall be willing to become our subjects, and live under our allegiance in the said colony, upon such terms, and for such estates, and upon such rents, reservations, and conditions, as the same may be lawfully granted, and as to the said Common Council, or the major part of them so present, shall seem fit and proper. Provided always, that no grants shall be made of any part of the said lands unto any person, being a member of the said corporation, or to any other person in trust, for the benefit of any member of the said corporation; and that no person having any estate or interest in law or equity, in any part of the said lands, shall be capable of being a member of the said corporation, during the continuance of such estate or interest. Provided also, that no greater quantity of lands be granted, either entirely or in parcels, to, or for the use, or in trust for any one person, than five hundred acres; and that all grants made contrary to the true intent and meaning hereof, shall be absolutely null and void. And we do hereby grant and ordain, that such person or persons for the time being, as shall be thereunto appointed by the said corporation, shall and may at all times, and from time to time hereafter, have full power and authority to administer and give the oaths appointed by an Act of Parliament made in the first year of the reign of our late royal father, to be taken instead of the oaths of allegiance and supremacy; and also the oath of abjuration, to all and every person and persons, which shall at any time be inhabiting or residing within our said colony; and in like cases to administer the solemn affirmation to any of the persons commonly called Quakers, in such manner as by the laws of our realm of Great Britain the same may be administered. And we do, of our further grace, certain knowledge and mere motion, grant, establish and ordain, for us, our heirs and successors, that the said corporation and their successors, shall have full power and authority, for and during the term of twenty-one years, to commence from the date of these our letters patents, to erect and constitute judicatures and courts of record, or other courts, to be held in the name of us, our heirs and successors, for the hearing and determining of all manner of crimes, offences, pleas, processes, plaints, actions, matters, causes and things whatsoever, arising or happening within the said province of Georgia, or between persons of Georgia; whether the same be criminal or civil, and whether the said crimes be capital or not capital, and whether the said pleas be real, personal, or mixed; and for awarding and making out executions thereupon; to which courts and judicatures, we do hereby, for us, our heirs and successors, give and grant full power and authority, from time to time, to administer oaths for the discovery of truth, in any matter in controversy, or depending before them, or the solemn affirmation to any of the persons commonly called Quakers, in such manner as by the laws of our realm of Great Britain the same may be administered. And our further will and pleasure is, that the said corporation, and their successors, do from time to time and at all times hereafter, register or cause to be registered all such leases, grants, plantings, conveyances, settlements and improvements whatsoever, as shall at any time hereafter be made, by, or in the name of the said corporation, of any lands, tenements or hereditaments, within the said province; and shall yearly send and transmit, or cause to be sent or transmitted, authentick accounts of such leases, grants, conveyances, settlements and improvements respectively, unto the auditor of the plantations for the time being, or his deputy, and also to our surveyor for the time being of our said province of South Carolina, to whom we do hereby grant full power and authority from time to time, as often as need shall require, to inspect and survey such of the said lands and premises as shall be demised, granted and settled, as aforesaid, which said survey and inspection, we do hereby declare, to be intended to ascertain the quit-rents which shall from time to time become due to us, our heirs and successors, according to the reservations herein before mentioned, and for no other purposes whatsoever; hereby, for us, our heirs and successors; strictly enjoining and commanding, that neither our or their surveyor, or any person whatsoever, under the pretext and color of making the said survey or inspection, shall take, demand, or receive, any gratuity, fee or reward, of, or from, any person or persons, inhabiting in the said colony, or from the said corporation, or Common Council of the same, on the pain of forfeiture of the said office or offices, and incurring our highest displeasure. Provided always, and our further will and pleasure is, that all leases, grants and conveyances to be made by or in the name of the said corporation, of any lands within the said province, or a memorial containing the substance and effect thereof, shall be registered with the auditor of the said plantations, of us, our heirs and successors, within the space of one year, to be computed from the date thereof, otherwise the same shall be void. And our further will and pleasure is, that the rents, issues, and all other profits, which shall at any time hereafter come to the said corporation, or the major part of them, which shall be present at any meeting for that purpose assembled, shall think will most improve and enlarge the said colony, and best answer the good purposes herein before mentioned, and for defraying all other charges about the same. And our will and pleasure is, that the said corporation, and their successors, shall, from time to time, give in to one of the principal secretaries of state, and to the commissioners of trade and plantations, accounts of the progresses of the said colony. And our will and pleasure is, that no act done at any meeting of the said Common Council of the said corporation, shall be effectual and valid, unless eight members, at least of the said Common Council, including the member who shall serve as chairman at the said meeting, be present, and the major part of them consenting thereunto. And our will and pleasure is, that the Common Council of the said corporation for the time being, or the major part of them, who shall be present, being assembled for that purpose, shall, from time to time, for, and during, and unto the full end and expiration of twenty-one years, to commence from the date of these our letters patents, have full power and authority to nominate, make, constitute, commission, ordain and appoint, by such name or names, stile or stiles, as to them shall seem meet and fitting, all and singular such governors, judges, magistrates, ministers and officers, civil and military, both by sea and land, within the said districts, as shall by them be thought fit and needful to be made or used for the said government of the said colony; save always, and except such officers only, as shall by us, our heirs and successors, be from time to time constituted and appointed, for the managing and collecting and receiving such revenues, as shall from time [to time] arise within the said province of Georgia, and become due to us, our heirs and successors. Provided always, and it is our will and pleasure, that every governor of the said province of Georgia, to be appointed by the Common Council of the said corporation, before he shall enter upon, or execute the said office of governor, shall be approved by us, our heirs, or successors, and shall take such oaths, and shall qualify himself in such manner in all respects, as any governor or commander in chief of any of our colonies or plantations in America, are by law required to do; and shall give good and sufficient security for observing the several acts of Parliament relating to trade and navigation; and to observe and obey all instructions that shall be sent to him by us, our heirs and successors, or any acting under our or their authority, pursuant to the said acts, or any of them. And we do, by these presents, for us, our heirs and successors, will, grant and ordain, that the said corporation and their successors, shall have full power, for, and during, and until the full end and term of twenty-one years, to commence from the date of these our letters patents, by any commander, or other officer or officers by them for that purpose, from time to time appointed, to train, instruct, exercise and govern, a militia, for the special defence and safety of our said colony, to assemble in martial array the inhabitants of the said colony, and to lead and conduct them, and with them to encounter, expulse, repel, resist and pursue, by force of arms, as well by sea as by land, within or without the limits of our said colony; and also to kill, slay and destroy, and conquer, by all fighting ways, enterprizes and means whatsoever, all and every such person or persons, as shall at any time hereafter, in any hostile manner, attempt or enterprize the destruction, invasion, detriment, or annoyance, of our said colony; and to use and exercise the martial law in time of actual war and invasion, or rebellion, in such cases where by law the same may be used or exercised; and also from time to time to erect forts, and fortify any place or places within our said colony, and the same to furnish with all necessary ammunition, provisions, and stores of war, for offence and defence, and so commit, from time to time, the custody or government of the same, to such person or persons as to them shall seem meet; and the said forts and fortifications to demolish at their pleasure; and to take and surprize, by all ways and means, all and every such person or persons, with their ship, arms, ammunition and other goods, as shall in an hostile manner invade, or attempt the invading, conquering or annoying of our said colony. And our will and pleasure is, and we do hereby, for us, our heirs and successors, declare and grant, that the governor and commander in chief of the province of South Carolina, of us, our heirs and successors, for the time being, shall, at all times hereafter, have the chief command of the militia of our said province hereby erected and established; and that such militia shall observe and obey all orders and directions that shall from time to time be given or sent to them, by the said governor or commander in chief, any thing in these presents before contained, to the contrary hereof, in any wise notwithstanding. And, of our more special grace, certain knowledge and mere motion, we have given and granted, and by these presents, for us, our heirs and successors, do give and grant unto the said corporation, and their successors, full power and authority to import and export their goods, at, and from any port or ports, that shall be appointed by us, our heirs and successors, within the said province of Georgia for that purpose, without being obliged to touch at any other port in South Carolina. And we do, by these presents, for us, our heirs and successors, will and declare, that from and after the determination of the said term of one and twenty years, such form of government and method of making laws, statutes and ordinances, for the better governing and ordering the said province of Georgia, and the inhabitants thereof, shall be established and observed within the same, as we, our heirs and successors, shall hereafter ordain and appoint, and shall be agreeable to law; and that, from and after the determination of the said term of one and twenty years, the governor of our said province of Georgia, and all officers civil and military within the same, shall from time to time be nominated, and constituted, and appointed by us, our heirs and successors. And lastly, we do hereby, for us, our heirs and successors, grant unto the said corporation, and their successors, that these our letters patents, or the enrolments or exemplification thereof, shall be in, and by all things, good, firm, valid, sufficient, and effectual in the law, according to the true intent and meaning thereof, and shall be taken, construed, and adjudged, in all courts, and elsewhere, in the most favourable and beneficial sense, and for the best advantage of the said corporation and their successors, any omission, imperfection, defect, matter or cause or thing whatsoever to the contrary in any wise notwithstanding. In witness we have caused these our letters to be made patents. Witness ourself at Westminster, the ninth day of June, in the fifth year of our reign.

By writ of privy seal.

COOKS.

The gracious purposes and ample privileges, contained in the foregoing Charter, are so obvious to every reader, that we need only say, they were suitable to a most generous and humane British monarch; and had the settlement of the colony of Georgia been carried on conformable thereto,[17] and no other restrictions or reservations made, than what are therein mentioned; [18] then would

---

17. The Plan the Trustees laid down is entirely conformable to the Intent of the Charter, namely to make Georgia a defensible Frontier, and a refuge to unfortunate persons.

18. *No other restrictions and reservations made etc.* Is it possible a Colony and Civil Government should subsist without some particular restrictions and reservations, not mentioned in the general provisions of the Charter? His Majesty thought fit to pass some laws since the Charter, whereby the Inhabitants are restrained from the use of Negroes, from the use of Rum, and from Trading with the Indians without Lycence; all which had the approbation

of the Attorney General the Board of Trade, and Privy Council: but it seems these men are for being under no restriction.

---

the colony, at this time, have been in a flourishing condition, answerable to all those glorious ends that were proposed and expected from it: But on the contrary, laws and restrictions being made, such as were never heard of in any British settlement, the colony is brought to the present melancholy situation.[19] But we shall say

---

19. *Such as were never heard of etc.* This is an open attack upon the prudence of his Majesty and Council, and an appeal to the Publick against him, for having past [passed] laws to the ruin of the Colony.

---

no more at present on this head, than what Mr. Oglethorpe said in Parliament relating to the charitable corporation, viz. [*Vide* Lond. Mag. p. 379.]: *The better the design was, the more those deserve to be punished who have disappointed the publick of reaping the benefits that might have accrued from it.*[20]

Inhabitants of all sorts, Roman Catholicks only excepted, from all parts of the world, were invited to possess this *promised land*,[21]

---

20. Since these laws and restrictions have disappointed the Publick from reaping the benfits that might have accrued from the Colony, and since they who made them deserve to be punished, the Reader will judge of the spirit of these men, and whether they themselves may not be punished for carrying their accusation so high.

21. *This promised land:* The Industrious Inhabitants and particular[ly] the foreigners have found it so: this low malicious sneer upon the Colony deserves contempt; Mr. Fitzwalter a Freeholder and gardiner expresly calls it so in a letter to the Trustees 16 Jan. 1734–5.

---

and large sums of money from the Parliament, as well as contributions from private and publick charity, were collected; the country was laid out as an *Earthly Paradise*, the soil far surpassing that of England; the air healthy, always serene, pleasant and temperate, never subject to excessive heat or cold, nor to sudden changes.

It was particularly set forth, and with a shew of reason enough, that this proposed settlement could not fail of succeeding, when the nation was so *bountiful;* the King so *gracious* [*Vide* a pamphlet, entitled, *A New and Accurate Account of the Provinces of South Carolina and Georgia.*]; the Trustees so *disinterested* and *honourable,* who had, for the benefit of mankind, given up that ease and indolence to which they were entitled by their fortunes and the too prevalent custom of their native country; and withal, being able, by seeing the mistakes and failures of other colonies, both to avoid and rectify them; and lastly, the universal report of Mr. Ogle-thorpe's matchless *humanity* and *generosity*, who was to conduct the first embarkation, and who was, in all appearance, to undergo the greatest hardships, without any other view than to succour the distressed; and, despising interest or riches, was to venture his life, his all, in establishing the intended settlement. *Glorious presages* of the future happiness of that colony! *Irresistible temptations* to those, whose genius or circumstances led them to leave their native country!

No wonder then, that great numbers of poor subjects, who lay under a cloud of misfortunes, embraced the opportunity of once more tasting liberty and happiness; that Jews, attracted by the temptation of inheritances, flocked over; that Germans, oppressed and dissatisfied at home, willingly joined in the adventure, some as settlers, and others as servants to the Trustees; and lastly, that great numbers of gentlemen [22] of some stock and fortune,[23] willingly expended part of the same, in purchasing servants,[24] tools, com-

---

22. *Great numbers of Gentlemen* etc. Lots above 50 acres were called Gen-tlemens lots, and those who took them assumed that Title, tho most of them were broken Tradesmen, and artisans: The whole number of this kind of gentry who took larger lots than 50 acres, were from the beginning of the Colony but 77, of which 20 Owners never set foot in the Colony, 3 never took up land, and 2 staid no time in it. So that deducting 25 from 77, there remains but 52, of whom 5 fled for felony and debt, and 9 died: which 14 deducted, leaves a remainder of only 38, some of whom went not from England, but joyned the Colony from other American Provinces. This is the boasted numbers of gentlemen, whom this writer says were *all* disappointed, tho he knows that some of them make no complaint at all, except of these complainants.

23. *Some Stock and fortune* etc. I don't believe there was one worth more than he could carry about him: at least Two of these 3 Authors were no sooner arrived than they desired subsistance from the stores, which was destined only for those who were sent on the charity.

24. What they call purchasing servants was only contracting with them, and they made a good hand of them by hiring them out to others at daily pay, whereby they maintained both servant and Master whilst their time lasted, in an extravagant manner of life. Among these was Patrick Tailfer, one of the authors of this scurrilous pamphlet.

When Lt. Col. Cochran came over from Georgia in April 1739 he acquainted the Trustees that it was a misfortune they ever admitted into the Colony such as call themselves Gentlemen, or any who carryed servants, for they were generally the idlest, giving an ill example to others, spending their money in Alehouses etc.

The same account was given to the Trustees by Robt. Howes a Freeholder. In june 1739, and "that it was a great misfortune the Scots left their Country Lots to live in town, where they set an example of extravagance, and brought in their servants to work, which lessened the Employment of the natural townsmen. That the Free Mason company met every Satturday at the Tavern, and reveled there till 2 a clock next morning, when they reeled home."

Col. Stephens gives the following account of these Freemasons annual procession 25 June 1739. "From Church they marched in solemn order to dinner at a Publick house: The warden, Dr. Tailfer (who likes pre-eminance as well as any man) attended by 4 or 5 wards[,] and red-ribbons in their bosoms, as badges of their several offices, took place formost: but the train that followed, amounted but to about half a dozen more, which some who are apt to burlesque the order turned into ridicule."

See more of the Scotch Gentrys behaviour p. 44 & 54.

---

modities and other necessaries, to *intitle* them to such respective proportions of land, as the Trustees had thought proper to determine,[25] and such liberties and properties as they had reason to

---

25. *Such respective portions of land* etc. This is said to make the reader believe the people had not the acres they desired: on the contrary they had as many as they applyed for, as far as 500 acres, which is the utmost the Charter allows to be granted to One Man.

---

expect from His Majesty's most gracious Charter: but how much they were all disappointed, the sequel will shew. The first thing that was done, was the circumscribing the rights and titles given by His Majesty, and making many other various restrictions, services and conditions, impossible for any human person to *perform;* [26] a few of which we shall here enumerate: In the first place, there was an excessive quit-rent laid upon the land,[27] being a great deal

---

26. They made no objections when they took their grants.
27. *An excessive quit-rent* etc. The Truth is here partially related: for none of the freehold lots (which are infinitely more numerous than the Land-holds) pay a farthing more than is paid in the other Colonies. This deceitfull and ambiguous manner of relating things runs through the whole pamphlet.

---

more than His Majesty's subjects in the other British colonies pay, viz. twenty shillings sterling for every hundred acres, to be paid yearly,[28] and if it, or any part thereof, should be behind and un-

---

28. This as has been said touches only the larger Grants; and they were to hold their land free of quitrent 10 compleat years. The oldest settler of these 3 Authors was not to commence paying quitrent till the year 1745. But surely, since industrious men keep a family and several children on 5

acres, it is no hard rent to pay 2·¼d for an acre of these gentlemens lots, after 10 years time to cultivate it.

paid by the space of six calendar months next after any day or payment on which the same became due, then the land was forfeited and returned to the Trustees,[29] as it likewise did upon fail-

29. *The land was forfeited* etc. Is not 6 months time for paying so inconsiderable a quit-Rent sufficient? Besides it was necessary to secure his Majesty's dutys.

ure in any of the following conditions, viz. one thousand mulberry trees always to be growing on every hundred acres,[30] no partnership or company to be entered into for making pot-ash,[31] not to assign or transfer the land,[32] or any part or parcel thereof, or any estate or

30. *One thousand Mulberry trees always to be growing* etc. This shews the care the Trustees had to introduce the silk, and the most proper and liklyest to succeed when required so severly [*sic*], yet they have the confidence to say the Trustees took none that was proper.

31. There was a set of persons who went over with intention to make pot ash, which being an expensive as well as advantagious undertaking, it was thought proper to grant them an exclusive lycense for a term of years, as is frequently done in England: but private men (not in company) were not hinderd to follow it. Besides the Lycence is expired as these writers know, who by the manner they relate it would have it thought that the Trustees would have no pot ash at all made.

32. *Not to assign* etc. Had this been allowed, there had nothing but buying and selling and jobbing their properties, been seen, and the lands had layn uncultivated, and 4 or 5 rich Carolinians would have bought up as many 50 acre lots as would amount to 500, and this Province designed for a frontier deprived of Inhabitants.

interest in the same, for any term of years; not to hire, keep, lodge, board or employ, within the limits of the province, any black or Negro; and if the person holding land should die without issue male, or his heirs at any time should die without issue male, in that case likewise, the whole land was forfeited and reverted to the Trustees; and if any part or parcel of any of the five hundred acre tracts, should remain not cultivated, cleared, planted and improved, after the space of eighteen years,[33] such part to return to the

33. This and all other forfeitures have been remitted, as these authors know.

Trustees. These were the chief restrictions in all the grants of lands, which appeared very hard even to strangers, who had not yet felt them,[34] and who were ignorant of the climate and nature of the

34. How could any one feel what was not to be felt till 1744 at the soonest? Mr. Anderson could not suffer by these restrictions till 1748.

place; but when any one complained of the hardships of them, to palliate the matter, it was given out, that Negroes were entirely useless and unprofitable, wine, silk, olives, gardens and manufactures for women and children, were the intended improvements of the colony,[35] that the restrictions of the rights of lands, were only temporary, to prevent the bartering or selling them by the unthinking people, at an undervalue,[36] and concerning the want

35. It is confessedly true that Negroes are not wanting for these purposes.
36. This is likewise true, and the Inhabitants have found it so: all those restrictions being taken off, except that of selling in their life time, which must not be suffered. see p. 27. note 8.

of male issue, it was asserted, that the Trustees, being duly petitioned would grant continuation of the land to the eldest daughter,[37] if any, &c. upon their good behavior [How precarious must this security be to such unfortunate persons, when their behaviour must be judged of by information and representation?]: [38] that

37. This true also, nor was it ever denied to those who applyed.
38. How should the Trustees judge of persons behaviour at that distance but by information and Representation? They have a Majestracy, a Court of Law, and a Trustee on the spot.

the *laws of England,* and the *administration of justice,* in the most impartial manner, and most adapted to the nature of *a free British government,* should be ever secured to the inhabitants.[39]

39. True also, consistent with a free American Colony, Inhabited by British Subjects: but are they less free for voluntarily submitting to local regulations?

The first of February, 1732-3, Mr. Oglethorpe arrived at Georgia with the first embarkation, consisting of forty families making upwards of one hundred persons, all brought over and supported at the publick charge. The first thing he did after he arrived in Georgia, was to *make* a kind of *solemn treaty* with a parcel of *fugitive Indians,* who had been formerly banished their own nation for some crimes and misdemeanours they had committed,[40] and

40. *a kind of solemn Treaty* etc. These Indians (whom they please to call

fugitives) are a very brave and prudent people, and the crime for which they were expelled, was cutting down a Popish Chappel, which the french were endeavouring to erect, with design to convert it into a Fort. They were proprietors of the land whereon Mr. Oglethorpe proposed to settle, and might have hindered his landing if they had pleased. They yeilded to him a great tract of land, and have ever since been usefull in preserving the friendship of divers other nations to Great Britain. Supposing they had leave from Carolina to settle there, which very likely is not true (since these Authors are capable of advancing for Truth any thing they please) Mr. Oglethorpe could not honestly dispossess them otherwise than by Treaty.

---

who had, some months before this, got liberty from the governor of South Carolina, to settle there. [They built a small number of huts [41] on a bluff called Yamacraw. Savannah now stands on the

---

41. *Small number of Huts* etc. Huts among the Indians are not like those in England built for a single family, but contain a much greater number of persons.

---

same bluff]. Some of these he afterwards carried home with him under the *title* of *kings* [42] &c. and all of them have been ever since maintained at the publick charge, at vast expense,[43] when many poor Christians were starving in the colony for want of bread; [44]

---

42. *Title of Kings* etc. One only was so entitled, which was Tomochachi, acknowledged king by all the neighbouring Indian Nations. They call the chief of every nation so, and the English every where allow it them.

43. *All of them have ever since been maintained at the publick charge at vast expence* etc. And so they must be: they are a kind of Swiss who fight on any side for pay, and if not engaged on ours, will go over to the French, who make the Indians much larger presents than we do, even as far as 2000£ at a time. All our Plantations are obliged to treat their friendly Indians after this manner, but the Trustees are more particularly obliged to it, as it is an Infant Colony, and so nearly situated both to the Spaniards and french. This being the case, it appears a malicious accusation of the Trustees to ascribe a fault to them in making the Indians an allowance, and this at a vast expence; when an unprejudiced man would be more disposed to believe they purchassed their friendship on the best terms they could.

44. *When many poor Christians* etc. Here is another malicious insinuation that the Trustees prefer the Indians to the English Inhabitants, whereas they were so far from letting these last starve for want of bread, that altho they were obliged by contract to maintain them one year only, yet they continued the same, to some a year more, to others two. But at length, being obliged to stop their hand, the idle, who whilst subsisted would not work, and had neg-

lected to make provision for themselves in time, abandoned the Colony crying out they were starved.

and we may safely affirm (and appeal to the storebooks for the truth
of it) that a larger sum of money has been expended for the support of those *useless vagrants*,[45] than ever was laid out [46] for the

45. *Idle vagrants* etc. All Indians hunt part of the year at a great distance,
but afterwards return home, they must be vagrants after this manner, or the
Indian trade would be worth nothing. The Indians here spoken of do the
same, and they are only called idle, to make the world believe we maintain
them in idleness.

46. *Than ever was laid out* etc. Tis no wonder that the necessary maintenance
of an Indian nation should cost more in 9 years and half than the encouragement of silk and wine in 2 years: for till the Mulberry trees were grown, and
the people were enterd on production of vines, which they were but lately
persuaded to, encouragements had no room given them. But this may be
affirmed, that encouragement has not been wanting when and where necessary.

encouragement of silk, wine, or any other manufacture in the
colony.

Secondly, he *prohibited* the *importation* of *rum*,[47] under pre-

47. *He prohibited the use of Rum* etc. What ever doubt may be raised of
the expediency of prohibiting Rum, it is sufficient that his Majesty and Council,
and the Board of trade approved it, and a law being past [passed] by his
Majesty to that purpose, the Trustees cannot repeal it. This law was made
at the Indians desire.

tence, that it was destructive to the constitution, and an incentive
to debauchery and idleness: However specious these pretences
might seem, a little experience soon convinced us, that this restriction was directly opposite to the well-being of the colony: for
in the first place, we were cut off from the most immediate and
probable way of exporting our timber (the only poor prospect of
export that we could ever flatter ourselves with) to the Sugar Islands, rum being the principal return they make: In the second
place, the experience of all the inhabitants of America will prove
the necessity of *qualifying water with some spirit,* and it is very
certain, that no province in America yields water, that such a
qualification is more necessary to, than Carolina and Georgia [48]

48. *the experience of all the Inhabitants* etc. What is here said of the water
of Savannah, is absolutely false, the town abounds with fine springs of water.
See Mr. Christies account of the Colony in print. There is besides a well of

excellent water. See Mr. Oglethorpes letter dated Dec. 1733. We have exceeding fine water at Savannah. Mr. Jones to Mr. Lyde 15 Sept. 1740

and the usefulness of this experiment has been sufficiently evident to all the inhabitants of Georgia who could procure *it,* and use *it* with moderation: A third reason which made this restriction very hurtful to the colony, was, that though the laws were in force against it (which put it in the power of magistrates to lay hardships upon every person who might be *otherwise* under *their resentment*) yet great quantities were imported, [Viz.: from Carolina and New England, who would take money only.] only with this difference, that, in place of barter or exchange, the ready money was drained from the inhabitants: and likewise, as it is *the nature of mankind* in general, and of the *common sort* in particular, more *eagerly* to desire, and more *immoderately* to use those things which are most restrained from them, such was the case with respect to rum in Georgia.

The third thing he did,[49] was regularly to *set out* to each free-

49. The intention of this paragraph is to expose Mr. Oglethorpe's judgment in laying out the town of Savannah, which others much commended.

holder in Savannah lots of fifty acres, in three distinct divisions, viz. the eighth part of one acre for a house and garden in the town; four acres and seven-eighths, at a small distance from town; and forty-five acres at a considerable remove from thence. No regard was had to the *quality* of the ground in the divisions,[50] so that

50. *No regard was had* etc. It could not be otherwise but that in laying out a regular town, some land would be worse than other, but it is certain many who had the best land cultivated nothing, being shopkeepers, Handy craftmen and the like, who knew nothing of it, and got more immediate Profit by their business than by cultivation.

some were altogether pine barren, and some swamp and morass, far surpassing the strength and ability of the planter: and indeed, what could be done at any rate, with such small parcels of land separate from one another: These lots were likewise shaped in long pointed triangles, which considerably increased the extent of inclosure, and rendered great part of each lot entirely useless. But these and many other hardships were scarcely felt by the few people that came there, so long as Mr. Oglethorpe staid, which was about fifteen months:[51] They worked hard indeed, in building

51. *But these and many other hardships* etc. It seems every thing right or wrong is with these men a hardship, altho they scarcely felt their hardships

for 15 months, nor long after, when in June 1736 the Grand jury declared they were truly sensible of the happiness they enjoyed, (vid. p. 16 of the preface) to which two of the Authors of this pamphlet subscribed their names; and when the third, Mr. Anderson, commended the prudent measures of the Trustees, and their honourable chalking out the ways and means of making the designs of the nation effectual. (vid. p. 15 of the preface) 15 June 1738[?].

---

some houses in town; but then they laboured in common, and were likewise assisted by Negroes from Carolina,[52] who did the heaviest work: But at Mr. Oglethorpe's going to England. [Before he departed, a vessel with about twenty families of Jews arrived,[53]

---

52. *And were likewise assisted by Negroes,* etc. There were then but 40 families there and it was necessary to make what hast[e] they could to build their houses.

53. *Twenty families of jews:* The whole number of souls were but 43. Mr. Oglethorpe was displeased at their coming, and took advice of Lawyers in Carolina whether he could not send them away, which they said he could not. They had a good Physitian with them and behaved so well as to their morals, peacableness and charity, that they were a reproach to the Christian Inhabitants.

---

all of whom had lots assigned them; and likewise a vessel with forty transported Irish convicts, whom he purchased, although they had been before refused at Jamaica, and who afterwards occasioned continual disturbances in the colony],[54] the growing fame of the colony

---

54. *Forty transported Irish Convicts whom he purchased* etc. The best and most human actions are by these malicious writers calumniated. That these Irish were Transports convict is more than we know, or that they were refused at Jamaica. Thousands of Irish at that time transported themselves to the Plantations, to be indented servants to Masters who should pay their passage, and these were probably of that sort, For the freight of such persons from Europe was at that time 5£ p head, and so much Mr. Oglethorpe paid the Master of the Vessel. It is farther to be observed, that these people arrived the first year the Colony was begun to be settled, when but 40 English capable to bear arms were yet come over, being the first embarkation that attended Mr. Oglethorpe, and they were judged an usefull recruit to assist those English in making their settlements. Take Mr. Oglethorpes account of this matter in his letter to the Trustees, dated from Savannah Dec. 1733.

"A sloop loaded with servants was forced in here through stress of weather, and want of victuals. Many of them were dead, 40 only remained. As they were likewise ready to perish through misery, I thought it an act of charity to buy them, which I did, giving 5£ a head. I gave one of them to each of the widows, which will render them able to cultivate their lands and maintain their families. I let each of the Magistrates have one at prime cost, that they might not be behind hand[s] in their gardens and Plantations by reason of their spending much of their time in the Publick Service. I have allotted Mr. La Fond 5 to help him in building a saw mill: 4 to the gardens, and 4 to the Island. I have drawn 200£ on you, being the payment for them."

was thereby greatly increased, so that, as it has been before observed, people, in abundance, from all parts of the world, flocked to Georgia.[55] Then they began to consider and endeavour, every one according to his genius or abilities, how they might best subsist themselves. Some, with great labour and expence,[56] essayed the

55. *from all parts of the world etc.* false, No foreigners, but perhapps some from Carolina and the neighbouring Provinces.
56. *Some with great labour and expense etc.* Few that ever the Trustees heard of, but perhaps Mr. Causton, attempted the making Tar.

making of tar [Mr. Causton, the Trustees' store keeper, mostly at their charge, made a tar kiln, which turned out to no advantage.]: This, as tis well known to the Trustees, never quitted costs: [57]

57. *Making of Tar etc.* Without the bounty no Tar would come from America. In Feb. 1735/6 there came from Georgia 64 hogsheads and 112 barrils of Tar which being sould did not quit freight and charges because for want of certificate from a proper officer the bounty was refused. Was it a fault to attempt usefull things?

Others tried to make plank and saw boards; which, by the great price they were obliged to sell them at, by reason of the great expence of white servants, was the chief means of ruining those who thought to procure a living by their buildings in town; [58] for boards

58. Sawyers and Carpenters were themselves Freeholders and built their own houses: those they built for others were at a fixt rate, and the general price of a house was 20£, which when let yeilded from 10 to 20£ a year. And Douglass one of the 3 Authors of this pamphlet let his house for half a year at 20£.

of all kinds could always be bought in Carolina, for half the price that they were able to sell them at; but few were capable to commission them from thence, and those, who were so, were prevented from doing it, upon pretence of discouraging the labour of white people in Georgia. Those who had numbers of servants and tracts of land in the county, went upon the planting of corn, peas, potatoes, &c., and the charge of these, who succeeded the best, so far exceeded the value of the produce, that it would have saved three fourths to have bought all from the Carolina market.[59] The fall-

59. Will it be believed that an industrious man whose land costs him nothing and whose labour is his own, cannot raise corn for himself as cheap as to buy it in another Province?

ing of timber was a task very unequal to the strength and constitution of white servants; and the hoeing the ground, they being exposed to the sultry heat of the sun, insupportable;[60] and it is well known, that this labour is one of the hardest upon the Negroes,[61] even though their constitutions are much stronger than

60. The Falling of timber etc is not too hard labour for white men, as is proved to the Trustees by several affidavits, and by the successfull labours of the Saltsburgers, who petitioned against Negroes.
61. Rice is the hardest labour for Negroes, yet even some of our white people have followed it.

white people, and the heat no way disagreeable nor hurtful to them; but in us it created inflammatory fevers of various kinds both continued and intermittent; wasting and tormenting fluxes, most excruciating cholicks, and dry belly-aches; tremors, vertigoes, palsies, and a long tra[i]n of painful and lingring nervous distempers,[62] which brought on to many a cessation both from work and

62. The Industrious make no such complaint.

life; especially as water without any qualification was the chief drink, and salt meat the only provisions that could be had or afforded: [63] And so general were these disorders, that during the

63. Tis false that water, without any qualification was their chief drink, for in six weeks 11 of our best workmen killed themselves with rum, and the people still continue the use of it, tho they have excellent bear [beer] brued [brewed] with molosses, and many drink madera wine. As to salt meat being the only provisions that could be had or afforded, if that were true at the peoples first landing and before they had time to raise corn and vegetables, it is no wonder: but this is so far from true that 5 days after the first embarkation arrived at Savannah, 1 Feb. 1732/3 there came for their use from Carolina 200 head of Cattle, besides hogs and rice. See Will. Milbury[?] letter dat. 6 Feb. 1732/3 from Savannah.

hot season, which lasts from March to October, hardly one half of the servants and working people were ever able to do their masters or themselves the least service; [64] and the yearly sickness of each

---

64. *during the hot season* etc. The falsity of this appears by the following affidavit. The Deposition of Lieut. Geo. Dunbar taken upon the holy Evangelists, before the Recorder of Frederica 20 Jan. 1738–9.

"This Deponent says, that he arrived in Georgia the beginning of June last with the first detachment of General Oglethorpes Regiment; and from that time to the beginning of August, all the carpenters of the said 3 companies, and a certain number of other soldiers were employed in building clapboard hutts for the said companies, and the other soldiers were employed in unloading vessels and boats loaded with clap-boards and other necessaries for building, and provisions of different kinds, often up to their necks in water: they were also employed in carrying clap boards etc. upon their backs to the camp, in clearing ground from Roots of Trees etc. for a Parade, Burning the wood and rubbish upon it, carrying of bricks and burning lime: and the artists who were excused from these works, wrought at their own trades without standing still by reason of heat. The hours of labour were from day light till between eleven and twelve, and from between one and two, and some times between two and three, till dark. All that time, the men kept so healthy, that often no man in the camp ailed in the least, and none died except one man, who came sick on board, and never worked at all: nor did I hear that any of the men made the heat a pretence for not working."

To the same purpose Lt. Hugh Mackay deposed 19 Jan. 1738/9 "that he had the charge of 17 Trust Servants 2 years, who worked very hard, and never lay by in summer by reason of the heat of the weather. That they worked willingly chearfully, and continued in good health: that their labour occasioned no illness among them, and when he left them 8 days ago they were all in good health, except one who was drownd by accident." Also Mr. John Cuthbert deposed, "that he planted 3 crops in Georgia, and verily believed a white servant might in 6 months of the year, after the land is cleared, raise as much corn, pease, potatoes, pompions, etc. as would be more than sufficient for his provisions and cloathing: and in the other 6 months may be employed in lumber: at which by this deponent's experience a white servant can at least earn 2 shillings sterl. p diem: Also that Hogs, cattle and Poultry, if taken care of, increase at a great rate, and with little expence." When Mr. Mcbane and Robt. Howes were in England they assured they worked in the hottest Days in the Summer, without inconvenience.

---

servant, generally speaking, cost his master as much as would have maintained a Negro for four years. These things were represented to the Trustees in summer 1735, in a petition for the use of Negroes, signed by about seventeen of the better sort of people in Savannah: In this petition there was also set forth the great disproportion betwixt the maintenance and cloathing of white servants and Negroes. This petition was carried to England and presented to the Trustees, by Mr. Hugh Stirling, an experienced planter in the colony; but no regard was had to it,[65] or to what he could say, and great resentment was [66] even shewn to Mr. Thompson, the

---

65. It could not be granted: his Majesty having past [passed] an act against Negroes in April preceeding.
66. Capt. Thompson is now here, let him be asked what resentment was ever shown him. The Capt. is himself against Negroes tho a freeholder.

---

master of the vessel in which it went.

Whilst we laboured under those difficulties in supporting ourselves, our *civil liberties* received a more *terrible* shock: For, instead of such a free government as we had reason to expect, and of being judged by the laws of our Mother Country, a *DICTATOR* [67] [Mr. Thomas Causton.] (under the title of Bailiff and

---

67. *a dictator* etc. None was greater with Mr. Causton than the chief author of this pamphlet whilst he remained in the Colony. The calumnious spirit of these men is such, that they deserve no credit to any thing they say.

Store-keeper, was appointed and left by Mr. Oglethorpe, at his departure, which was in April, 1734) whose *will* and *pleasure* were the only laws in Georgia: In regard to this magistrate, the others were entirely nominal, and in a manner but cyphers: Sometimes he would ask in publick their opinion, in order to have the pleasure of showing his power by contradicting them. He would often threaten juries, and especially when their verdicts did not agree with his inclination or humour. And in order the more fully to establish his *absolute* authority,[68] the store and disposal of the

---

68. Here they insinuate that Mr. Oglethorpe purposely chose him out to tyrannise the people, but read the following paragraph in a letter from Mr. Beaufain of Carolina wrote about that time to Mr. Simond 23 Jan. 1733/4 "He (Mr. Oglethorpe) enters in every particular, and hears with the greatest patience and good nature every one who apply's to him."
This Mr. Causton was found a man of good parts, and spirit, and knew accounts all which was necessary to meet in a man who in Mr. Oglethorpes absence had charge of a new settlement.

---

provisions, money, and publick places of trust, were committed to him; by which alteration in his state and circumstances, he became in a manner *infatuated,* being before that a person of no substance or character, having come over with Mr. Oglethorpe amongst the first forty, and left England upon account of something committed by him concerning His Majesty's duties: [69] However, he was fit enough for a great many purposes,[70] being a person naturally *proud,*

---

69. *And left England* etc. This is what the Trustees have no reason to believe.
70. *He was fit enough for* etc. Mr. Oglethorpe must be blackened at any rate: but can any man believe he chose out Mr. Causton for these bad qualities?

---

covetous, cunning, and *deceitful,* and would bring his designs about by all possible ways and means.

As his *power* increased, so did his *pride, haughtiness,* and *cruelty;* insomuch, that he caused eight freeholders with an officer, to attend at the door of the court, every day it sat, with their guns and bayonets, and they were commanded, by his orders, to *rest their firelocks* as soon as he appeared; which made people in some manner afraid to speak their minds, or juries to act as their consciences directed them. He was seldom or never uncovered on the bench, not even when an oath was administered; [71] and being perfectly

---

71. *He was seldom or never uncovered* etc. Was it his duty to be so? or is it credible he would not uncover when Oathes were administered?

---

intoxicated with power and pride, he threatened every person without distinction, rich and poor, strangers and inhabitants, who in the least opposed his *arbitrary* proceedings [72] or claimed their

---

72. *his arbitrary proceedings* etc. "When I was there, was [at] the Quarter Sesssions: when appeared a great many gentlemen, being summoned as Grand Jury men from all parts of the settlement, to whom Mr. Causton gave a very handsome charge, and then proceeded to business, where causes were tryed, and in my judgment very impartially, without the jargon or confused quirks of the lawyers, and without cost or charges, and yet in my opinion consonant to reason and equity, which I take to be the foundation of all Laws. Mr. Causton has there a great deal of business, and is very much fatigued from morning till night by the impertinences of some people, and who seem to exclaim against him, tho I believe without cause." See Mr. Saml. Eveleighs letter from Charlestown 19 Oct. 1734.

---

just rights and privileges, with the stocks, whipping-post, and logg-house, and many times put those threatenings into execution; so that the Georgia stocks, whipping-post, and logg-house, soon were famous in Carolina, and every where else in America, where the name of the Province was heard of, and the very thoughts of coming to the colony became a terror to people's minds.[73] And now

73. False, for at this time people flocked to the Colony from Carolina, New York, and other Provinces. See more p. 40 note 1.

the province of Carolina, who had, in private and publick donations, given us upwards of 1300l. sterling, seeing these things, and how the publick money was thrown away, began to despise the colony, and, out of a regard to the welfare of their fellow creatures, persuaded everybody they could from settling in it.[74] That this

74. And now the Province of Carolina etc. We would not lessen the generous benefactions of Carolina, but at the time the Authors speak of that Province had given but 464·18·2 Sterling. But they continued after this time to assist the Colony, tho these authors pretend they were now set against it. There is no colour for saying the publick money was thrown away at this time, neither the Carolinians or Inhabitants had any such thought. At this time every body was busie in settling themselves, and the Magistrates in pushing on publick buildings, surveying the peoples lots, providing provisions for them etc there was enough to do with the Trustees Cash without leaving any to be squandered. As to the Carolinians discouraging their fellow Creatures from settling in the Colony, they did not begin to do so early, that came afterwards upon a jealousie that Georgia would succeed in the Indian trade, and out do them therein, and upon his Majesty's passing a law against admitting their rum into Georgia. But at this time they considered Georgia as a strong barrier, and this very year their assembly in a memorial to his Majesty thanked him for erecting this Province.

absolute power might be exercised without the least interruption, the other magistrates were such, that they either were unable or incapable to oppose it: It is true, in December 1734, Mr. Causton met with a little interruption; for the Trustees then sent over to Savannah one Mr. Gordon, as Chief Magistrate,[75] who, being a

75. It is true, in December 1734 etc. These Authors lye for lying sake: Mr. Gordon was 1st Magistrate, from the first dis-embarkation 1 feby. 1732–3. In Nove. 1733 he returned to England to be cut for a fistula, and gave a very good account of the Colony, and Mr. Oglethorpes indefatagableness in carrying on the affairs of the Province, keeping peace, supplying the stores with provisions, encouraging the faint hearted etc. He returned to Georgia 31 Oct. 1734 and arrived there December following. In March 1734–5 he saild again for England contrary to his duty and Covenant being without leave of the Trustees or acquainting them therewith. He was a conceited unstable man, and his purpose in returning, was, as it afterwards appeard, to set up a punch house in London. The courtship paid him by such [as] had personal enmity with Mr. Causton pleased his vanity, and he undertook to expose their pretended grievances to the Trustees, yet never came near them

till sent to, and then he deliverd to them complaints from several against Mr. Causton, which Mr. Oglethorpe (who in June 1734 was returnd to England) promised to enquire into at his return to Georgia whither he saild 14 Oct. 1735, but did not arrive till 5 feb. 1735/6 soon after which he heard every mans complaint and found them frivelous and vexatious.

person of a very winning behaviour, affable and fluent in speech, soon got the good will of every body, and a great many of the people laid their grievances and hardships open to him, which seemed a little to eclipse Mr. Causton; but he soon found out an expedient to remove this adversary, viz. by refusing him provisions from the store, which in a little time rendered him incapable to support himself and family, whereby he was obliged, after about six weeks' stay, to leave the place,[76] in order, as he said, to represent our griev-

76. *by refusing him provisions from the Store* etc. Another plain lie: for on the 7th. May 1735 Mr. Gordon wrote to the Trustees as follows: "My endeavours do not proceed from any personal peak to Mr. Causton, with whom I declare I never had the least difference; On the contrary, Mr. Causton was so kind to offer me the arrears due to me from the stores, which would have amounted to between 20 and 30£ but I chose rather to leave my affairs in some disorder etc."

ances to the Trustees, and soon after returned to London; but he did not perform his promise, for what reason we shall not pretend to determine; and some time thereafter, he either resigned, or was dismissed from his office of First Bailiff, and Mr. Causton was appointed in his stead. As to Mr. Henry Parker, who was appointed Third Bailiff when Mr. Gordon came over, he was, in the first place, a man who had nothing to support himself and large family but his day labour, which was sawing,[77] and consequently, as soon

77. Mr. Hen. Parker was of a genteel trade in London, a linnen draper, and no sawyer, as here represented.

as his time was otherwise employed, he must be entirely dependant on the store for his subsistence: In the second place, he was a man of no education;[78] so that Mr. Causton soon moulded him to his

78. *He was a man of no education* etc. Yet better than that of a sawyer, or of David Douglass one of these Authors who is but a shopkeeper, and at present a writer to a merchant at Charlestown, who but for charity would dismiss him for insufficiency. Col. Stephens account of him is, 7. Dec. 1737. "Mr. Parker, one of the Magistrates, at my request came, and eat a bit[e] with me at dinner; and as I had from a pretty long observation of him, as well formerly as of late, conceived a good opinion of him, for an honest plain well meaning Man, and one whom I apprehended has as good a share of

common understanding as most of his neighbours, I wished to have the more intimacy with him."

Again: (Col. Stephens letter 21 feby. 1737/8) "Mr. Parker the only Magistrate on the Bench, shewed himself a man of ready apprehension and good judgment."

Again (letter 19 May 1739) "Mr. Parker has in his station as well as I could observe acquitted himself like a good Magistrate, and an honest man, having strict justice in his aim at all times, and his good understanding will not easily misguide him." There is much more to this purpose, and of his courage not to be terrified from pursuing what he thinks is just, like a right honest man.

---

own liking, and infused into him what notions he pleased: Thirdly, he was, and is, an *absolute* slave to liquor [79] and he who plies him most with it (which Causton always took care to do, and whose example has been since followed by his successor Jones) [80] has him,

---

79. never upon business
80. Mr. Dobel, lately returned to Georgia, declared this to be absolutely false, and that Mr. Jones is a patern to all men for sobriety. It is the constant practice of these Authors to malign ever[y] man who supports the Government of the Province on the Trustees Plan.

---

right or wrong, on his side. As to Mr. Christie, the Recorder, he was easily overruled by the other two; and the same practice was always continued; for he who was appointed Third Bailiff after Gordon's dismission or resignation, was one Darn, nigh seventy years of age, crazed both in body and mind, who died not long after his appointment; [81] and his successor, R. Gilbert, could neither read nor write; [82] so that Causton, had never after Gor-

---

81. crazed both in body and mind etc. The Trustees never heard this before: neither did he die soon after his appointment: for he was appointed 3. Sept. 1735, and died not till 1 July 1737.
82. Robt. Gilbert was a bold and honest man, and the people were well pleased with him.

---

don's departure, any opposition made by the other magistrates to his *arbitrary* proceedings. If we should allow ourselves to enter into a detail of the particular instances of such proceedings, we should exceed much our proposed bounds: We shall therefore confine ourselves to two only, which may serve as a specimen of the many others. ONE is, that of Captain Joseph Watson: This person, having incurred Mr. Causton's displeasure, [83] was indicted for stir-

---

83. *having incurred Mr. Caustons displeasure* etc. Not on Mr. Causton's own but the publick account. On the 19 Oct. 1734 Mr. Eveleigh of Carolina wrote

thus to Mr. Oglethorpe: "Watson has been drunk almost ever since you went away: I was credibly informed he has been so three weeks successively, but yet whilst I was there he kept himself sober, especially in the day time. He rails very much against you, my self, and the whole Province of Georgia, and says he has seen the ruin of two new Colonies and doubts not but he shall see the third. He kept Skee drunk in his store for a fortnight together, and when he went away publickly said, that he had done his business for him, and he died soon after. This came to the ears of *Stitchee*, who came to Yamacraw with a design to kill him, but he made his escape by breaking through the end of his store, and he in his rage killed justice Musgrove's slave, and persists in his resolution to kill Watson, if he can find him."

See also Mr. Christie's letter to Mr. Oglethorpe 14 Dec. 1734: "Watson has behaved very ill since your departure, and has committed several irregularities, has beat the Indians, presented a gun of Mrs. Musgrove, proved very dissafected to the Colony and unfit for a trader: the Indians are full of resentment against him" Mr. Causton gave the Trustees a full account of all this affair in his letter to the Trustees dat. 16 Jany. 1734–5 but tis too long to incert here, as also the Grand Juries verdict against Watson for the murder of Skee, and divers notices of this bad man.

---

ring up animosities in the minds of the Indians, &c. tending to the ruin and subversion of the colony. Upon his trial, the jury, in their verdict, found him only guilty of some unguarded expressions [84]

---

84. This is a false account: they found him guilty of [illegible word] but recommended him to mercy as [a] lunatick, and as such he was confined, partly also out of good nature lest the Indians should murder him.

He was also found guilty of a design to shoot Mrs. Musgrove and fined for it.

(although twice returned and hectored by Mr. Causton, who acted both as witness and judge in the matter) and verbally recommended him, by their foreman, to the mercy of the court, imagining or supposing he might be a lunatick; (however, as it afterwards appeared, it was represented to the Trustees, that the jury found him guilty of lunacy in their verdict) whereupon he was immediately confined by Mr. Causton (although sufficient bail was offered) [85] and kept prisoner near three years, without any sentence. But, as we are informed, this affair now lies before a proper judicature,[86] we shall say no more of it.

The *other* instance is that of Mr. Odingsell,[87] who was an in-

---

85. His bail would have been taken if he would have engaged [illegible word] should not leave the town.
86. The Trustees know of no judicature before which this affair lies.
87. *The other instance* etc. Every thing these fellows write is with gall: Capt. Odingsells was a very good benefactor even so late as April 1734, and no

doubt was received as all other strangers were with great sevility; how ever it be, the Trustees never heard this story concerning him, possibly the guard on duty might not know him at that unseasonable hour, and speak roughly to him, but tis not credible he should fear being put in the stocks, which could not be but by the Magistrates orders, who would never have granted one to their friend and benefactor, a person of character and who bore a commission; and made them a friendly visit. No Country affords instances of such barbarity.

---

habitant of Carolina, and had been a great benefactor to the infant colony of Georgia, having given several head of cattle and other valuable contributions, towards the promoting it. This person having come to Savannah to see how the colony succeeded, after he had been there a few days, being abroad some time after it was night, as he was going to his lodgings, was taken up in the street for a stroller, carried to the guard-house, and threatened with the stocks and whipping-post; the terror and fright of which (he being a mild and peaceable man) threw him into a *high fever* with a *strong delirium,* crying out to every person who came near him, that they were come to carry him to the whipping-post; and after lying two or three days in this distracted condition, he was carried aboard his boat in order to be sent home, and died in the way somewhere about Dawfuskee Sound.

Thus, while the nation at home was amused with the fame of the happiness and flourishing of the colony, and of its being *free from lawyers of any kind,* the poor miserable settlers and inhabitants were exposed to as *arbitrary* a government as Turkey or Muscovy ever felt. Very looks were criminal, and the grand sin of *withstanding,* or any way *opposing* authority, (as it was called, when any person insisted upon his just rights and privileges) was punished without mercy.[88] Nevertheless, we bore all these things

---

88. All this that is interlined, is only false and malicious oratory. If by arbitrary Government they mean the 2 instances above given of Watson and Odingsel[l] treatment they are no proof at all the first case being misrepresented, the other false: had there been more, these Defamers would not have failed to mention them. But why all this dirt thrown on a man who never used them personally ill, and who has been out of the Magistracy ever since June 1738? unless it be to make the world believe he and the other Magistrates committed these pretended irregularities by the Trustees orders.

---

patiently, in full hopes that the Trustees' eyes would soon be opened, and then our grievances be redressed, and still continued exhausting our substance in pursuing an impracticable scheme, namely, cultivating land to advantage in such a climate with white servants only,[89] not doubting, but that the Parliament, who yearly

---

89. *An impracticable scheme etc.* No impracticable scheme to the Industrious Saltsburghers and other Germans, nor to the laborious English. turn to p. 9 of the preface note 1. and p. 10, 11. See also p. 3 of the narrative, and the state of the Colony upon Oath, where the subscribers desire only white servants. See also the petitions of the Saltsburgers, and the settlers at Darien against Negroes.

---

repeated their bounty, would make up our damages: but alas! their bounty was applied in Georgia, rather to the hurt than benefit of the colony, as we shall here briefly relate. First, a light-house was set about; but, before the frame was erected, it was almost half rotten, and has not been carried on any farther,[90] nor never even

---

90. The light house was finished many years ago, and proved the saving of many ships: the Trustees foresaw the necessity of repairing it and gave orders for it, but a violent storm threw it down. A new one better than the old one is at this time erected.

---

covered, which has likewise greatly contributed to its decay; and now that lofty fabrick, so highly useful to vessels which make that coast, is either fallen or must fall very soon. Logg-houses and prisons of various sorts were built and erased successively, and most part of them were fitter for dungeons [91] in the Spanish inquisition than

---

91. Will people believe prisons were built merely for pleasure and building sake? Were the prison (for there is but one) a dungeon, there would not be so many escapes of prisoners as have happened.

British goals. Irons, whipping-posts, gibbets [It was a very usual thing with General Oglethorpe, when any persons had incurred his displeasure, to threaten to hang them], &c. were provided, to keep the inhabitants in perpetual terror; for innocence was no protection: and for some time there were more imprisonments, whippings, &c. of white people, in that *colony of liberty,* than in all British America besides.[92] Corn-mills, saw-mills, publick roads, Trustees

---

92. Men who write after this inflaming rate, shew they mean more to raise the passions, than give plain truth. It had been more candid to say that whipping Posts etc were set up to aw the wicked, than to keep the Inhabitants in general in perpetual terror. Is there any country where such things are not done? The Trustees never received any complaint of this kind from the Inhabitants except from one who ran away in their debt.

plantations (as they were called) wells and forts, in different places, were all set about, but, as is evident from the event, with no design to serve the publick, but only to amuse the world, and maintain some creatures who assisted in keeping their neighbours in subjection; for few or none of these things were ever brought to perfection; some of them were left off half finished, and of those that were finished, some were erased (being found of no service) and others fell of themselves for want of proper care.[93] To carry on the

---

93. *with no design to serve the publick* etc. It is acknowledged publick works were set about, but why was it only to amuse the publick? Several were perfected, and more had been, if the Trustees had been sufficiently in cash for such purposes. An expensive saw mill was sent from England and erected, which would have proved of great service to the Inhabitants in sawing timber and plank, but an unexpected flud washed it away, could this be intended only to amuse the publick or maintain creatures to keep others in subjection? or were the forts erected, the light house, the publick garden, the Townhouse etc built for no other end? roads and passages were made through woods, bridges made etc were these intended for no real use? and was it a fault to discontinue any works (tho we know of none such) when found unnecessary?

---

manufactures of silk and wine, a garden was planted with mulberries and vines, which was to be a nursery to supply the rest of the province: [94] But this was as far from answering the proposed end,

---

94. *To carry on the Manufactures of silk* etc. All that is said here of the publick garden is malicious and false. It has answered the end proposed, for there have been 100,000 [180,000?] mulberry plants in it at a time, which the Inhabitants were supply'd with from time to time. The land is indeed pine barren but this defaming author (Hugh Anderson) who had the care of the garden, confest in his letter to the Trustees dated 10 Aug. 1737 "that the soil is very proper to serve as a mulberry nursery for the Colony, it being much the advan- of a planter to bring his trees from a barren and worse soil to a rich and better."

---

as every thing else was; for it is situated upon one of the most barren spots of land in the colony, being only a large hill of dry sand: Great sums of money were thrown away upon it from year to year, to no purpose: This was remonstrated to the Trustees; and they seemed to be sensible of the error, and gave orders to chuse another spot of ground; but the *ruling powers* in Georgia took no notice thereof. And now, after so great time and charge, there are not so many mulberry trees in all the province of Georgia, as many one of the Carolina planters have upon their plantations; nor so much silk made there in one year, as many of those planters do make: [95] Nor could they ever, in that garden, raise one vine [96] to the perfection of bearing fruit. And here it

---

95. *And now* etc. This monstrous assertion is confuted by the Accounts sent over to the Trustees, and by 45£ of silk made in the year they write of, and now at the Trustees Office, 8£ of it excepted which was made the year before, and we are told double or treble the quantity will be sent next year.
96. *Nor could they ever in that garden raise one vine* etc. Here again is a notorious untruth: on the 16 March 1736–7, Mrs. Stanley who returned to England to ly in, acquainted the Trustees, that the vines in the publick garden succeeded extreamly well, and produced very large grapes. And why should they not, when the very same pine barren land produced a bewtifull large portugal grape, as big as a mans thumb, almost pelucid, and bunches exceeding big: that one shoot growing from the root of a bearing vine was as big as a walking cane and ran to 14 foot length: all which was without using any manure or art, other than planting and pruning. See Col. Stephens journal 6 dec. 1737.

---

may be observed, that the silk, Mr. O——pe carried over for a present to Queen CAROLINE, was most of it, if not all, made in Carolina.[97] Though no proper measures were ever taken for advancing the silk and wine manufactures; [98] yet private persons

---

97. Were this observation true (as it is very unfairly represented) to what purpose is it told, except to reflect on Mr. Oglethorpes sincerity? Would they have it thought that silk cannot be produced or made in Georgia? The Fact was that: in 1735 Mr. Oglethorpe brought over a small parcel of silk, equally fine with any made in Italy. This was shewn to the Queen not as the growth of Georgia, but wound in Georgia, as it actually was, and to shew how skilfull a Piedmontese we had procured to settle there and carry on the silk manufacture. Every body knows, that the white mulberry tree, (the only proper sort for the worm) requires 6, 7 or 8 years to come to the necessary perfection for producing leaves to feed the worm, and the Colony had then been inhabited but 2 years and a half, so that the trees that had begun to be planted were not then in sufficient forwardness, and Mr. Oglethorpe had too much sense and honour to offer at imposing on her Majesty. That it was wound by our Italian his own letters shew.
98. *No proper methods were taken for advancing the silk & wine manufactures* etc. What properer methods than to give bounties? The Trustees as soon as it was judged necessary gave a bounty of 4 shill. sterl. p pound on silk balls or cocons, and pay 2 shill. p pound on winding. They paid a sallary to the Italians and furnished them with all they wanted, houses, horses, servants, provisions etc. as they from time to time required them, and this bounty has greatly advanced the industry of the Inhabitants to follow the silk. Then as to encouraging the wine, there was no occasion for it until it was found that it would probably succeeded, which depended on the tryall the people

should make of the soil, and as soon as this appeared, *De Leon* above mentioned was advanced 200£, of which Mr. Oglethorpe immediately paid him 100£, but paid the rest by smaller sums, being desirous first to see how faithfully that jew would perform his covenants.

---

made several assays towards the culture of European grapes; but even such attempts met with no suitable encouragement from Mr. Oglethorpe, as will appear from the following fact. Abraham De Leon, a Jew, who had been many years a vineron in Portugal, and a freeholder in Savannah, cultivated several kinds of grapes in his garden, and, amongst others, the Porto and Malaga to great perfection; [99] of this he sent home an attested account to the Board of

---

99. It seems that now pine barren land can furnish grapes to great perfection, which the Authors denyed before, for this land is the same with that of the publick garden.

Trustees, proposing further, *that if they would lend him, upon such security as he offered,* two hundred pounds sterling, *for three years without interest, that he would employ the said sum, with a further stock of his own, in sending to Portugal, and bringing over vines and vinerons; and that he should be bound to repay the money in three years, and to have growing within the colony forty thousand such vines, which he would furnish the freeholders with at moderate rates.*

The Trustees were satisfied with the security, and accepted the proposal, and wrote him, that they had remitted the two hundred pounds by Mr. Oglethorpe for his use; which he did not deny, when applied to by the said Leon for the same, but said, that he could not advance more than twenty or thirty pounds, in regard he had other uses for the money; and so that design dropped.[100]

---

100. *And so that design droped.* It must drop when this man ran away for fear of the Spaniards: but as to others, who by his example took to planting vines, the design goes on with great alacrity and success, and some wine has already been made the last year.

In February, 1735–6, Mr. Og——pe arrived in Georgia, for the second time, with great numbers of people, in order to settle to the southward, where he soon after carried them. Upon the Island of St. Simons he settled a town, which he called Frederica; and about five miles distance from thence, towards the sea, he placed the independant company which he removed from Port Royal in Carolina, their former station. On one of the branches of the Alatamaha he settled the Highlanders, in a village which was called

Darien. Then he settled a fort on Cumberland, which he named St. Andrews; and some time after he caused a garrison of about fifty men to be placed upon a sandy island (without fresh water) in the mouth of St. John's River, opposite to a Spanish lookout, where possession was kept for about six months, and several fortifications built; but at last he was obliged to abandon it, after several people had lost their lives by the inconveniences of the place, besides great sums of money thrown away in vain.[101]

---

101. *But at last he was obliged to abandon it* etc. He drew off his men by Treaty with the Spaniards, not for want of water, or by reason of many mens dying there, not one dying that the Trustees know of. Neither was much money thrown away there. It is the constant method of these Calumniators to mingle falsities with truth, and give an invidious turn to every thing.

Whilst things thus passed in the southern part of the province, Mr. Causton was not idle at Savannah; and one would have thought, that he made it his particular design further to exasperate the people of Carolina: He stopped their boats who were going up to New-Windsor in South Carolina; and not content with that, he caused them to be searched, and whatever rum was found therein, was directly staved, in pursuance of an Act, as he alleged, entitled, *An Act against the Importation of Rum into the Colony of Georgia.*[102] To complain of this, and to represent the bad state

---

102. Here the truth is told, but not the whole truth. He did stop and search their boats, and his Majesties Act against importing Rum into the Colony authorised him so to do. The case was, that in the midst of the Savannah River, just opposite to Savannah town, lyes Hutchinson Island, dividing the river into two channels. The island itself belonged to Georgia, and consequently the inner channel between that and the town, but the outward channel next to Carolina was allowed to her. The Carolinians (who might with the same ease pass the outward channel where none molested them as the inner one) chose nevertheless that next to Savannah, for no other reason than for opportunities to run their Rum into the town, and therefore Mr. Causton stopt and searched their boats. From this and divers other passages in this book it appears plain that these venal writers have sold their pens to the Carolinians, by whose contributions this pamphlet was first printed in Charlestown.

---

of the Indian trade, a committee, from the Assembly of South Carolina, arrived at Savannah in July 1736, where Mr. Og——pe then was: But their coming was of little consequence; for after this the differences and animosities betwixt the two provinces rather increased than diminished; and we shall only observe, that one thing is certain, that, ever since Mr. Ogle——pe intermeddled in the Indian trade, it has decayed apace, and at this time is almost intirely *good for nothing* either to the one or the other province.[103]

103. Prodigious assertion! See the State of the Colony upon Oath. The Carolinians trade as freely with the Georgia Indians as do the Georgians themselves. Nay 'what the latter get is carried to Charlestown and there sold and shipt for Europe. If it be true that their trade had decayd a pace, they may thank themselves, as appears by the following extract from Mr. Eveleigh's letter to Mr. Oglethorpe dated 20. Nov. 1734. from Charlestown. "The Assembly lately met and past [passed] a law which was ratified last Satturday, wherein they have put a duty on all skins and Furrs, light as well as heavie of 6 pence p skin, and an addition of 51£ p head p lycence, which is a burthen too great for them to bear. I endeavoured while this act was passing to shew them the disadvantage it would be to this Province, that it would drive the whole trade to Virginia, Cape Fear and Georgia. I demonstrated that it would be 50,000£ or more out of this Provinces way, and do believe it will be as much in the way of Georgia. However plausible the introduction of this act may appear, yet I do assure you it was levelled against me and other persons concerned in the trade, and they did expect to ruin the Traders, so that they may take the Indian trade into a company."

To the same purpose the same gentleman wrote to Mr. Will. Jeffrys of Bristol on the 4th. July 1735 from Savannah, in manner following: "I told them (the Assembly of Carolina) that I could make it appear as plain as any of Euclids Elements that it would drive away the trade to this place. I can assure you that after all, they (the Georgians) can trade with the Creeks, Chickesaws, and Cherokees from this place 20 to 25 p cent cheaper than they can from Charlestown, not withstanding the encouragement they talk of giving."

Thus while the province of Carolina resented the bad treatment they had met with from the leading powers in Georgia, against the colony in general; the poor inhabitants were doubly unfortunate, being ill looked upon by their nearest neighbours and friends, for the actings of their Governors, while they themselves were still the greatest sufferers by those very actings.

Whilst Mr. O——pe staid in Georgia, great complaints were made against the *arbitrary* proceedings of Mr. Causton; but to no purpose: [104] Likewise several persons endeavoured to shew the im-

104. The character Mr. John Wesley (tho his enemy) gave of Mr. Causton at his return to England Sept. 1735 was, that he was a passionate man, but resolution was necessary to repress the insolence of many of the people. And Mr. Eveleigh of Carolina (a very unprejudiced gentleman) wrote thus from Savannah to Mr. Oglethorpe 16th. May 1735. "I found the people very much divided here like Court and Country: the Magistrates and the better sort, as I take it, on one side; the Populasy, if I may so call them, on the

other, with a few of the better sort. I find if any person wants anything of Mr. Causton, and he refuses them, tho it be unreasonable and contrary to his Instructions, they presently turn Grumbletonians, and side and herd with one another, as in the Corpeal body, if there is a wound in the leg, all the malignant humours will incredibly fly to that place. If a person has a tryal with another, the Loser immediately exlaims: nay I observed when I was last here, that after a Tryal, both Parties were dissatisfyed and both reflected chiefly on Mr. Causton, for as he is the chief Magistrate, all the reproaches are levelled at him. Mr. Causton has his faults as all men have, but I must assure you 'tis the common vogue, that he was the most capable of such an office of any man in the Province when you went." See more, p. 33 note. 4.

---

possibility of the colony's succeeding, according to its then present constitution: but if this was done in his hearing, he either always browbeat the person, or evaded the discourse; if by letters, he never made any answer to them; even although he had given publick orders, that every person should give in their grievances and complaints to him in writing, and that he would consider and answer the same.[105] But that we might not be entirely ignorant of his

---

105. *But if this was done in his hearing* etc. Mr. Beaufain of Carolina gave a very different character of Mr. Oglethorpes behaviour, in his letter to Mr. Simond Merchant in London: "The settling of Georgia is what Mr. Oglethorpe has so entirely at heart, that every thought and action of his is directed to that favourite object: he is taken up in town with the political and civil part of the administration, the business of Grants, the settling and providing new Inhabitants, keeping a good order among the people; he enters into every particular, and hears with the greatest patience and good nature any one who apply's to him."

Again, Mr. Cha. Wesley, at his return to England in December 1736, acquainted the Trustees, "That every one of the complaints against Mr. Causton, were found by Mr. Oglethorpe at his arrival absolutely frivelous:"

And Mr. Mcbane of Darien who the same month came to England to procure Scotch servants declared that "a fair hearing had been given to all the complaints made against Mr. Causton's administration, and this by Mr. Oglethorpe in open Court, and all present said there never were more groundless accusations."

---

thoughts, Mr. Causton, who always spoke his sentiments, publickly declared, *that we had neither lands, rights, or possessions;* that *the Trustees gave, and that the Trustees could freely take away:* [106] And

---

106. Impossible that Mr. Causton should say, for the peoples grants were as secure to them as any other man's[?] property in any country.

---

again, when he was told that the light-house wanted a few spike nails to fasten some of its braces which were loose, and which might occasion the downfal of the whole fabrick; he answered, *that he would say as Mr. Oglethorpe said, it might fall and be d——d.*[107]

---

107. The whole spirit of this book being one entire invective and defamation, these scandals deserve no credit. What motive could Mr. Oglethorpe or Mr. Causton have to wish so usefull and costly a work as this light house should fail [fall?]?

Mr. Oglethorpe staid in Georgia until November 1736, most of which time he spent to the southward, and then embarked for England, leaving Mr. Causton with the same authority he had formerly invested him with, and in the same power he then exercised, and the colony under the same difficulties and hardships.

In March thereafter, we had advice of the Spaniards' intentions of attacking the colony from the Havana. This put the whole province in great consternation, especially the town of Savannah; they having neither fort, battery,[108] or any other place to shelter them-

---

108. *neither Fort, Battery,* etc. Battery they had, but no Fort, which being an expensive work, Mr. Causton could not presume to concur therein, having neither orders, nor money for such purpose, nor any Ingeneer to conduct it: nevertheless, such was the fear and obstinacy of the people, that he was obliged to set men at work at 7£ currency to each man p month, which amounted to 515£ sterl. before he received the Trustees orders to stop the work, which was ill judged and un-necessary, as will appear by the Trustees letter to him 11 August 1737 wherein they wrote as follows: "The Trustees are apprehensive that the expences which have been run into upon account of the Fort will exceed their establishment, and as such the people were very much in the wrong for thinking of putting them to any expences which the Trustees think improper. You was in the wrong to comply at all in the beginning, but what makes it something excusable in you was the terrour of the people might have been under; and you was much in the right to insist upon not going further in it. The cutting down the wood was a great folly, for that wood was a better defence than any Fort they could erect by the garden: such a Fort would be of no use but by commanding the river, which might have been better defended from the Guard house, Battery, and guns in the wood: the town would have been as open to an Enemy over land, as if no such Fort had been. The real defence of the Town is the woods and the swamps, and a few men who know the country, assisted by the Indians, might have made a much better defence in the woods, than in the Fort, since thereby they could have prevented an Enemy from coming to the town, which they could not by defending the Fort, and Savannah is as strong by the swamps and the river which surround it, as any town in America, tho fortified. For Fortifications without a garrison are no defence, and the same garrison that would defend a Fort, can keep the Passes of the swamps. Capt. Macpherson judged extreamly right, and the whole scheme of the Fort, seems

more to be a design to draw money from the Publick Store, than any defence against an Enemy.

selves in, in case of any actual attack; therefore they immediately set about building a wooden fort, and all sorts of people laboured continually until it was in some measure finished; only Mr. Causton never came to work, but did all he could to retard it, making light of the information, although it was sent express by Commodore Dent, with a letter directed to the Commander in Chief of Georgia; and has since been put out of all manner of doubt, the Spaniards having at that time four thousand men embarqued, and ready to sail, if an extraordinary accident had not prevented them [They were detained eight days at the Havana, by contrary winds (the land forces being on board all that time) at the end of which there came orders from Old Spain, to forbear hostilities, the Convention being then agreed upon]. People now seeing the little care that was likely to be taken in case of a real attack; and likewise finding, to their cost, that the improvement of land was a vain and fruitless labour with white servants only, and with such restrictions, and precarious titles, many began to withdraw, and leave the colony, and very little was planted this season.[109]

109. *People now seeing the little care likely to be taken* etc. Here again everything is summed up to cast dirt on the Trustees and the Magistrates, by these defamers: such repetitions are frequent. Notwithstanding this allarm of the Spaniards and these pretended grievances, there left the Colony but 32 persons of all ages and sexes during the whole year, several of whom fled for debt, or crimes.

And now to make our subjection the more complete, a new kind of tyranny was this summer [1737] begun to be imposed upon us,[110] for Mr. John Wesly [Wesley], who had come over, and was received by us as a clergyman of the Church of England,[111] soon

110. *And now to make out subjection the more compleat* etc. Here is a fresh scandal cast on the Trustees as if they sent Mr. Wesley over to enslave the people. When he went over he had not discovered in England that folly he since was guilty of, and had he not left the colony of his own accord, the Trustees would have recalled him on account of his behaviour whilst in the Province.
111. All this tedious Account of Mr. Wesley is impertinent.

discovered that his aim was to enslave our *minds,* as a necessary preparative for enslaving our *bodies.* The attendances upon prayers, meetings and sermons inculcated by him, so frequently, and at improper hours,[112] inconsistent with necessary labour, especially in

---

112. *The attendance upon prayers* etc. These Scotch Dissenters who did not attend the church service could find no inconvenience from Mr. Wesleys prayers. They had amusements they liked better. Patrick Tailfer one of these authors with some of his crew, did on a Sunday whilst others were at church, break into the Publick garden, threatened to beat the gardiner who was a german, and made destruction there.

---

an infant colony, tended to propagate a spirit of indolence, and of hypocrisy, amongst the most abandoned; it being much easier for such persons, by an affected shew of religion, and adherence to Mr. Wesly's [Wesley] novelties, to be provided, by his procurement from the public Stores, than to use that industry which *true* religion recommends: Nor indeed could the reverend gentleman conceal the designs he was so full of, having frequently declared, that he never desired to see Georgia *a rich,* but *a religious* [According to his system.] colony.[113]

---

113. These words if true (for we have no other authority to believe it but the pen of these defamers) were probably spoken by way of comparison without intention to prejudice either of the points or propositions in question: it is very familiar in language, and denotes only a preference of one thing to another. Certainly poverty with religion is better than Riches without Religion, but no body can reasonably infer from this speech, that Mr. Wesley would be sorry to see the colony both rich and religious.

At last, all persons of any consideration came to look upon him as a Roman Catholick, for which the following reasons seemed pretty convincing. 1st, Under an affected strict adherence to the Church of England, he most unmercifully damned all Dissenters of whatever denomination, who were never admitted to communicate with him, until they first gave up their faith and principles entirely to his moulding and direction, and, in confirmation thereof, declared their belief of the invalidity of their former baptism, and then to receive a new one from him: This was done publickly on the persons of Richard Turner, carpenter, and his son. Another instance was that of William Gaff, who had once communicated, and always conformed to his regulations, but was at last found out by Mr. Wesly [Wesley] to have been baptized by a Presbyterian Dissenter, the same thing was proposed to him; but

Mr. Gaff, not inclinable to go that length, was ever thereafter excluded from the communion.[114]

---

114. *Mr. Gough* [Goff] *not inclinable to go that length* etc. Nevertheless so fond of him as to run away with him to Carolina.

2*dly*, While all Dissenters (whereof a considerable number was in the colony) were thus unmercifully damned, and shut out from religious ordinances, contrary to that spirit of moderation and tenderness which the Church of England shew towards them; persons suspected to be Roman Catholicks were received and caressed by him as his First Rate Saints.[115]

---

115. We know but of one person then in the Colony suspected to be a Roman Catholick, who was a silver smith, and I think is since dead.

3*dly*, A third confirmatiton of this suspicion arose from his endeavours to establish confession, penance, mortifications, mixing wine with water in the sacrament, and suppressing, in the administration of the sacrament, the explanation adjoined to the words of communicating by the Church of England, to shew that they mean a feeding on Christ by faith, saying no more than "the body of Christ; the blood of Christ;" by appointing deaconesses, with sundry other innovations, which he called Apostolic Constitutions.

4*thly*, As there is always a strict connexion betwixt Popery and Slavery; so the design of all this fine scheme seemed to the most judicious, to be calculated to debase and depress the minds of the people, to break any spirit of liberty, and humble them with fastings, penances, drinking of water, and a thorough subjection to the spiritual jurisdiction which he asserted was to be established in his person; and when this should be accomplished, the minds of people would be equally prepared for the receiving civil or ecclesiastical tyranny.[116]

---

116. These declaimers can it seems see through a Mill Stone. The judicious men who discovered this fine scheme are only themselves. As the generality of the World are not apprized that the Trustees have no advantage, nor possibility of making any, from the Trust they are engaged in, these insinuations are flung out to make it believed, that the Trustees have very bad designs in view, when they shall have reduced the Inhabitants into a slavish condition.

All Jesuitical arts were made use of to bring the well concerted scheme [117] to perfection; families were divided in parties; spies

117. *the well concerted scheme* etc. The only schemers are these fellows, who make mountains of mole hills, and pass their dreams on the world for realities.

were engaged in many houses, and the servants of others bribed and decoyed to let him into all the secrets of the families they belonged to; nay, those who had given themselves up to his spiritual guidance (more especially women) were obliged to discover to him their most secret actions, nay even their thoughts and the subject of their dreams: At the same time he gave charge to juries; gave his opinion in all civil causes that came before the court: Nor could we imagine what all this would end in: Complain we might; but to no purpose; and Mr. Causton and he went *hand in hand*.

But the merciful providence of GOD disappoints frequently those designs that are laid deepest in human prudence.[118]

118. What a solemn observation is here upon a ridiculous fact!

Mr. Wesly [Wesley] at this time repulsed Mrs. Sophia Williamson, niece to Mr. Causton, from the sacrament. This young lady was by her friends put under the ghostly care of Mr. Wesly,[119] who

119. A Fact not truly related neither, for it was not Mr. Wesley who made the proposal of marriage, but Mr. Causton made it to him in behalf of his niece, who was not then averse to it. I only mention this to observe these writers are not always well informed, and that if they can but catch up the end of a story, it is sufficient ground work for them to make a frightfull picture, By adding circumstances thereto without regard to truth, or even probability, as has already been shown in divers other cases.

was pleased to make proposals of marriage to her: these she always rejected; and in some little time married Mr. William Williamson, of Savannah, much contrary to Mr. Wesly's inclinations: After the said marriage, Mr. Wesly used all means to create a misunderstanding betwixt Mrs. Williamson and her husband, by persuading her, that Mr. Williamson had no right to regulate her behaviour as to conversing with him, or attending meetings as formerly; but at last finding he could gain nothing upon her, and that Mr. Williamson had forbad him any conversation with his wife out of his presence; he took the aforesaid means, by repelling her from the Holy Communion, of shewing his resentment. Mr. Williamson thought himself well founded in an action of damages; and Mr.

Wesly (being no longer supported by Mr. Causton, who was highly nettled at the affront put upon his niece, and could now declaim as fluently against spiritual tyranny as any person) was indicted before a Grand Jury of forty-four freeholders, and thirteen indictments were found against him; one concerned Mr. Williamson and his spouse; the others concerning the grievances we felt by his measures, and the exercise of his ecclesiastical functions, as above related: These last were given in to the magistrates, to be by them laid before the Trustees, that these our grievances might, in time coming, be properly redressed, (we having no other jurisdiction, either civil or ecclesiastical, that we could make application to;) Then the Grand Jury began to consider and think, that as it was not probable a greater number of the *better sort* of people could ever be legally met together; so this was a fit time to represent their grievances and hardships to the Trustees: [120] Which they did in the following manner.

---

120. *Then the Grand jury began to consider* etc. The town of Savannah was at this time fallen into faction, as appears by Col. Stephens letter to the Trustees dated 20 dec. 1737 where speaking of this Grand Jury, he says: "After a charge given them to enquire into all Offences, and this affair of Mr. Wesleys among the rest, They not only made a Presentment against *him*, But also drew up a long representation of grievances (as they judged them) wherein they were as free with Mr. Causton as any one. And now open defyance seemed to be given out by Mr. Wesley on one part, and the Magistrates on the other, most of the malecontents according to Mr. Wesley; And many others (I must say, of the best note and distinction) strenuously adhering to the magistrates, resolving at all adventures to support them in the exercise of their Authority, for the preservation of the whole, not withstanding any personal pique, which possibly might exist against either of them. In this miserable state I found the town divided at my arrival: and how great soever Mr. Wesley's resentment against Mr. Causton's family was, it was really some to see it shewn in abetting an angry set of people against the civil magistrates, whom they appeared to overthrow at any rate."

The same turbulent disposition reigned at this time in the South, where a worthy gentleman and very Improving Landholder, Willm. Horton Esq, military Commander of Frederica was most unjustly try'd for felony, for only employing a boat 2 days to a Capt. of his Majesties sloop, upon the colonies affairs, and that by consent of one of the owners the boat, without the knowledge of the other owner who was not then on the spot. In a word, there have been some in the Colony, from the beginning, restless under their Magistrates.

It may be proper here to acquaint the Reader how this mutinous disposition arose: Take it in Col. Stephens own words, extracted from his letter to the Trustees dated from Savannah 19 Jany. 1737/8—"I never thought my self better employed than in endeavouring to allay those heats grown so violent between neighbours, and doing my best to quell that cursed spirit of Faction and Party lately sprung up among them, from the seeds of sedition sown by a very few, whom no power of Goverment can please, but such as they themselves are at the head of, and whose great aim has been to become popular, by first raising jealousies in weak minds of such innovations in their liberties, and such arbitrary Goverment, as was never before thought of, and then cajoling them into an opinion, that if they wou'd stand firm together in opposing this imaginary Tyrany, they would not doubt but carry their point, and become a free people. From hence arose that open opposition given to Magistrates in the Execution of their office, whom they treated with scorn and contempt." In a subsequent letter dated 27 feb. 1737/8 he writes—"What remains principally an eye sore with me at present, is to see the same knot of Scotch Landholders, in the Country, now residing here, with one only Englishman joyning them, continue undesolved. The names of those of most significance among them I mentioned in my last [Patrick Mackay, Hugh Sterling, William Stirling, Patrick Tailfer, Andrew Grant, Robert Williams]. They adhere closely together (which is national with them in all Countries) and seldom fail meeting at a Tavern every night, 8 or 10 or more, where they always sing the same tune, and whatever strangers come to town, some of these soon get acquainted with them, who too often (I fear) go away under bad impressions of the Colony." Of these men, Mr. Tho. Jones wrote thus to Mr. Lyde 15 Sept. 1740. "What has been the greatest bane to this part of the Colony has been a company of proud, idle and turbulent spirited Scotch, who arrived at Savannah about 6 years ago: most of them had no visible way of subsisting (accounting labour unbecoming gentlemen) besides a few unhappy servants (whom they had persuaded to accompany them[)], but whose labour (letting them out to hire[)], they were supported in their idleness and extravagance for some years. But those servants indentures being expired, Poverty began to stare them in the face, yet would not stoop to any thing which they imagined unbecoming gentlemen (tho some of them in raggs[)], but kept their daily perambulation on the parade, priding themselves in their fine shapes, tho they could not of their clothes, and kept up daily their meetings at the Tavern, where they combined not only to raise discontents among the drunken idle part of the Inhabitants (who were now left to provide for themselves) but contrived also several falshoods which have been industriously spread in England, representing this Colony as unfruitfull and unhealthfull, therefore not worth the regard of the Government. Their views therein could be no other, than, if these falshoods were credited, the Goverment would yeild up Georgia to the Spaniards, and then they would have a fair pretence for a recompence of the loss of their Estates in Georgia, which they expected to receive, without any enquiries what Improvments they had made on the lands granted them. What has contributed much towards the support of this Society, has been the allyance with Mr. Robert Williams (our Countryman) by *Patrick Tailfer*, a surgeon marrying Mr. Williams sister. Tailfer who a little before had narrowly escaped on a Tryal for the murther of his servant, was then come into tolerable practice (having no other that profest [professed] any tolerable skill in surgery at Savannah) and being the only person of the Club that could command any money, was their chief Dictator. Mr. Williams was in partnership with his brother at St. Christophers, who carried on a trade to Guinea for Negro Slaves. Notwithstanding the Act which past [passed] soon after the establishment of this Colony, against Negro Slaves therein, yet those Scotch gentlemen prevaild with Mr. Williams to joyn with them in an attempt to procure the repeal of that Act, which he the more readily concurred in from the prospect he had of having the monopoly of Negroes brought into the Colony, if they could have the law repealed.

Accordingly in the beginning of the year 1739, This doughty Club formed a Memorial representing the difficulties the Planters in this Colony laboured under, for want of Negroe Slaves, and prevaild with some of the honest labourious (but unthinking) people to sign the same. There was not one of those Scotch contrivers who had so much as one Acre of land, and I am very certain that none among them (Tailfer excepted) could pay the purchasse of one Negroe, nor even pay the debts contracted by them in this Colony. This Representation was sent to England by Mr. Williams, in order to be laid before the Trustees, which together with the Trustees answer thereto, I doubt not you have seen in your publick papers, therefore shall not add on that head.

Three or four Scotch families (who I find to be well affected to the British Constitution) after their arrival in Georgia, seldom associated with the rest of their Countrymen, but took to planting, or followed other occupations, wherein they have been very successfull, and are usefull people in the Colony: but the others (who on all occasions, discover an Inveteracy to the present Goverment, finding fault with all the measures that have been taken since the Revolution, excepting during the few years of Lord Bolingbrokes Ministry) continued in town, where they drest [dressed] gay, set up a St. Andrews Club, a Free Masons Club and other Tipling Societies, which they have kept up to this time (from what fund they are supported in this expencive way of living is yet a secret and only guessed at). This has proved the ruin of several young, vain, and unexperienced people, who arrived in Georgia, by being either admitted Members of their societies, or by following the same example of Luxury. Every one of this Scotch Club (one Douglass excepted) kept his concubine publickly, by whom they have had a number of spurious children now living. Your friend Robert Williams and his brother (when adopted members of St. Andrews) followed the same example. They have at all times shewn their to, and contempt of Religion, which at length broke out into a rage. Since our Minister Mr. Whitfeild found fault with their setting up horse races this summer (when we were in danger of being invaded by the Enemy), and had also both in publick and private endeavoured to persuade them to part with, or marry their concubines, promising to provide for and educate their spurious children: in which he was seconded by Mr. Maclaud (the presbiterian Minister at Darien) who came to Savannah for that purpose, and used his utmost endeavours to persuade his Countrymen, but could not prevail with them.

"An Abstract of the Representation of the Grand Jury of Savannah, to the Honorable the Trustees.

"We the Grand Jury, duly sworn on the 22d of the last month, and having divers matters laid before us, which, we humbly conceive, cannot properly be presented to this court, because several of the said matters touch the proceedings of the magistrates of the said court, and contain sundry articles, setting forth many publick necessities and hardships, which can only be remedied by your Honours' authority: Therefore, we the said Grand Jury having examined several witnesses, do, upon our oaths, represent to your Honours the following *grievances, hardships,* and *necessities.*

"That as the inhabitants of this town and county have been and are still subject to many inconveniences, for want of a body of the laws and constitutions of this province; [121] it being exceeding diffi-

---

121. *for want of a body of the laws* etc. They had the laws of England for their guide, which one would think sufficient for Grand jury's.

---

cult in many cases, both for grand and petit juries, to discharge in a proper manner the great duties that are incumbent on them by their oaths; so we hope your Honours will assist us, that we may be enabled well and truly to execute our duties as aforesaid.

"That Thomas Causton, by his *arbitrary* proceedings, hath endeavoured to render the power and proceedings of Grand Juries ineffectual, especially this Grand Jury, by intruding upon it when inclosed and about business, and using the members thereof with great haughtiness and ill nature, and threatening to dissolve them.[122]

---

122. *using the members with great haughtyness* etc. The Trustees know nothing of this, but it was in the power of the Court to dissolve them if it thought fit.

"That the said Thomas Causton, by his office of Storekeeper, hath the dangerous power in his hands of alluring weak-minded people to comply with unjust measures; [123] and also overawing

---

123. If it was in Mr. Caustons power to do these things as storekeeper, it was equally in the power of any other storekeeper to do the same, so the peoples condition would not have been mended. They made the same complaint of

his Successor Mr. Tho. Jones, for the little time he held it, and even after he kept only a private store. Besides were he so arbitrary a man as here represented, he might have the Storekeeper equally under his Influence as He is supposed to have had the other magistrates.

---

others from making just complaints and representations to your Honours; and the known *implacability* of the said Causton, and his frequent *threatening* of such people, is to many weak-minded, though well disposed persons, a strong bulwark against their seeking redress, by making proper complaints and just representations to you their *benefactors, patrons,* and *protectors.*

"That the said Causton has made great advancements on provisions and goods sold out of the Trustees' store to the inhabitants,[124] contrary to Mr. Oglethorpe's promise when he first set-

---

124. *That the said Causton has made great advancement* etc. The Trustees Publick Store was principally erected for the support of their servants, and such as went over at the Trustees charge, with whom they contracted to find [sic] them one year in provisions gratis, and to whom it was continued a year or more longer as their wants required. This set of men had therefore no cause of complaint whether the stores were sold dear or cheap since they had them for nothing. The other set of men who went over, had no demand whatever, they going at their own expence: nevertheless, because it might happen that some of these might want assistance, the Trustees directed to supply them from the store for money or upon credit at prime cost, (which included freight and loss) and accordingly in two years time, no less than 800£ was advanced them in provisions and goods, and the ungratefull Authors of this Pamphlet were of the number.

That Mr. Causton made too great advancements on these provisions and goods is not known to the Trustees, and indeed very improbable, because there were private stores where persons might furnish themselves, if it was found that they sold cheaper than Mr. Causton, which is so true, that the Private Storekeeper fell out among themselves upon this very account. There is a remarkable account of this in one of the private storekeepers letters to the Trustees (Mr. Brownfeild) dated from Savannah 6. March 1735/6, who writes—

"I had leave to go up to Savannah on the 13. feby. in order to settle my own little affairs. I found there a Cargoe of Goods consigned to me from Mr. Tuckwell, and had the favour of putting them into your Honours Magazine for some days, till I could get a proper House to remove them into. Several of the Freeholders told me that the town was already overstocked with Goods, and trade in general at a very low Ebb. I could not help being a little surprised at what they said but upon diligent enquiry found it too true. The present Shopkeepers have used such extortion, partly by taking advantage of the peoples necessities, and partly through the extravagant prices they themselves paid for goods from Carolina, that they are generally hated; but more particularly for their having taken out executions, and imprisoned the persons indebted to them after two or three months credit. These means have been chiefly used by a number of Scotch Gentlemen [David Douglass, one of the Authors of this pamphlet, Ja. Houston, Tho. Baillie, Andrew Grant etc.], who arrived here soon after Mr. Oglethorpe went for England in 1734. Instead of improving their lands, they fell into trade, and thereby dispirited the poor Inhabitants of Savannah from any attempts that way. When they had engrossed most part of the Trade, they advanced their prices, and by fair outward pretences drew abundance of people into debt, soon after which they threatened to serve executions in order to get houses and lands morgaged [mortgaged] to them, and Succeeded with a few weak men. But others are here, who have lived independent of the Trading people, by keeping out of debt, and they have made the most Improvments upon their Lands."

---

tled this colony, and contrary, as we apprehended, to your Honours' good intentions, and greatly detrimental to the prosperity of the colony; and that he hath refused to pay the publick debts otherwise than in provisions at those dear rates, and sometimes bad and unwholsome, out of the publick store, whereby the inhabitants were *greatly* distressed, and some have been obliged to leave the province.

"That whereas one John White, who had been committed for felony, at the suit of William Aglionby, and he the said Aglionby was bound to prosecute the same at next court: Notwithstanding he the said White was removed before that time by a warrant under the hand and seal of Thomas Christie, and as we think, by the advice and command of Thomas Causton; [125] by which means

---

125. Mr. Christie was Recorder, and if he committed anything irregular; it ought not to be attributed to another, without better proof than *as we think* especially by a Grand jury to the Chief Magistrate.

---

we imagine the criminal has escaped justice, to the great encouragement of enormous offenders, contrary, as we conceive, to the laws of our country, to the peace of our Sovereign Lord the King, his Crown and Dignity, and particularly to the welfare of this your colony.

"That the said Causton did greatly discourage the inhabitants of this town and county, in the measures they had taken for the defence and safety of this place in the late alarm from the Spaniards; [126] for although almost every body, masters and servants,

---

126. *That the said Mr. Causton* etc. See all this paragraph answered note 1. p. 41.

---

laboured continually in making a fort to defend themselves, in case of necessity; yet he the said Causton never came nigh the work, but by his words and behaviour did all he could to prevent it; until at last the people were obliged to leave off the work unfinished, contrary to the welfare and safety of this colony.

"That the said Causton hath greatly prevented and discouraged the cultivation of lands,[127] by his hindering people to settle on

---

127. *That the said Causton* etc. This is a most unjust accusation of Mr. Causton as the papers at the Trustees Office make appear.

---

the tracts that were allotted to them by the Trustees; whereby several people have been greatly distressed, and some almost ruined, contrary (as we humbly conceive) to your Honours good intention, and the principal part of your glorious undertaking.

"That the said Thomas Causton, in order to colour his illegal proceedings, hath uttered words to this or the like purpose,— *We do not stand upon our feet; we do not know either our laws or liberties, nor what the Trustees intend; a magistrate cannot act to strict forms, but may dismiss matters of petty felony in the easiest manner;* [128] thereby claiming to himself (as we humbly con-

---

128. *We do not stand* etc. The Trustees do not believe that Mr. Causton ever utterd such speeches, or claimed a dispensing power: on the contrary They find that his adherence to the Trustees orders made him many enemys, and that he underwent the Scandal of many bad tongues for vigorously maintaining the Publick Peace. This the very Foreman of the present Grand jury owned some time before in a letter to the Trustees 6 March 1735/6 in the following words: "With respect to the magistracy, there have certainly been very warm measures in order to preserve the publick peace: but here are a set of people who come under pretence of seeing the town, stay in it till they are found guilty of some enormity, and those have been punished in an exemplary manner; upon their leaving a place where Criminals are so severely handled, they cannot be supposed to speak well of it."

---

ceive) a dispensing power, fatal to the liberties of British subjects, and contrary, &c.

"The want of publick roads hath been greatly detrimental to many who have settlements at any distance from this place; [129] and

---

129. *The want of Publick Roads* etc. Publick Roads were certainly necessary, and the Trustees made divers at a great expence, as one from Savannah to Augusta (near 200 miles) being a path cut through the woods, so that horsemen can now ride thither, only there are some bad places which ought to be causewayd and made good, which for want of money has not yet been done: they also made a pathway from Savannah to Darien 90 miles, so that

droves of Cattle past [passed] it from one town to tother. And nearer the town a western road was cut, bridges laid etc. which by Mr. Tho. [Thomas] Stephens account cost 700£.

---

some have lost, and are still liable to loose great part of their crops, through the difficulty of passing to and from their plantations.

"That the great want of servants, in this town and county, doth render the freeholders thereof incapable of proceeding with proper vigour in the cultivating their lands; [130] and as the Honourable

---

130. *That the great want of servants* etc. It may here be observed that the idle gentry in Savannah town, could not as yet persuade the people that it was safe or necessary to admit of Negroes, for all the Grand jury desired, was to be lent white Servants, with the help of whom, they intimate, the Free-holders would be capable to proceed with proper vigour in cultivating their lands. They could not but be good judges of this, since the Colony had now been inhabited 4 years and a half. Had the Inhabitants cultivated one for tother in common as did the industrious Saltsburghers (who never desired the assistance of Servants) our English, in the general, would have wanted no white Servants, but the idleness of some, and the pride of others who put on the character of gentlemen, occasion'd this demand of Servants, of whom a very great number were sent before the year was out.

James Oglethorpe, Esq; did generously promise, that your Honours would be pleased to give this colony continual assistance, by sending over servants to the said freeholders, at reasonable rates: therefore, we do, with all humility, lay before your Honours the great and general want of servants in this town and county; not doubting your timely assistance therein.

"That the town of Savannah stands in the utmost need of having a good wharf and crane,[131] for the conveniency of both strangers

---

131. Accordingly a good wharf and Crane was built, and Servants appointed at the Trustees charge to work at it.

---

and inhabitants, they being at *double* pains and costs in landing and getting their goods up the bluff.

"That the light-house of Tybee, which, with great labour and (as we humbly conceive) vast expence to your Honours, remains unfinished and uncovered; [132] by reason of which, that most neces-

---

132. *That the light house* etc. This Presentment was very proper, and the Trustees gave early orders to repair and preserve it; It fell last year, before expected, being blown down by a violent storm, but orders were sent to prepare a new one some time before, and by the last accounts received, it must be erected by this time.

sary and lofty structure is subject to all the injuries of weather, and may totally decay, if not in time prevented, which will be greatly detrimental to the trade, navigation, and welfare of this colony.

"That the inhabitants of this town and county are at vast expence in time of sickness, especially they who have most servants; it being a general misfortune, that, during the *hot season* of the year, hardly one half of the servants are able to do their masters any work, by reason of the *violent* sicknesses; [133] which hath very much prevented the inhabitants from making improvements.

"It is without the least personal resentment to Mr. Causton,[134]

---

133. The common sickness at certain Seasons of the Year is the Ague, but to say that half the servants are not able to work during the hot season on account of Sickness, is we believe an exageration. We have repeated, and I think uncontradicted accounts, that there is not in all America so healthy a town as Savannah.

134. Is it possible to have no personal Resentment against Mr. Causton, if guilty of the heavy charges laid against him in this Presentment? As to the words grievances, hardships, subersion [subversion] of laws and liberties, the complaints are so groundless, and so often repeated by a Set of Malecontents, who like no Magistrates that are not chosen by themselves, nor any Government which is not of their own framing, that the Magistrates and Trustees shew too much lenity in forbearing to treat Such mutinous Spirits with the severity they deserve. It is observable, that after Mr. Causton was removed from the Magistracy, he grew a favourite to them, and particularly to the Foreman of this Grand jury (who had been Mr. Oglethorpes domestick servant) and all their malice was turnd against his Successor.

---

or any other person, that we do, with the most profound respect and duty, lay before your Honours the foregoing *grievances, hardships,* and *necessities;* and it is not the persons or personal infirmities of any of the magistrates we blame; but such of their actions and words as (we humbly conceive) tends to the subversion of our laws and liberties; and we are firmly persuaded, that Mr. Causton would not have impanneled this Grand Jury, on an affair that so nearly concerned him as that of his niece's did, if he had not believed the several persons of this Grand Jury to be men of integrity, and no way prejudiced against him; and as we the said Grand Jury are, for the time being, appointed for the solemn representation of truth, we humbly hope your Honours will consider this our representation, as proceeding from a strict, impartial, and sound enquiry.

"In witness, &c. ——— This first day of September, 1737."

The original of this was signed by all the forty-four, and sent home; but was taken no notice of by the Trustees,[135] for anything

---

135. *But was taken no notice of* etc. Mr. Causton was removed the following year, which was sufficient notice, this being their principal aim.

---

ever we heard; and we hope it will appear evident to every judicious reader, that this jury was neither *byassed* nor *intimidated* by Causton, to the prejudice of any person whatsoever, as Mr. Wesly asserts in his Journal printed at Bristol, 1739. He likewise says, there were a professed atheist and deist in the number; but for our parts we know of neither: [136] But a man of Mr. Wesly's

---

136. *Ther[e] was a professed atheist and deist in the number* etc. Whether any Atheist was among them we know not: but the Trustees are well assured there were two Deists at that time there viz. Mr. Aglienby[?] and Andrew Duchee. The former died in August 1738, of whom Col. Stephens wrote in his journal of 24th that month, that "his character were better forgot than remembered to his Infamy. That having a smattering of the law, he made use of that talent, being a great adviser among divers of our late Malecontents, most of whom had forsaken him Seeing their Error. He was so far from making any Improvment, that he discouraged many others from it, and in most matters of controversie, took part against the Civil Magistrates, a Stirrer up of ill blood, and a great Devotee to Rum. Tis said that using it to excess, brought a flux on him which carryd him off. During his sickness Mr. Whitfeild offered to do his duty in prayer etc. but he refused any such assistance, denyed any Mediator, and dyed a profest Deist."

As to Andrew Duchee, Col. Stephens wrote that he was a proffest Deist, and attempted to make others so, in so much that the Magistrates refused to put apprentices to him. He was in the first class of Malecontents, a harranger of the mob, an opposer of the Civil magistrates, and all authority, and still continues so. All this the Authors of this pamphlet know to be true, being then in Savannah.

---

principles, who makes no scruple of writing wilful falshoods (as may be seen by any body that compares this *Narrative* with his *Journal*) [137] and of damning every person of a contrary opinion

---

137. *Who makes no Scruple* etc. The comparing this narrative with Mr. Wesley's or any other mans account can be no proof of his falshoods, the narrative being itself full of untruths.

---

with himself; may, without hesitation, give people what appellations come in his head: However, this put an end to any further prosecution of Mr. Wesly's schemes; for soon after this, he departed the colony privately by night, and went to Charlestown, and from thence to England.

Mr. Wesly had address enough (as he says in his forementioned

Journal) to persuade several persons who were members of the Grand Jury, to retract (by some paper which he drew up for them to sign) their former sentiments; [138] but this, if it was at all,[139] proceeded entirely from the solemn assurances [140] which he gave them,

---

138. *Mr. Wesley had address enough* etc. There were no less than 9 or 10 who retracted, but I suppose he did not own in his journal that he prevaild on them so to do by using any Address.
139. *if it was at all:* Why make a supposition of what they know to be true?
140. *proceeded entirely from the solemn assurances* etc. This Grand Jury is said p. 44 to consist of the better sort of people, but tis no good character of them to say that any number of them retracted, that is, denied the truth, for future considerations.

---

that his main design home was to represent the grievances and oppressions which the poor colony laboured under; and upon this account was charged with divers letters and papers from private persons, relating to the colony; which he undertook faithfully to deliver: But as we have since found, that all Mr. Oglethorpe's interest was employed to protect Mr. Wesly; [141] it is no wonder those

---

141. Where, or how have they found this? It seems Mr. Oglethorpes name is on every occasion to be used right or wrong to defame him. Mr. Wesley had no occasion for protection, for he never designed to return again to the Colony, where if he committed any male-practices he ought to be tryed. At his return to England, he waited on the Trustees but once, where he met with so cool reception that he never came again. He was an inveterate Enemy to Mr. Causton, yet Mr. Oglethorpe is here represented his Protector, who before was complained of patronizing Causton. Such is the inconsistency of these Lybellers.

---

promises were never fulfilled; nor indeed could it ever be ascertained, that even the private letters, which he carried, were so much as delivered.

On the other hand, Mr. Causton ever after bore a mortal hatred to the members of this Grand Jury, and took every opportunity to shew his resentment; [142] and we doubt not but he prevailed upon three or four of them to a recantation, having either terrified or starved them into a compliance: But we bore these things the more patiently,[143] as being satisfied the Trustees were gentlemen

---

142. *On the other hand* etc. I have taken notice (note 4 p. 48) that many of them were afterwards great friends with Mr. Causton.
143. *But We bore* etc. The Authors of this pamphlet had no pretence to complain against him for any injury done them.

who had our interest at heart, and who would hear and redress our grievances in due time; and that Mr. O———pe might still be a friend to the colony; but at last we heard he had procured a regiment for its defence, of which he was made Colonel; [144] and that

144. *But at last* etc. Was Mr. Oglethorpes procuring a Regiment for defence of the Colony, any argument that he might not be a friend to it?

he was likewise made General and Commander in Chief over all His Majesty's forces in South Carolina and Georgia. This news was confirmed by William Stephens, Esq; who was sent over as Trustees' Secretary to represent the state and condition of the colony as it really was, and to assist and consult with the magistrates: But Mr. Causton soon found the means to bring over the old gentleman to his interest, or at least to acquiesce in every thing he said or did; for he had still the command of the cash and stores, and Mr. Stephens had nothing to live upon but his salary, which he could stop the payment of at pleasure; so our Secretary remained passive until Causton's government ended.[145]

145. *This news was confirmed by Will. Stephens Esq* etc. This paragraph is put in to blacken the character of a gentleman of Strict honour, piety and virtue, but because he on all occasions endeavours to support the Civil Magistry, and the execution of the Trustees Orders, tho with the greatest lenity and Temper, therefore he is an object of these fellows malice. He is a gentleman of ancient extraction in the Isle of Wight, in which he served for Member in divers Parliaments, but by a Series of misfortunes (not of his own incurring) became reduced in his fortune, and from his good opinion of the Trustees went over their Secretary in Georgia and became a considerable Landholder there. He was directed to send over a journal of every days proceedings, and give an account of what ever was material for the Trustees to know, which duty he faithfully discharged, to the great disatisfaction of the turbulent spirits ther[e]. He was by his Office independent of Mr. Causton, and by his character above being influenced by him; nor could Mr. Causton stop his sallary, the same being settled and appropriated to him by the Trustees Estimated Expences. Mr. Causton was removed in 1738, yet the malecontents continue to use this worthy gentleman very ill, which shows that his concurrence with Causton in every thing he said and did (which yet is a false assertion) whilst he had the command of the Stores, was not the true cause of these mens not liking him, but that he gave right information of their characters, practices and designs.

At last Mr. Oglethorpe comes over for the third time, in September [1738], with the remainder of his regiment; the other part having come with Colonel Cochran in May: But alas! this regiment was of no service, otherwise than to strengthen us in case of an attack; for we could neither furnish them in cloathes, provisions, nor any one thing they wanted: [146] And to put us out of all hopes

---

146. *But alas! this Regiment* etc. Neither the Colony, or the Trustees were to furnish the Regiment with clothes, provisions, or any thing, it being on the military establishment, So this Alas! might have been spared: nevertheless provisions, workmen, boats etc. were advanced by the Magistrates to the value of 1900£ which was afterwards repaid.

---

of bettering our condition, Mr. Oglethorpe was pleased to declare in the court-house of Savannah, that, as long as he had any thing to do with the colony, there should neither be allowance of Negroes nor alteration in the titles of land; and if any such thing should happen, he would have no further concern with it.[147] The people, thus seeing there was no hope of redress, left the colony daily; [148] and the Trustees' credit receiving a great shock by their re-

---

147. *Mr. Oglethorpe was pleased to declare* etc. He knew too well the danger of allowing Negroes, that there was a law against them, and that the Trustees were of the same mind with himself.

148. *Left the Colony daily* etc. We know but of 44 men women and children who left the Colony this year 1738, occasioned not by hardships from their Governours, but partly by the severest drought that had happened in the memory of man and which equally affected the other colonies, so that the people did not see half their crops, and partly by the orders given to shut the Trustees store to all but their servants, it not being reasonable to feed any longer the idle and lazy who for some years lived upon it.

Of these Col. Stephens writes—"I confess it was matter of concern to me for a while, to observe how many people have deserted this place within some months past, but upon due consideration since, I can think of it with content, when I reflect on the character of many of them, whom I am confident no Country will be the better for: Many of them Run-aways from hence, idle and of no use to the Community, nevertheless great Exclaimers against the Publick Proceedings here, where they helped to make an Outcry whilst they staid: and I am fully convinced twould be happy for the Colony if it were entirely weeded of all such mischievous Plants got into it. Some few indeed are gone off, not to be ranked among these, but even in them the greatest loss sustained is in so many sencible [fencible?] men, for otherwise, they were not prone to cultivate land, But mostly carpenters, smiths, or such like, who found their work began not to carry the same wages as formerly, or could not readily find employment at their trades, and therefore went (as most tradesmen will) where they thought they could earn more: and the same reason will bring them back again."

fusing Mr. Causton's certified accompts, and an entire stop being put to the publick store; many poor wretches died of hunger: [149] For

---

149. none died of hunger, it is a most injurious slander

---

at this time Mr. Causton was turned out of all his places, and the store was ordered to be sold, in order, as was said, to pay off the Trustees' debts. One Thomas Jones, a favourite of Mr. Oglethorpe, whose character we shall have occasion to give afterwards, was put in his place, as Cash and Store-keeper, only with a different title, viz. that of Magazine-Keeper; for none but the Trustees' servants were to be supplied from it: [150] But the contrary soon appeared;

---

150. *was put in his place* etc. When Mr. Causton was removed from his place of Storekeeper, it was necessary that some person should succeed him till the remainder of the stores were consumed, and there being accounts to make up with Causton, Mr. Jones was appointed being the person who best understood Accounts and a man of acknowledged just character. The Trustees never gave him the name of Magazine keeper, tho he was truly so when he by Col. Oglethorpes order took in stores for his Regiment after the Trustees had done keeping a store, and for which there was an account between him and the Colonel: and after he and Col. Stephens by Col. Oglethorpes direction set up a private store on their own accounts, to keep down the exorbitant prices of other private Storekeepers, who took the advantage of the Trustees putting down their publick One. But take Col. Stephens plain and full account of this affair in his own words 20. November 1740. "One thing I cannot pass over, without immediately applying my self to explain, which through the accusation of Benj. Adams, and the false light that I humbly conceive he has represented them in, I fear he has created some displeasure against Mr. Jones and me (one or both of us) as if a Publick Store had been carred on here, notwithstanding the Trustees express order to the contrary: which is so daring a fault that I should think unpardonable, if it appeared really so as I take it he desired it should. Mr. Jones is gone to wait on the General, at Frederica, in order to adjust accounts with his Excellency, and seperate those that belong to the Army, from such as relate properly to the Trust. In his absence therefore I venture to unfold these things a little as far as I can knowingly, and shall leave it to him to add what more he thinks needfull, when he returns.

When we received the last Estimate, the General was then at Savannah, and by his direction appointed 3 Chandlers for retailing provisions, and other necessaries to supply the wants of the Inhabitants; directing also that no provisions etc. should for the future be issued by us than to those Chaundlers, unless to ships or vessels that put in here, and required larger quantities than they could be supplyed with by them, and also for boats and pettiaguas employed in the service of the Colony, and Indians. The 3 following were named by the General to be supplyed by us on Credit with all necessary provisions, etc., which they were to retail at a moderate proffit, viz. Harry Loyd, Widow Weddel, and John Pye, and to pay weekly, as they vended the same. They were supplyed with butter at 6 pence, the same to be by them sold at not exceeding 7½ p [pence] pound: Cheese at 5 pence to be sold at 6 pence: Molasses at 17 pence p gallon to be sold at 20 pence: Sugar at 4 pence to be sold at 6 pence, and other goods in like manner. Harry Loyd was entrusted with about 10 or 12£ worth of goods, which he soon made spoil of, and faild in payment: Mrs. Weddel soon after marryed, and left off keeping shop: John Pye went to the Southward, and his wife would follow that trade no longer. These Chaundlers failing, Mr. Woodrose and Mr. Penrose advanced the prices of all such goods to so high a rate, that butter and candles which generally had been sold from 6 pence to 8 pence p pound, were sold by them at 12 pence each pound. It was then found necessary, in order to supply the German servants [The Trustees now paid them in money], and other poor Inhabitants, to buy a Cargo brought from New York, and ever since, butter has been sold for 6 pence, never exceeding 7 pence, and candles the same: flour of the best 9/ and never exceeding 9/6 p cwt.: biscuit from 9/6 to 10: meat from 1·½ to 2 pence p pound. The Indian and Carolina troops passing and repassing here this year, and the Generals own Regiment in the South, occasioning great demands of all kinds of provision, which they could not at all times be readily provided with, it was thought necessary by the General that when any vessels with provisions from the North Colonies called here, we should by no means let them slip, if their Cargoes could be purchased at a reasonable rate. As soon as Mr. Jones returns from Frederica, the Receipts and Issues of such provisions, are intended to be laid before their Honours, whereby twill appear, that provisions of most kinds have been issued 20 p cent cheaper, than we find it to have been ever before. The Rule has been, in bread and flowr (which are the two main Articles) to advance 6 pence p hundred weight to answer loss and damage, and other goods in proportion: by these means of coming to a reasonable Market, and being defended from Monopolizers, many of the Common people of this town have found it their Interest to live here, notwithstanding the temptation they daily meet with from our false brethren of the Club, to try their fortune elsewhere."

Notwithstanding the evident advantage this private store was of to the people, yet through the clamour of the other store keepers, and in obedience to the Trustees orders, these Gentlemen were obliged to put it down the following year. It had been so confidently asserted by the Malecontents that they made use of the Trustees Cash to serve their private Ends, and such pains was taken to pass this falsity on the World, that the Trustees thought it necessary to give those orders, which being submitted to, flung the Inhabitants into great distress as Col. Stephens foretold it would, and as appears by the following passages in his journal.

Monday 20 July 1741. "Some of our discontented people having made complaints that the Publick Stores were made a place of Retail, to the injury and discouragement of divers of our Inhabitants who kept private shops,

'Twas determined to put an entire stop to the delivering any goods by sale for the future: the effect of which would soon be seen. To set this matter in a true light, it may be needfull to look back to my letter of the 20. November last, where in some measure I set forth the occasion of any provisions being bought, and the use made of them: which had such an Effect, that Monolopizers [sic] thereby were constrained from oppressing the Common people, and prevented from driving many more out of the Colony, by their setting exorbitant prices on what they Sold. This was most notoriously evident. At the same time, divers of these now complaining Storekeepers, who were not of substance to buy a large Stock, were furnished at any time with what they asked, that could by spared out of the Publick Magazine, at the very price within a trifle of what they were at first bought at: so that as to my own part, instead of making any profit, I am not without apprehensions of being a sufferer. And it ought likewise to be noted, that these Retailers of goods so purchased, sold them out again under our noses at 20 p cent profit, so that it might have been hoped all were pleased. But since tis now become a practice among such as are instigated by our Ruling Cabal, to exclaim against every thing that is done by those whom the Trust employs, it is high time to lay aside all farther concern, how, or which way Provisions are to be had at the easiest rate, and to force Benefits on such as are averse to receive them: One misfortune however seems unavoidable, viz. that whereof all without exception must be now precluded from dealing at the Publick Magazine in any kind, many well disposed people will be Sufferers, who have already applyed in vain, not without tears, but must share the common chance with their neighbours, and get what they stand in need of, on such terms as they can elsewhere."

Accordingly so it happened, for on the 11. August following he wrote to the Trustees—"Many people of the town had now sufficient experience what advantage they had acquired by their clamour and Out-cry against Provisions being delivered out the Stores, whereof such profit was made as they thought fit to set forth: for now they found to their cost that they must pay a much greater price, so that they [their] Cry was turned: heavy complaints made by the accusers, at our refusing to supply them cheaper, and ridiculous threats that they would send to the Government of Carolina, to assist them in their needs. All which I gave little heed to, for what would it avail to endeavour at humouring a set of people, who were determined to be pleased with nothing we could do? And I was with good reason grown averse to any more retailing work at the Stores, more especially knowing The Trust's opinion therein, which nothing should occasion us to vary from, but the misery which came on our people, by the exorbitant prices at that time imposed on them by monolopizers [sic], when this Relief was provided for *their* Sakes. It was a little surprizing to me to find Mr. *Fallowfeild* in this number asking provisions of us, who had been, and yet was a violent exclaimer against all we did: He telling me, that the price of flowr among our private Storekeepers was risen to 16 shillings p hundred, and that not good, wherefore he should take it kindly. I told him that divers species were growing very scarce with us, having purchassed none for some time past, and we were obliged to keep a reasonable quantity for many contingent demands which we were lyable to for the publick service. Nevertheless, at length I condescended to let him have a Cask of Rice, and a small quantity of flowr for the present exigence of his family (upon credit too) thinking therein I heaped coals of fire on his head."

for the *Sola* bills that were sent over, were ordered to be issued out in the names of William Stephens, Esq; Mr. Thomas Christie and Mr. Thomas Jones, or any two of them; but the other two, agreeing together, entirely excluded Christie, and paid them to whom, and for what purpose they thought convenient: They bought New York cargoes, and any other commodities that could be got in quantities, and put them into the magazine, where they were sold out by Jones in wholesale and retail, for ready money, *at exorbitant rates.*[151] This trade they have carried on ever since, to

151. Note 5th explains this whole affair to the confusion of these consummate slanderers.

their vast advantage; but to the no small distress of the poor people, who are obliged to give at the rate almost of cent. per cent. for their provisions.[152] Thus, under the colour of *no store,* these two

152. All a lye from first to last

keep as open a one as ever Causton did; and, by having the publick money at their disposal, the payment of all salaries and pensions coming through their hands, they are become as *absolute;* with this difference, that Mr. Causton's power, in every respect, extended over the whole colony when it was most populous and money most plenty; but *theirs* seems only to affect the *wretched* remains of Savannah.

We might have imagined, that the Trustees were somewhat moved with our repeated complaints,[153] and that Mr. Causton's

153. Hugh Anderson as he had no reason, so he never complained of Mr. Causton to the Trustees whilst in the Colony, with whom he was in friendship, but having sold his pen he writes as others would have him.

removal was owing thereto: But alas! in this we were mistaken; nothing (as ever we could understand) was laid to his charge on our account; and it was of small benefit to us, whether the mismanagement of money, which was the reason of his dismission, lies at his or Mr. Oglethorpe's door:[154] And we *cannot but* here take notice,

154. Always a fling at Mr. Oglethorpe

that Mr. Causton's case fortifies the common observation, *that those who prostitute themselves to carry on illegal and oppressive schemes, when they have once stuck in the mire, they are forsaken by their employers, and despised by all the world besides.*

Mr. Oglethorpe staid not long at Savannah, his common residence being at Frederica, where they had, in imitation of us, built a few houses, and cleared some land; but, finding planting not answer, they left it off,[155] and as soon as the regiment came, almost every body betook themselves to the keeping publick houses; [156] and in this manner do the few that now remain live.[157]

---

155. Settlers in any place need no imitation for building themselves houses.
156. False: houses were particularly lycensed there, and planting goes on. See pref. p. 9. and they are now going on the silk.
157. *the few that now remain.* The number of householders there when at the highest in 1738 were but 54, and in August 1741 which is the latest account they were 43. The difference of 11 is not much in 3 years time. Some died, others for various reasons changed their minds and removed, and some who go to seek work in Carolina return. The nearness of that Province makes this a frequent practice.

All the publick work being put a stop to, and clearing of land being found impracticable, by which most of us had ruined ourselves; we were in a miserable condition; and all hope from Mr. Oglethorpe being at an end, we could hardly tell what to do: But still thinking, the Trustees might be ignorant or misinformed of the present condition of the colony, we at last resolved to set forth our grievances in a short and general Representation, to be signed by all the freeholders in the colony; of which the following is an exact copy.

"To the Honorable the Trustees for Establishing the Colony of Georgia in America.

"May it please your Honors,

"We whose names are underwritten, being all settlers, freeholders, and inhabitants in the province of Georgia, and being sensible of the great pains and care exerted by you, in endeavouring to settle this colony, since it has been under your protection and management; do unanimously join to lay before you, with the utmost regret, the following particulars: But in the first place, we must beg leave to observe, that it has afforded us a great deal of concern and uneasiness, that former representations made to you, of the same nature, have not been thought worthy of due consideration, nor even of an answer. We have most of us settled in this colony, in pursuance of the description and recommendation given of it by you in Britain; and, from the experience of residing here several years, do find that it is impossible that the measures, hitherto laid down and pursued for making it a colony can succeed. None of all those, who have planted their land, have been able to raise sufficient produce to maintain their families in bread kind only,[158] even

158. *None of all those* etc. A false assertion. See the notes on p. 9. 10. and 11. of the preface: and Mr. Cuthberts affidavit, note 1. on p. 32. As also what is remarked p. 3.

though as much application and industry have been exerted to bring it about, as could be done by men engaged in an affair on which they believed the welfare of themselves and posterity so much depended, and which they imagined required more than ordinary pains to make succeed; so that by the accumulated expences every year, of provisions, cloathing, and medicines, for themselves, families, and servants, several hath expended all their money, nay even run considerably in debt, and so been obliged to leave off planting and making further improvements;[159] and those, who

159. It was not their improvements ran them in debt but their extravagancies. In a letter of Mr. Robert Parker to the Trustees in the year 1734, there is the following paragraph—"We have about 30 or 40 Free Masons: they have a fine supper every Satturday night and often 2 or 3 in the week besides; where such an expence can be born I am at a loss to know. One night among other disorders, they went to the Guard, cut the Capt. down the head, and disarmed the rest, carrying the Arms away. When they came to reflect on it on the morrow, to make things up, they called a lodge at night, and admitted Gough the Captain a Free Mason, so I suppose the thing dropt."
Mr. Gordon also wrote to the Trustees 7. May 1735 that at several Feastings and Clubs, 15 or 16£ Sterl. had been spent. See more of these peoples behaviour p. 26. 44.

continue, are daily exhausting more and more of their money, and some daily increasing their debt, without a *possibility* of being reimbursed, according to the *present* constitution. This being now the general *state of the colony*, it must be obvious that people cannot subsist by their land, according to the present establishment; and this being a truth resulting from trial, practice, and experience, cannot be contradicted by any *theoretical* scheme, or reasoning.[160] The land then, according to the present constitution, not

160. It is acknowledge[d] that people who will not work themselves, and have not money to hire servants cannot subsist according to the present Estab-

lishment; neither can they subsist under any Establishment. But Tryal, practice and experience shews that industrious men can do it, witness the Saltsburgers and some English. This very month (March 1741/2) arrived a letter from Mr. Boltzius the Saltsburg Minister to Mr. Hen. Newman[,] Secretary to the Society[,] for promoting Christian knowledge, that God had prospered them with so good a harvest, that they had corn to spare for the Saltsburgers whom the Trustees sent over last year.

being capable to maintain the settlers here, they must unavoidably have recourse to and depend upon trade: But to our *woful experience* likewise, the same causes, that prevented the first, obstruct the latter; for though the situation of this place is exceeding well adapted for trade, and, if it was encouraged, might be much more improved by the inhabitants; yet the difficulties and restrictions, which we *hitherto have,* and *at present do* labour under, debar us of that advantage: Timber is the only thing we have here which we might export,[161] and notwithstanding we are obliged

161. *Timber is the only thing we have here we might export* etc. This is false, for numbers of skins are brought down by the Indian Traders, but for want of shipping at Savannah they are carred forward to Charlestown.

to fall it in planting our land, yet we cannot manufacture it for a foreign market, but at double the expence of other colonies; as for instance, the river of May, which is but twenty miles from us, with the allowance of Negroes, load vessels with that commodity at one half of the price that we can do; and what should induce persons to bring ships here, when they can be loaded at one half of the expence so near us; therefore the timber on the land is only a continual charge to the possessors of it, though of very great advantage in all the northern colonies, where Negroes are allowed, and consequently labour cheap. We do not in the least doubt, but that in time, silk and wine may be produced here, especially the former; but since the cultivation of land, with white servants only, cannot raise provisions for our families,[162] as before mentioned,

162. This falsity is continually repeated: but has been frequently confuted in the notes.

therefore it is likewise impossible to carry on these manufactures according to the *present* constitution. It is very well known, that Carolina can raise every thing that this colony can; and they, having their labour so much cheaper, will always ruin our market, unless we are in some measure on a footing with them; [163] and as,

163. *It is very well known* etc. This argument holds where the 2 Provinces cultivate the same produces: but as Georgia is not designed to follow the

business of Rice, so Carolina does not follow silk and wine because they get most by rice, wherefore cheapness of labour in Carolina through the use of Negroes, is of no prejudice to the raising the intended produces [products] in Georgia.

in both, the land is worn out in four or five years, and then fit for nothing but pasture; we must be always at a great deal more expence than they in clearing new land for planting. The importation of the necessaries of life come to us at the most *extravagant* rate: [164]

164. The truly Industrious have the necessaries of life of their own raising (clothes excepted) viz. corn, Cattle, hoggs, poultry, garden stuff pease, potatoes, pumkins etc.

Merchants in general, especially of England, not being willing to supply the settlers here with goods upon commission, because no person here can make them any security of their lands or improvements,[165] as is very often practised in other places to pro-

165. Some Merchants of England do supply the Settlers with goods on Commission: Mr. Pytt and Tuckwell supply Mr. Brownfeild: but to supply the people with Negroes would indeed require the giving lands for security, but if there were no other reason than the throwing the peoples propertie into Negro Merchants hands from whence they Seldom or never get out, this were sufficient reason not to admit of alienations.

mote trade, when some of the employer's money is laid out in necessary buildings and improvements fitting for the trade intended, without which it cannot be carried on: The benefit of importation therefore is all to *transient* persons, who do not lay out any money amongst us; but, on the contrary, carry every penny out of the place; [166] and the chief reason for their enhancing the price is, be-

166. *carry every penny out of the place etc.* This would not be if the people were industrious.

cause they cannot get any goods here either on freight or purchase for another market: If the advantage accruing from importation centered in the inhabitants, the profit thereof would naturally circulate amongst us, and be laid out in improvements in the colony. Your Honours, we imagine, are not insensible of the numbers that have left this province, not being able to support themselves and families any longer; [167] and those still remaining, who had money

167. *your honours we imagine are not insensible etc.* See this answered p. 41. note 2. p. 51. note 3.

of their own, and credit with their friends, have laid out most of the *former* in improvements, and lost the *latter* for doing it on such precarious titles.[168] And upon account of the present establishment,

168. *And those still remaining etc.* This is spoken in general, of all remaining, which is not true, for very few improved land, or laid much money out thereon, but they soon chose to live in town and turn shopkeepers or left the Colony, not caring to work with their own hands as did many of the poorer sort. The others spent most of their money and time in taverns and ale houses. As to losing their credit with their friends on account of their precarious Titles, this could not be with such as resolved to keep their lands, for their Titles were absolute secure to them, and so it is reasonable to believe they thought themselves, otherwise they would not have taken up grants, to the conditions of which no objections were made by any for some years, nor until the Scotch Club of pretended Gentry took it into their heads to clamour for the use of Negroes, and in order to obtain them of merchants, to dispute the validity of their grants, that they might have leave to morgage their lands for security to those Merchants.

not above two or three persons, except those brought on charity, and servants sent by you, have come here for the space of two years past, either to *settle* land, or *encourage* trade; [169] neither do we

169. *Not above 2 or 3 etc.* The fewer of this kind of people come, the better, for this kind of gentry are the plague of the place. As to the inferiour sort many come daily and are desirous of Freehold lotts. In the last letter wrote by Col. Stephens to the Trustees dated Nov. 1741 he told them all the known vacant lots in Savannah were filled up, and there were others ready to take the lots of those who had left the Colony, if they could obtain them, so that he beleived in a little time the town would be as full as ever. But if none had come for the space of 2 years past it would be no wonder, since the Scotch gentry made it their business to write into all Countries to their friends to discourage every body from settling in Georgia, in spight [spite] that the Trustees would not give them Negroes; hoping that their own abandoning the place would be justified by the fewness of those who should remain behind. They had the confidence frequently to threaten the Trustees themselves with their intention to do this, and there are abundant instances in the Trustees Office of their actual attempts that way, too numerous to be here inserted: nay they had the impudence to harrangue the poor Inhabitants (before themselves went away) and advise them to follow their example, and when gone to Carolina, discouraged every one they met with, who happened to pass through Charlestown or be there on business, from returning to the Colony.

hear of any such likely to come until we are on better terms. It is true, His Majesty has been graciously pleased to grant a regiment for the defence of this province and our neighbouring colony, which, indeed, will very much assist us in defending ourselves against all enemies; but, otherwise, does not in the least contribute to our support; for all that part of their pay, which is expended here, is laid out with transient people, and our neighbours in Carolina, who are capable to supply them with provisions and other necessaries at a moderate price, which we, as before observed, are not at all capable to do upon the present establishment. This then being our present condition, it is obvious what the consequences must be.

"But we for our parts have entirely relied on, and confided in your good intentions, believing you would redress any grievances that should appear; and now, by our long experience, from industry and continual application to improvement of land here, do find it impossible to pursue it, or even to subsist ourselves any longer, according to the *present* nature of the constitution; [170] and like-

170. Some falsity always trumped up.

wise believing you will agree to those measures that are found from experience capable to make this colony succeed, and to promote which we have consumed our money, time, and labour; we do, from a sincere regard to its welfare, and in duty both to you and ourselves, beg leave to lay before your immediate consideration the two following chief causes of these our present misfortunes, and this *deplorable* State of the Colony, and which, we are certain, if granted, would be an infallible remedy for both.

"1st. The want of a free title, or fee-simple, to our lands; [171]

171. *The want of a free Title* etc. It has been taken notice before that what they call a Free title or Fee Simple, is only desired that they may morgage their lands to Negro Merchants; there may be other reasons why they clamour for it. Creditors may hope thereby to be paid their debts or get the land in their possession; and many idle people may hope to sell their properties to Carolinians (who are too desirous of getting them) and then abandon the Colony. As it would be impolitick in the Trustees to grant this, so it is very unreasonable to be required; there have been such alterations in the Tenures made from time, that Col. Stephens has frequently acquainted the Trustees, the sober part of the Inhabitants are well satisfied, and Capt. Horton now here, who is a Landholder and has as much reason to desire a good Title as any, by reason of his family and great Improvments, avers that no reasonable man can desire a better or fuller Title.

which, if granted, would both induce great numbers of new settlers to come amongst us, and likewise encourage those who remain here, chearfully to proceed in making further improvements, as well to retrieve their sunk fortunes, as to make provisions for their posterity.

"2d. The want of the use of Negroes, with proper limitations; [172]

---

172. *The want of the use of Negroes with proper limitations* etc. Experience has shewn in Carolina, Jamaica, etc. that no limitation of Negroes takes effect, and this the gentlemen of Carolina themselves acknowledge. But the arguments why no Negroes should be suffered in Georgia are so strong and so many, that it is needless to repeat them here. The opinions of Col. Oglethorpe, the Magistrates, Col. Stephens, Capt. Thompson, Mr. Christie, Capt. Horton (the 4 last Land and freeholders) Capt. Dempsy, and Governor Glen of Carolina are against Negroes, and the town of Ebenezar and Darien petitioned against them.

---

which, if granted, would both occasion great numbers of white people to come here, and also render us capable to subsist ourselves, by raising provisions upon our lands, until we could make some produce fit for export, and in some measure to ballance our importation. We are very sensible of the inconveniences and mischiefs that have already, and do daily arise from an unlimited use of Negroes; but we are as sensible, that these may be prevented by a due limitation, such as so many to each white man, or so many to such a quantity of land, or in any other manner which your Honours shall think most proper.

"By granting us, gentlemen, these two particulars, and such other privileges as His Majesty's most dutiful subjects in America enjoy, you will not only prevent our impending ruin, but, we are fully satisfied, also will soon make this the most flourishing colony possessed by His Majesty in America, and your memories will be *perpetuated* to all future ages, our latest posterity *sounding* your praises, as their first founders, patrons, and guardians; but if, by denying us these privileges, we ourselves and families are not only ruined, but even our posterity likewise; you will always be mentioned as the *cause* and *authors* of all their misfortunes and calamities; which we hope will never happen.

We are,

with all due respect,

Your Honors' most dutiful

and obedient servants.

"Savannah, Decemb. 9, 1738.

Henry Parker,
his
Robert R G Gilbert,
mark
Thomas Christie,

Magistrates.

Robert Williams,
Samuel Mercer,
Patrick Grhame,
David Douglass,
Thomas Bailie,
Hugh Anderson,
James Williams,
Edward Jenkins,
Thomas Ormston,
Joseph Wardrope,
George Bunckle,
Adam Loyer,
Peter Joubart,
John Burton,
Robert Hows,
William Meers,
Thomas Salter,
James Bailow,
James Anderson,
Thomas Trip,
Samuel Holms,
James Muer,
William Parker,
John Grhame,
James Papot,
John Smith,
William Calvert,
Stephen Marrauld,
Richard Mellechamp,
Isaac Young, sen.
James Dormer,
William Carter,
Henry Moulton,
Jacob Watts,
Henry Manley,
Thomas Young,
Thomas Cross,

Richard Davis,
Thomas Tibbet,
James Dean,
Donald Stewart,
John Dudding,
William Ewen,
Henry Loyd,
John Amory,
James Houston,
Isaac Young,
Robert Hanks,
Archibald Glen,
Thomas Neal,
Stephen Tarrien,
James Smith,
Samuel Ward,
Pierre Morelle,
John Desborough, jun.
John Fallowfield,
John Brownfield,
William Woodroofe,
Patrick Tailfer,
Andrew Grant,
Samuel Parker,
Stephen Mounfoord,
David Gender,
James Chainsae,
James Landry,
Lewis Stamon,
William Starflichet,
Simon Rieuwere,
John Young,
Samuel Lacy,
Peter Baillow,
Peter Emry,
William Elbert,
William Greenfield,
Christopher Greenfield,
Thomas Young, sen.
Henry Green,
Peter Tector,
Hugh Frazer,

John Sallie,
James Carwells,
John Lyndall,
Joseph Fitzwater,
Elisha Foster,
Walter Fox,
John Penrose,
David Snook,
Edward Townsend,
John Desborough,
—— Gorsand,
Andrew Duchee,
James Gallway,
John Kelly,
Joseph Stanley,
Edward Bush,
Benjamin Adams,
Charles Britain,

John Rae,
William Coltbred,
Thomas Wattle,
Thomas Bailie,
James Corneck,
James Burnside,
John Teasdale,
Giles Becon,
Francis Brooks,
John Clark,
George Rush,
Andrew Walker,
John Miller,
Thomas Andrews,
William Sterling,
Thomas Gantlet,
Richard Rogers.

In all 117.

This Representation was signed with the greatest willingness by the above one hundred and seventeen freeholders in the county of Savannah,[173] and only a very few of the General's favourites de-

173. *This representation was signed etc.* Every one knows how easie tis to get hands to any petition, and for artfull men to draw in the poor and unwary: besides they were made believe that Col. Oglethorpe would himself approve and sign it.

clined to subscribe the same, so strong appeared to all of them the truths contained, and the *absolute* necessity of such an application. The Jews applied for liberty to sign with us; but we did not think it proper to join them in any of our measures: [174] We

174. *The jews applyed for liberty to sign it etc.* This I do not believe, for why should they be refused, being Freeholders? In a subsequent application they gladly admitted them to sign. Besides, to swell the number to 117 they got the hands of some who were no freeholders, tho they pass them all on the Reader for such. On the 10 Nov. 1740[,] 13 of this number changed their minds.

likewise did not allow widows and orphans to subscribe; because, as the Representation contained the absolute necessities of the colony, it might be objected to us, that they were no proper judges. As for the people of Ebenezer, the subscribers did particularly appoint some of their number to wait upon Mr. Boltzius, their pastor, and to shew him the Representation; which was done; and Mr. Boltzius declared, that the Saltzburghers were equally dissatisfied with their rights and restrictions as the other freeholders, and he doubted not their willingness to join in petitioning for redress, engaging to consult them, and to bring their answer; which he never did; and being thereafter questioned thereupon by Mr. Anderson (one of the persons commissioned to commune with him as is above related) in the presence of several gentlemen, he the said Boltzius, after some frivolous excuses, confessed, that the honourable Mr. Oglethorpe had both given them satisfaction, and engaged him to write home to Germany for a further supply of his country-men.[175]

---

175. *As for the people of Ebenezar etc.* This whole paragraph is an imposition on the Publick; The Saltsburghers in all their letters (not only to the Trustees but private correspondents and friends) exprest [expressed] themselves thoroughly satisfyed with their condition, and in their petition, signed by their whole body, (which these Pamphleers have artfully conceald from the Publick) exprest themselves as follows: "This being so that neither the hot summer season nor any thing else hinders us from work in the ground, we wish to lead a quiet and peacable life at our place: We humbly beseach the Honble. Trustees not to allow that any Negroes might be brought to our place, or in our neighborhood, knowing by experience that houses and gardens will be robbed always by them, and white people are in danger of life because of them, besides other great inconveniencies. Likewise we humbly beseech not to allow to any person the liberty of buying up lands in our place, by which, if granted, it would happen that by Bad and turbulent neighbours our Congregation would be spoilt, and poor harmless people troubled and opprest." This petition was signed the 13 March 1738/9, and occasiond by the Representation mention p. 53.

This gentleman (we observe it with regret) has been made the instrument of imposing upon many British subjects, by publishing journals and letters (to which we refer) most inconsistent with truth.[176]

---

176. It is an outrage scarce to be paraleled thus to defame the character of Mr. Boltzius. There is not a person in the Colony more eminent and more esteemed for piety, integrity and prudence than this clergyman: his letters and journals wrote in the German language for the use of his Countrymen, and his letters to his friends in England are constantly full of praises to God and thanks to the Trustees for the happy condition the Saltsburghers are in, and all who come from the Province and have seen them, declare the same. On the 18 Sept. 1740 Mr. Jones gave an account of these people in a private letter to Mr. Ja. Lyde of London, as follows: "I know of no other settlement in this Colony more desirable, except Ebenezar, a town on the river Savannah

at 35 miles distance from hence (Savannah), inhabited by Saltsburghers and other Germans, under the Pastoral care of Mr. Bolzius and Mr. Gronau, who are discreet worthy men. The town is neatly built, the situation exceeding pleasant; they consist of 60 families or upwards. They live in the greatest harmony with their Ministers, and with one another as one family. They have no idle, drunken, or profligate people among them, but are industrious, many grown wealthy, and their industry has been blessed with remarkable and uncommon successs, to the envy of their Carolina neighbours, having great plenty of all the necessary conveniencies of life (except clothing) within themselves, and supply this town and other neighbouring places, with bread kind, as also beef, pork, veal, poultry etc. Many artifices have been used to gain over these Germans and the Darien people to go on with the discontented Party here in petitioning for Negroes, and since they could not be prevaild on, letters have been writ to them from England endeavouring to intimidate them into a complyance, threatning, that if they did not come into the Scheme proposed, the Spaniards would destroy them all, and the Goverment would not concern themselves with supporting this Colony. Mr. Bolzius shewed me a letter writ to him by one of the Scotch Club, who went from hence to England, and takes upon himself to be their chief Manager in London.["]

Neither did we admit of servants to sign the same, lest it should be objected, that they were under the influence of their masters. By this our conduct it will appear to every person of impartiality, how far we were from using arts [*Vide* Trustees' answer.] to extort by clamour a redress of our grievances.

A COPY of the Representation was immediately sent to Frederica, and another to Darien: The last was sent to Mr. John More McIntosh, and under the same cover a letter to Mr. Benjamin McIntosh: But the first kept up the other's letter, and sent his own with the Representation to the General; who immediately despatched Lieutenant George Dunbar [177] (who speaks the Highland

177. Lieut. Geo. Dunbar is a gentleman of good sence and experience in the Colony: a landholder, and made an affidavit against the necessity of employing Negroes.

language, and has a very fluent and artful way of talking) who, with the assistance of More McIntosh, and promise to the poor people of cattle (which they afterwards got) with several other considerations,[178] soon persuaded them to sign a paper, the design of

178. *promises to the poor people of cattle* etc. There was a loan made them of 200£ to purchase cattle, but this was made them many months after they had petitioned against the use of Negroes, and soon after they paid back part of the money. Here is a great disingenuity in so representing the matter,

as if the cattle were given them by way of bribe. As to the several considerations that induced these people to reject the Representation for Negroes, these declaimers would probably have mentioned them if there were any. The Trustees know of none.

which, they were told, was to oppose the people of Savannah, who, being enemies to the General, were petitioning against him. As for their leader McIntosh, he was immediately set up in a store, and plentifully supplied with all kinds of goods,[179] and has often de-

179. *As for their leader Macintosh* etc. If he set up a store (which is unknown to the Trustees) it was at his own cost, for in the Accounts sent to the Trustees there is no article of money advanced or given to him on such account.

clared, *that if, by acting as he did, he could live well himself, he did not care what became of the rest of the colony; and as for his children, they might go wander in the woods with the Indians.*[180]

180. *That if by acting as he did* etc. The character given of this brave gentleman by Col. Stephens 4 feb. 1737-8 (being then at Darien where the Trustees orderd him to go and inspect the place) will not allow us to think him capable of so vile expressions. His account of him was—"He is indeed a carefull and discreet man." Before the Representation for Negroes was made, he had the care of the Trust Servants at Darien, the supply of whom with necessaries it was his business to provide for, and from hence these Declaimers may have taken occasion to say that he was set up in a store because he opposed their measures. He had a wife and six children, and tis not credible he should have so little concern for them as here represented. On 11. July 1740 Col. Stephens giving an account of the loss our people sustained at Mousa [Moosa] repeats his good character of him in the following words: "The most bloody part of all fell to the unhappy share of our good people at Darien, who almost all to a man engaged under the command of their Leader John Mackintosh More, a worthy carefull Director among his people at home, and who now shewed himself as valiant in the feild of Battle, where calling on his men and followers to follow his example, they made such work with their broad swords as the Spaniards cannot easily forget." He is now a prisoner in Spain, but if ever he returns will probably call these writers to account for so vilanously defaming his character.

As soon as it was heard that the Representation was come to Frederica, the inhabitants were called together, and told, *that the people of Savannah were going to throw off the government of the Trustees, and had associated together for that purpose; and therefore advised them to beware of any snare that might be laid by these people, which if they were caught it would ruin them.* And thus was the design of the Representation quashed both in Darien and

Frederica.[181] Some time after this a copy of the Representation was sent to Mr. Oglethorpe, together with the following letter, which was wrote by an anonymous author; [182] which we think is partly an

---

181. *And thus was the design of the Representation quashed* etc. Capt. Horton now here, averrs that the Inhabitants of Frederica put into his hand a petition against negroes, which he returned to them as needless to present to the Trustees, they not being disposed to allow of Negroes and thereby hazard the safety of the Colony, neither having it in their power as the king had past [passed] a law against it. This these authors conceal.

182. The anonymus author, was Hugh Anderson, the principal Author of this pamphlet. Why he here conceals it I dont know, unless to make his Readers believe that more persons are discontented than really are.

---

explanation of the Representation, and likewise a *true* view of the situation of the colony at that time, with the character Mr. Oglethorpe then bore in it; and for these reasons we here insert it: It was directed,

"*To the Honorable James Oglethorpe, Esq.; General and Commander in Chief over all His Majesty's Forces in South Carolina and Georgia, &c. _____ at Frederica.*

"Sir, It is the common misfortune of all who act in the higher stations of life, to be surrounded with flatterers, who consult rather the humours, passions and prejudices of their patrons, than their honour and interest: This should induce every person in such station, who regards his own honour, interest, or fame, to lend an open and attentive ear to truth, in whatever shape or from whatever hand delivered. I who use this freedom with your Excellency, being an anonymous author, have no other byass, motive, or interest in view, further than as I am a member of the colony, and a well-wisher to the happiness of society, unless a real and sincere regard to your honour and welfare, and an earnest desire to restore you to that quiet of mind and the now suspended affections of the people, which the present state of affairs must necessarily deprive you of; it is not therefore of consequence to enquire *who* writes, but *what* is wrote: I am, sir, a Plain Dealer, and shall, with the greatest respect, use you with more *sincerity* than *ceremony;* and if my arguments can attain the desired effect, you will, I doubt not, think me your and the colony's real friend. When a skilful physician would relieve his patient of a disease, he traces it from the beginning, and examines the sources and progress of it, in order that, by finding out the cause, he may the more certainly apply a remedy: In the body politick the same process is necessary to effect a cure. The present languishing and almost desperate condition of the affairs of this province, is too obvious to your Excellency to need a description: Be pleased then, laying aside prepossession and prejudice, to retire unto yourself, and examine impartially whence the present misfortunes take rise; in order to which, let me present your Excellency with a view of the nation's designs in establishing this colony; and indeed they were and are nothing unsuitable to a British or Roman spirit; to wit, *the establishing a strong and numerous settlement as a barrier and safeguard of British America: to employ those persons in effecting this end who were least useful at home, and others who, from the reasonableness of the proposals, should voluntarily profer their service; to restore liberty and happiness to those who, oppressed by the common misfortunes of mankind, were groaning under the consequences of those misfortunes, and incapable to serve themselves or country at home: and lastly, to set afoot such new manufactures as might be most useful to support the colony, or tend to rectify the ballance of trade of Great Britain with neighbouring nations.* A design truly great, founded on the justest policy, and practicable: To suggest that any low private design was ever laid down, that might tend to make the adventurers slaves, or, at best, tenants at will; or that it was a concert to leave the industry and substance of the settlers exposed to satisfy the ambition or covetousness of an after governor, or any particular courtier or party; or to imagine that the honourable Board of Trustees, or any of them, could be capable of such a concert; I say, sir, that such a thought were impious. What wonder then, if numbers of persons, encouraged by His Majesty's most ample rights and privileges granted in His Royal Charter to the honourable Trustees, for the behalf of the inhabitants; from the beautiful description of the *fertility* of the soil and *happiness* of the climate; and lastly, from a view that Mr. Oglethorpe, a gentleman of the greatest humanity and generosity, was willing to sacrifice his ease, and all those pleasures and enjoyments which his easy circumstances of life *intitled* him to, in order to be the *patron* and *father* of the distressed, and the *distinguished friend* of his country, society, and human nature; I say, sir, no wonder if numbers, upon those views, embarked [183] their persons, families and fates in

---

183. *If numbers on those views, embark'd* etc. how few the numbers see p. 26. note 1.

such an adventure. Shall any thing then intervene to render such a noble design abortive, and frustrate those of their expected happiness, or your Excellency of your deserved honour? God forbid!

"This colony consists of two sorts of people; either those whom the publick sent over and supported, or *volunteers* [By this word was meant those persons who settled in Georgia upon their own expense], who were not burthensom to the publick: [184] Both now

---

184. *Volunteers who were not burthensome to the publick:* They were by contract not to be burthensome to the publick, but they proved so, many obtaining loans from the stores, and others advanced money, which they went away, without repaying. Hugh Anderson and Patrick Tailfer (two of these authors[)] had loans from the stores.

I look upon in the same light; as either party have exhausted their support or private stocks, in endeavouring to prosecute the intended plan; but it shall suffice for my argument, that so many of each kind have applied themselves to this purpose, as are sufficient to confirm the experiment, that it is impossible for us, with British or foreign servants, to afford the lowest necessaries of life, much less to increase our stocks, or defray the many exigencies and disappointments that this soil and climate are *inevitably* exposed to: This I take to be granted; and would to God the success of the colony depended on the laying the most *satisfying* proof of it! And as for persons who, from selfish views, have imposed upon the credulity of the honourable Trustees,[185] by representing things in

---

185. *As for persons who from selfish views* etc. What selfish views could persons settled in the Colony, and occupying land, have to give false representations of the Colony, which must have been so much to their own hurt? Or what interest could others who have no Interest in the Colony to represent it in false colours? Or what Interest could the Trustees have in concealment of the truth from them?

---

colours distant from truth, it were superfluous to curse them. I do not say, but in time manufactures may be founded more suitable to the strength and constitution of British servants,[186] that might sup-

---

186. *in time Manufactures may be founded* etc. What more suitable to the strength and constitution of British Servants than raising silk and wine, which these writers know there was a progress making in, when they published this book.

---

port and enrich the colony; I heartily pray for that happy period. And should then condemn and dissent from any who would *not* be content with the *present* regulation; but as in the *interim* production of necessaries is *absolutely* requisite, and under the *present* establishment impracticable; [187] it follows of course, that either the scheme must be *altered,* or the design *abandoned:* At the first it was a trial, now it is an experiment,[188] and certainly no man or so-

187. This falsity is so often repeated that it became nausious. See note 1. on preface, p. 9. 10. 11. 12.

188. *now it is an experiment:* It is only true with respect to these Authors and their idle associates; if men will spend their substance extravagantly, there is no living any where long.

ciety need be ashamed to own, that from *unforeseen* emergencies their *hypothesis* did misgive; and no person of judgment would censure, for want of success, where the proposal was probable; but all the world would exclaim against that person or society who, through mistaken notions of honour or positiveness of temper, would persist in pushing an experiment *contrary to all probability,* to the ruin of the adventurers. How many *methods* may be found out by the wisdom of the Trustees, for remedying *this* inconvenience, I know not; *one* only occurs to me, which is, the *admitting* a certain number of Negroes, sufficient to ease the white servants from *those* labours that are most fatal to a *British constitution.* I am very sensible of the inconveniences of an *unlimited* use of them in a frontier colony; but am as sensible, that *those* inconveniences may be prevented by prudent *regulations;* [189] and their

189. It has been experienced that no regulations of Negroes are of force in the Colonies where they are admitted. This was confirmed to me by Mr. Beaufain a Carolina gentleman.

admission for executing the more laborious parts of culture, made the means to *attract* numbers of white servants, who would otherwise fly the place as a *purgatory* or *charnelhouse.*[190] If our labour

190. *Made the means to attract white servants etc.* On the contrary it is a known case that Negroes, where admitted, root out the white Inhabitants, for the Owners employ them in all their works. When I mentioned this to Mr. Crockat a Carolina Merchant and asked him what must become of our white labourers and handicraft people? he answered, they might go to Carolina where they wanted white men, and those who remaind with us might be overseers of the Negroes. As to white Servants flying the place as a purgatory or Charnel house, few honest ones do it, except such as are ill used by their Masters: of these Mr. Jones wrote 1. July 1741 as follows: "Many of the other German servants bound by Indenture to serve some of the Freeholders in this Colony, have by their ill usage (of which there has been repeated complaints) deserted their Masters Service. The Carolina temper of procuring

Slaves and treating them with barbarity seems to be very prevalent with us: I mention this the rather, that if any foreigners or others, Servants, should be sent over, the honble. Trustees might give such orders therein, as would prevent this Inconvenience for the future." Col. Stephens gives a remarkable instance of this cruelty to two Dutch Servants, in his journal 24 Oct. 1741. This is the only reason why honest White Servants fly the Colony as a purgatory or charnel house.

---

and toil is not capable of producing mere necessaries by *cultivation of land,* much less by *trade*: For as all the neighbouring colonies, by reason of their Negroes, prosecute all branches of it at a sixth part of the expence we can; [191] they would forever preclude us of

---

191. *at a Sixth part* etc. This is another false assertion. See Capt. Dunbar's affidavit, who swears that Negroes are but about one third less than the expence of white mens Labour in S. Carolina, and that their work is proportionably worse done. Besides, these fellows omit the prime cost of a Negroe, which is 20 or 30 pound Sterl. which must be repaid the Merchant in case of death or escape.

---

any benefit therefrom. And supposing, what cannot be admitted, that the nation would consent to give a *perpetual* fund for making up *all those* deficiencies, what benefit could ever accrue to the nation? or what to the settlers but a present bare sustenance? and what the certain consequence but the bequeathing a numerous legacy of orphans to the care of Providence, since no period of time can be affixed when such a support would enable us to provide for ourselves? A second reason which disables us to improve, either by land or trade, is our *want of credit:* [192] You know very well that

---

192. *Want of credit* etc. This explains the reason and is indeed the sole reason why they clamour for liberty to sell: If they may sell, they may morgage, and having raised a little money by cheating the lender, run away. But what Merchant would lend Negroes on the security of 50 uncultivated acres, or even 500 which is the most the Trustees can grant to any one man? especially to an idle kind of gentry who by extravagance had run out their substance? The honest freeholders, who meant to abide in the Colony, and not to run away were well contented without the permission to sell their property.

---

both the mercantile and the mechanick part of mankind live more by *credit* than *stock;* and the man, who has a probable scheme of improving credit, is naturally intitled to it: As we have no stock further to dispense, either in cultivation or trade, we are reduced to need the support of credit,[193] which the present restrictions of

---

193. *We are reduced* etc. entirely by their own extravagances.

our legal rights and titles to our land deprive us of: It is true, indeed, the Trustees have assured us, *that those and other restrictions are only temporary, and for the welfare of the first settlement, until a proper body of laws, which was upon the carpet, should be perfected;* [194] and I am far from disputing the reasonableness of

---

194. *That these and other restrictions are only temporary* etc. They have found it so, to the satisfaction of all who are acquainted with it, except such as nothing will satisfy. Capt. Horton now here assured the Trustees that in this matter they have granted more than the people when he came over, desired him to ask for.

---

that resolution, while either the *publick* support or *private* stocks kept us from needing credit; but that now the case is altered, the necessity of removing those restrictions is arrived, to preserve the remains of the colony not *yet* dissolved, and far too late for hundreds, whom *necessity* has dispersed in *other* corners of the world: [195] This is a truth, sir, too obvious to need *further* enlargement.

"Hence it is clear, we can insist on demanding our privileges, as British subjects, from the Trustees' promises,[196] but we likewise

---

195. *Far too late for hundreds* etc. Another probable falsity. The Trustees began gradually to extend the Tenures in 1739, all forfeitures were forgiven, and notification given to absent persons to return and put in their claims. It was not necessity that drove hundreds away, but idleness, disappointments, and new schemes of living: debt, want of health, and avoidance of punishment for crimes committed, and in some a fear of the Spaniards during the War. As for such as were industrious, they frequently go and return, as they find work.

196. *We can insist on demanding our privileges* etc. The privileges as British Subjects have never been denied them, but if they mean the restrictions, they were under by their grants, these were such as they voluntarily submitted to, and were for some years approved of by the Inhabitants. These writers know how much the Trustees have done to remove them, but it seems nothing will satisfy them whilst denied Negroes.

---

claim them as *law, justice* and *property.* Your Excellency was pleased, in the court house of Savannah, to use a comparison, to satisfy the minds of the people, of a man, who would lend his horse, but not his saddle, which one refusing, another accepted of: This, I humbly take it, no ways meets the case; the King's Majesty was owner both of horse and saddle, of lands and rights, and gave us both, in his Charter; we ask but what is *there* given us. The re-

liance on the publick faith brought us to this colony; and to endeavour to obviate, or disappoint the effects of *those* promises,[197]

---

197. *Those promises* etc. The promises made the people, have been faithfully kept: but the promises made by these people, which are the Covenants
made with them in their Grants, have not been kept.

---

which tempted us here, were to justify the decoying us to misery,
under the sanction of the *royal authority;* than which nothing
could be more injurious to the *fountain of honour*. I shall suppose, that, were full and ample rights given, *some* idle persons,
who had no *judgment* to value, or inclination to improve their
properties, no *affections* for their families or relations, might dispose of their rights for a *glass of rum;* but I absolutely deny, that
the colony could lose by such an exchange: I own such persons were
much safer, *if bound,* than *at liberty,*[198] but, where the *affection*

---

198. *I shall suppose* etc. Here is a fair confession that idle people ought to
be bound: now this is the character of most of the English who went away, and
yet they were bound only by such Covenants as themselves consented to.

---

of the parent and the *reason of the man* die, the person is a fitter
inhabitant for *Moorfields* than Georgia. I must notice further, that
not only are parents incapable, for *want of credit,* to provide for
themselves, being necessitated to dispose of their servants for want
of provisions; [199] but, if they could, only their eldest son could
reap the benefit; their younger children, however numerous, are
left to be fed by Him who *feeds the ravens*,[200] and if they have no

---

199. It has been shown that industrious men can provide for themselves, and
therefore need no credit, and many such have Servants and maintain them.
In the State of the Colony upon Oath, the Subscribers thereto desire white
servants. On the 26 April 1738, Samuel Davidson an industrious Freeholder at
Frederica wrote to John Gilbert as follows: "If you fancy to come over to us,
I must beg of you to get all the servants you can, and be carefull of them
at Sea, for they will bring you money, or enable you to live handsomly on
your plantation."

200. *Their younger children* etc. Another false assertion: for if their children
are Orphans, they are maintain'd by the Trustees: if grown up may have
lands given them: None need be left to be fed by the ravens, if able and
willing to work, and is it not the case in all Countries as well as Georgia, that
the younger children of poor families or small estates, have little or no
provision made for them?

children, their labour and substance descends to strangers: How, sir, could you, or indeed any *free-born* spirit, brook such a tenure? [201] Are not our younger children, and daughters, equally

---

201. *Their labour descend to Strangers* etc. They may now bequeath to whom they please. But before this, such alterations were made in their Tenures, as fully satisfyed Capt. Horton a Landholder, who was empowered by the people to express their desires.

---

entitled to our bowels and affections? And does human nature end with our first-born, and not extend itself to the rest of our progeny and more distant relations? And is it not inverting the law of nature, that the eldest son should not only enjoy a double portion, but exclude all the younger children? and having an interest *independent* of the parents', how natural is it he should withdraw that obedience and subjection which proceeds from *paternal* authority and *filial* dependance! The Trustees are but a channel to convey to us the King's rights. and *cannot* in law or equity, and, I dare say, *will not* abridge those rights. Can we suppose that we are singled out for a *state of misery* and *servitude,* and that so many honourable personages are instruments of it? Far be the thoughts from us! The genius of the British nation, so remarkably zealous for *liberty* and the *rights of mankind,* will never suffer British subjects, who have not fled their country for crimes, but voluntarily profered their service, and risqued their ALL, upon the confidence of the *publick faith,* and the *Trustees' honour,* to accomplish a settlement upon the *most dangerous* point of His Majesty's dominions; I say, it will never allow such to be deprived of *publick* promises of the *natural* liberties of British subjects. As we are on a frontier, where our lives and fortunes may more frequently come into dispute than other people's, our privileges and supports should be proportionately greater; for who would venture his life to secure *no property,* or fight to secure to himself *poverty* and *misery;* and no doubt our cunning and vigilant adversaries, the French and Spaniards would know how to make their own advantage: The King has been very gracious, and your endeavours generous and useful, in procuring a regiment for our protection; but let me add a truth equally certain, that only the flourishing of the colony can support that regiment; and not only the *support* of the soldiers, but your own *honour, glory,* and *reputation* are *intermixed* with the *fate of the colony,* and must *stand* or *fall* with *it.*

"To come closer to the point, please to consider the *consequences* of refusing the Representation of the colony, whereof your Excellency, as one of the Honourable Board will be furnished with a copy, and how these consequences may affect the Colony, the Nation, the Trustees, the Military Establishment in this province, the Indians, and your Excellency.

"As to the COLONY, the deferring hitherto the necessary relief has already *too tragically* affected it, by dispersing a great part of the inhabitants; the remainder, in a languishing condition, supported more with *faint hopes,* and a *continued reliance* on the honour of the nation and Trustees, than *victuals;* while want and meagre famine guard the door of many, and render them equally incapable to stay or go: [202] The town, so beautifully situated, to

---

202. *the deferring hitherto the necessary relief* etc. It was in truth the too long continuance of relief that made the people idle, and the Malecontents persuasions that if they did not cultivate but joyn with them, they would procure them Negroes to labour in their stead, and the Trustees would be obliged to grant them. Want and meager famine guarding doors, and the being incapable to stay or go are pathetick Rhetorical flights to move the Readers passions, but false, and contradictory to what they before asserted that hundreds were gone away.

---

the honour of the contriver, bearing the most visible signs of *decay* and *mortality,* before it is *fully born;* and the once cultivated plantations, now overgrown with weeds and brush, are so many *hic jacets* of such and such persons and families! [203] I wish it were

---

203. *The once cultivated plantations* etc. The Trustees have a better account of the plantations of those who are industrious: but tis no wonder the plantations of those who are gone away, or abandon'd them are overgrown with weeds and brush. It is wrote over, that if these idle deserters could be induced to quit their lands and holdings, or forfeited, that there are others ready to take them, of a more industrial character.

---

possible to draw a veil over this *tragick* scene! But, sir, our case is more *clamant* than a *thousand tongues,* and will reach the ears, and pierce the hearts of every TRUE BRITON. If such the effects of *delay,* what will the *total dissolution* of the colony produce? Such a body of miserable people, orphans, and suppliants, will be heard by the *justice of the nation;* and if it shall appear, that the too positively adhering to an impracticable scheme, and the refusing those obvious means, that would answer the proposed end, or withholding those just rights which we are *entitled* to, have been the cause, we should have right to recover damages from the authors of our miseries.[204] In all places where settlements were

204. *And if it should appear* etc. The Trustees have confidence that these things will never appear, and have no apprehensions from this menace of the peoples recovering damages from them.

attempted by the English, and found untenable, the settlers were taken home upon publick charge, their losses recompensed, and they made otherwise useful to the community; while we are neither allowed to do for ourselves here, or elsewhere.[205] As to the second

205. *While we are neither allowed* etc. Impudent assertion! None have been hindered from using their industry, on the contrary several bounties have been given, money advanced etc. to provoke them to it, and the good consequence thereof has been found in many.

point, how the NATION would be affected by it; it is first obvious, that all the noble *ends* and *advantages* they proposed are lost, and sums of money expended to no purpose, but to inform the French and Spaniards of the importance of a pass, which they would not fail to possess.[206] It were impossible to make a second settle-

206. *which they would not fail to possess.* This is certainly true if the Colony be abandoned, which the Authors labour to bring about by representing it as abandoned already, and by persuading all who remain to leave it, as well as all who might be disposed to joyn it, not to go.

ment upon the present plan; and if it is to be altered in the favours of others, why not of us who have risqued and spent our *all* in the *adventure?* How the Trustees may be affected by it in all respects, I shall not say; a parliamentary enquiry into their management, I no ways question but they could entirely satisfy; but all good men will regret, that so honourable a body should lose that glory and fame, which the prosperous success of the colony would have crowned them with. I have formerly asserted, that only the flourishing state of the colony can support the MILITARY; and indeed, without a colony, it were easier to maintain a garrison in Tangier on the coast of Africa, than in the south of Georgia. One regiment would *little* suffice to withstand the enemy; and yet so small an handful may be reduced to *discontent, straits,* and *wants,* notwithstanding all the bounty of a King or *prudence* of a General. As to the INDIANS; what could we expect less than being scorned and despised? That they should immediately fall in with the tempting proffers of the French and Spaniards, and so Great Britain cut off from that valuable branch of the Indians' trade? For how indeed could they expect *execution of treaties,* or *protection* from people, who, *without* the force of any enemy, could *not* preserve their *own* schemes of government from falling to pieces? How the tragedy must affect YOUR EXCELLENCY, would be presumption in me to determine: I only know, that to see those you honour with the name of *children,* in *want* and *misery;* that *settlement,* which should have *perpetuated* your name to posterity with the *greatest* honour; become the *foil* of all your great undertakings; and the *expectations* of all the world, from your promising endeavours; *setting* in a *cloud* and *obscurity,* must affect your Excellency in a way suitable to your human and generous disposition.

"Sir, we still *love, honour,* and *respect* you (whatever low, selfishminded persons, the bane of society, may surmise to the contrary) and will continue to do so, while we can have any *hopes* of your pursuing measures consistent with *our prosperity:* But, sir, *smiles* cannot be expected amidst *disappointments* and *wants;* and there is no altering the course of nature: *Love* and *gratitude* are the tribute of favours and *protection,* and *resentment* the consequence of *injuries* received; and in *disappointments* of this nature, much more reasonably than in those of *love,* do the contrary passions take place in the same degree. What then remains, but that you embrace those obvious measures, that will *retrieve* our desperate affairs; *restore* to us, in Mr. Oglethorpe, our father and protector, whose honour and affection was depended upon; *secure* to yourself a society that loves and honours you, and who will always be ready to sacrifice both life and fortune to your honour and protection; and your name with blessings will be *perpetuated.* If in this I have, by a *sincere* and *well-meant* freedom, given offence, I heartily ask pardon; none was intended: And I only request, that, while *truth* keeps the stage, the *author* may be allowed to remain *incog.* behind the scenes.

"I am, SIR, your, &c.
"THE PLAIN-DEALER."

This year there was promised a bounty of two shillings sterling on every bushel of corn, and one shilling on every bushel of pease and potatoes, raised in the county of Savannah: this induced some few to plant; but they were miserably deceived; for few or none of them ever received their full bounty, and not many any part thereof (although, if they had received it twice over, it could not have answered the end:) [207] People being thus, by a chain of disappoint-

---

207. *This year there was promised a bounty* etc. The year here meant was 1739. There is in this account a very unfair concealment of the truth, for the case was this: The bounty was promised by Col. Oglethorpe, unknown to the Trustees, who having made no provision for it in their Estimate of Expences for that year, The Cashier had no money in his hands to pay it, but what was saved upon other articles. As far as that went he paid the bounty, to such as had a just demand; but to several who owed more to the Trustees than their claym amounted to, were left unpaid, and from others who owed less, so much was deducted, and only the overplus paid them, all which must be allowed to be just. The money not holding out, some claymants drew upon the Trustees, who when they were informed of the promised bounty, paid their bills, and gave direction for paying the remaining Claymants.

Tis said here, that if the people had received the bounty twice over, it could not have answered the End: but Mr. Tho. Stephens told me 13. Oct. 1739, that if but 1 Shilling p bushel, bounty upon corn were given to the people, to last till the Silk became an exportable commodity, it was likely the people would stay. He did not then know, neither did the Trustees that 2 Shillings bounty on corn, 1 Shilling on potatoes and pease per bushel, bounty was promised.

---

ments and miseries, most of them rendered incapable to subsist, and, toward the end of this summer, beginning to despair of having any favourable answer to their Representation, or hopes of redress, left the colony faster than ever,[208] and, when the answer (or rather

---

208. *beginning to dispair* etc. In 1738 they write that the people left the Colony daily, yet only 44 did so: see p. 51. and the reason and character of them note 3. Here, in 1739 they say, they left the Colony faster than ever, and it seems they were in great hast to do so, when they would not wait for the Trustees answer to their representation. The whole number who went away in 1739, men women and children, were 47, and here I must observe, that at all times, the far greater number of those who went were out of the Single town of Savannah, the seat of the Factioners, and nearest to Carolina, Ebenezar excepted from whence none went at all. Of those who went this year, Col. Stephens writes, March 29, 1739. "Savannah began indeed now to grow thinner apace of people, nevertheless 'twas aparent, that the generality of those who went off, were either such as being one size above the lowest Rank of people had formed wrong notions to themselves of growing wealthy a little sooner, than the ordinary circumstances of a new founded Colony will readily admit of; or else they were people really of no value for promoting the publick welfare by their Industry and honest labour."

On the 19 May following he writes, "I cant depart from what I before asserted, that the greatest part by far of those that are gone, are not to be wished for again, very few of such as are really valuable being among them."

Again 23 July following, speaking of those who remaind, he says of the others, "They of another disposition, always most clamorous tho far less worth regarding, have sought for better fare in another Province, where I am mistaken if they find they can support themselves better, unless they take more pains to live by their labour, than they did here."

denial) came over, they went in such numbers, that the whole province of South Carolina was overspread with them, and in and about the town of Charlestown alone, this autumn, about fifty Georgians died in misery and want, most of whom were buried at the publick charge.[209]

209. When the answer or rather denyal came over etc. Here is a very exagerated Account of the persons who went away: I have before observed that we know of no more than 47. They acknowledge that the Trustees answer arrived in September, yet in October following Col. Stephens wrote that the number of people in Savannah town alone capable of bearing arms was near 200. They say they went in such numbers that the whole Province of South Carolina was overspread with them, but how 47 persons should overspread a whole Colony is hard to imagine. They also say that in and about Charlestown alone, above 50 Georgians dy'd this Autumn in misery and want, which must be false, for in the Register of that town sent by themselves to the Trustees, there were but 59 Georgians deceased in the Province from the first Settlement of Georgia feby. 1732–3 to feby. 1740–1, in which time it may be supposed that they might have died in Georgia, as well as in Carolina.

If there were more than the above mentioned 47 that went, they were Travellers or Inmates of whom the Trustees have no account.

In September, a printed paper, intitled, *An Answer to the Representation, &c.,* was sent over, and arrived at Savannah, and of which this is an exact copy.

"The Answer of the Trustees for establishing the Colony of Georgia, in America, to the Representation from the inhabitants of Savannah, the 9th of December, 1738, for altering the tenure of the lands, and introducing negroes into Georgia.

"To the Magistrates of the town of Savannah, in the province of Georgia.

"The Trustees for establishing the colony of Georgia in America, have received, by the hands of Mr. Benjamin Ball of London, merchant, an attested copy of a Representation, signed by you the magistrates, and many of the inhabitants of Savannah, on the 9th of December last, for altering the tenure of the lands, and introducing Negroes into the province, transmitted from thence by Mr. Robert Williams.

"The Trustees are not surprised to find unwary people drawn in by crafty men, to join in a design of *extorting by clamour* from the Trustees, an alteration in the Fundamental Laws, framed for the preservation of the people, from those very designs.

"But the Trustees cannot but express their astonishment, that you the magistrates, appointed by them to be guardians of the people, by putting those laws in execution, should so far forget your duty, as to put yourselves at the head of this attempt.

"However, they direct you to give the complainants this answer from the Trustees, that they should deem themselves very unfit for the trust reposed in them by His Majesty on their behalf, if they could be prevailed upon, by such an irrational attempt, to give up a constitution, framed with the greatest caution for the preservation of liberty and property; and of which the laws against the use of slaves, and for the entail of lands, are the surest foundations.

"And the Trustees are the more confirmed in their opinion of the unreasonableness of this demand, that they have received petitions from the Darien, and other parts of the province, representing the inconvenience and danger, which must arise to the good people of the province from the introduction of Negroes. And as the Trustees themselves are fully convinced, that besides the hazard attending that introduction, it would destroy all industry among the white inhabitants; and that, by giving them a power to alien their lands, the colony would soon be too like its neighbours, void of white inhabitants, filled with blacks, and reduced to be the precarious property of a few, equally exposed to domestick treachery, and foreign invasion; and therefore the Trustees cannot be supposed to be in any disposition of granting this request; and, if they have not before this signified their dislike of it, this delay is to be imputed to no other motives, but the hopes they had conceived, that time and experience would bring the complainants to a better mind: And the Trustees readily join issue with them in their appeal to posterity, who shall judge between them, who were their best friends; those, who endeavoured to preserve for them a property in their lands, by tying up the hands of their unthrifty progenitors; or they, who wanted a power to mortgage or alien them: Who were the best friends of the colony, those who with great labour and cost had endeavoured to form a colony of His Majesty's subjects, and persecuted Protestants from other parts of Europe, had placed them on a fruitful soil, and strove to secure them in their possessions, by those arts which naturally tend to keep the colony full of useful and industrious people, capable both to cultivate and defend it; or those, who, to gratify the greedy and ambitious views of a few Negro merchants, would put it into their power to become sole owners of the province, by introducing their baneful commodity; which, it is well known by sad experience, has brought our neighbour colonies to the brink of ruin, by driving out their white inhabitants, who were their glory and strength, to make room for black, who are now become the terror of their unadvised masters.

"Signed by order of the Trustees,

this 20th day of June, 1739.

"BENJ. MARTYN, *Secretary.*"

We shall not in this place detain the reader, to shew the absurdity and insufficiency of the reasons made use of in the above paper, or how improperly it is called *An Answer to the Representation;* but refer them to the whole tenor of this Narrative: [210]

---

210. *The absurdity and insufficiency of the reasons* etc. These are hard words to use of a set of Noblemen and Gentlemen their Masters, and shew what respect these fellows bear to Authority. The Reader will judge whether the answer is absurd, or rather clear and full to the point. What they please to call only a paper, was a Corporate Act, deliberatly considered, and signed in form by the Secretary. The reference they make to the whole tenour of their Narrative must appear very impudent to those who take the pains to read the notes, which (to use the softest words) shew that the Narrative is not to be rely'd on.

The Reader will observe the contempt they threw upon an authentick Resolution of the Trustees signed by their Secretary, in calling it only a paper.

With this paper came over new commissions for magistrates, viz. Messrs. Thomas Christie, First, John Fallowfield, Second, and Thomas Jones, Third, Bailiffs, and Mr. William Williamson, Recorder: And, as if the inhabitants had not been sufficiently punished before, by the *arbitrary* government of Causton, the two offices of Store-keeper and Magistrate were again joined in one person,[211] which infallibly renders him (whoever he is) *absolute*

---

211. *The two Offices of Store keeper and Magistrate* etc. The Publick Stores were put down in 1738, and Mr. Jones was appointed only to take care of what should remain therein till disposed of, and was sent for the immediate

relief of the Inhabitants who might for a time be distrest [distressed] thereby. This was well known to these Authors, tho they write in the present tence [tense], as if the publick store continued in June 1741. Besides, whether continued or not, these Landholders had no right to be supplyed there out.

---

in Savannah; and indeed, if the miseries and hardships of the people could have received any addition, they must have done so from the person appointed to execute those offices, namely, Mr. Thomas Jones, Third Bailiff, as before mentioned, who surpassed Mr. Causton in every thing that was *bad*, without having any one of his *good* qualifications: [212] And, that he might the more easily gov-

---

212. *Who Surpassed Mr. Causton* etc. Mr. Jones made himself many Enemies by his hot and passionate temper, but they who personally know him, affirm that he is a sober able and just Man, and so the Trustees have found him.

---

ern at pleasure, Mr. Oglethorpe thought proper to supersede the commissions of Messrs. Thomas Christie and William Williamson,[213] and continued Mr. Henry Parker as First Magistrate, being sure he was a person that would always be in the interest of whoever was Store-keeper,[214] and, having no other magistrate to cope with, but Mr. Fallowfield, they were certain of overruling him, though his sentiments were never so just; [215] and, when the Gen-

---

213. *That he might more easily govern at pleasure, Mr. Oglethorpe* etc. It seems Mr. Oglethorpe is always to be blamed for bad designs: how do they know he superseaded the Commissions here mentioned, that Mr. Jones might more easily govern at pleasure? The truth was, he had solid objections against both Christie and Williamson, and suspended their being sworn into their offices until the Trustees further pleasure was known, after he had given his reasons for so doing. The first had not cleared his accompts [accounts] with the Trustees, and had favoured the escape of one of Mr. Caustons Clerks, whilst the Accounts of his Master were under examination: the other had refused to accept the Recordership unless he might not be turnd out at will, and also appoint a deputy. The Trustees therefore approved of what Mr. Oglethorpe did in that affair.

214. *continued Mr. Hen. Parker as first Magistrate, being Sure* etc. It was necessary to continue him since Mr. Christies commission was suspended. As to Mr. Parkers being always in the Interest of whoever was Store keeper, it is certain he never was in Mr. Jones Interest but at variance with him from first to last. On the contrary, he was so much a friend to Mr. Causton, tho turnd out, as to be bound for him.

215. *Tho his (Mr. Fallowfeilds) Sentiments* etc. This Fallowfeild was a very Troublesome Magistrate, and obstructor of justice. He became the head of

the remaining Malecontents, even to the exposing his brethren on the Bench, and Signing petitions against the whole Constitution of the Government, his Majesties laws, and against the Trustees themselves, for which he is deservedly turned out.

eral heard that some people justly complained, that the Trustees' commissions were of none effect, he threatened an armed force, if they refused to comply.[216]

216. We have only these defamers word for this.

William Stephens, Esq; Messrs. Thomas Christie and Thomas Jones, were likewise appointed to inspect into Causton's accounts; but Christie was altogether rejected by the other two; nor did they ever do any thing to the purpose: Indeed, Jones would sometimes hector and domineer over Causton, in as haughty a manner as ever he had formerly done over the meanest person in Savannah.

Although the Trustees say, in their *Answer* to the Representation, *that they should think themselves very unfit for the trust reposed in them, should they, by an irrational attempt, alter the entail of lands;* yet not one month after we had received the aforesaid answer, over comes the following paper, viz.[217]

217. *Altho the Trustees* etc. It seems nothing the Trustees did, could please them. They complained before of restrictions, and now they were begun to be enlarged they are censured: but they gave no cause for this sneer. The irrational attempt they would not allow of was the peoples selling their lands in their life time, and this they have rigidly adhered to. It was a principal demand of the representation, and the Trustees had this in their view to reply to. As to other restrictions in the tenure, they always intended to enlarge them as the circumstances of the Colony should admit thereof, and this is confest [confessed] by the publishers of this Lybel p. 66. fig. 2.

"*The Resolutions of the Trustees for establishing the Colony of Georgia, in America, in Common Council assembled this 28th day of August, in the year of our Lord* 1739; *relating to the grants and tenure of lands within the said Colony.*

"Whereas the Common Council of the said Trustees, assembled for that purpose, in the name of the corporation of the said Trustees, and under their common seal, have, in pursuance of His Majesty's most gracious letters patent, and in execution of the trusts thereby reposed in them, granted and conveyed divers portions of the lands, tenements, and hereditaments in the said letters patent mentioned, to many of His Majesty's loving subjects, natural born, and denizens, and others willing to become his subjects, and to live under allegiance to His Majesty in the said colony, to hold to them respectively, and to the heirs male of their respective bodies, lawfully begotten, or to be begotten, under the several rents, reservations, conditions, and provisoes therein contained; and whereas it hath been represented to the said Trustees, that many of the persons, to whom such grants have been made, have no issue male of their respective bodies, and that an alteration in the grants and tenure of the said lands, upon failure of such issue, and likewise a known certain provision for the widows of tenants in tail male, would not only encourage all such persons chearfully to go on with their several improvements, but also be an *inducement* and *means* of inviting divers other persons to resort to, and settle in the said colony, and greatly tend to the cultivation of the lands, the increase of the people, and the defence, strength, and security of the said colony; which the said Trustees most earnestly desire to promote, as far as in them lies: It is therefore this day unanimously resolved by the Common Council of the said corporation, assembled for that purpose, that the grants of lands or tenements within the said colony heretofore made, and hereafter to be made by the said Trustees to any person or persons whatsoever, shall be altered, made, and established in manner and form following; that is to say, that

"If tenant in tail male of lands or tenements in the said colony, not having done or suffered any act, matter, or thing, whereby his estate therein may be forfeited or determined, shall happen to die, leaving a widow and one or more child or children; that then, and in such case, the widow of such tenant shall hold and enjoy the dwelling-house and garden (if any such there be) and one moiety of such lands and tenements, for and during the term of her life; the said moiety to be set out and divided, in case the parties interested therein do not agree within the space of three months, by the magistrates of the town-court in Georgia nearest thereunto, or any one of them. And in case such division be made by one of such magistrates only, then any person or persons finding him, her, or themselves aggrieved thereby, may, within the space of three months, appeal to the other three magistrates of the said town-court, whose determination thereof shall be final. And if such tenant shall happen to die, leaving only a widow, and no child or children, then that such widow shall hold and enjoy the said dwelling-house, garden, and all such lands and tenements, for and during the term of her life. And in case the widow of any such tenant, whether he die without issue by her or not, shall marry again after his decease, then such person, to whom she shall be so married, shall, within the space of twelve months after such marriage, give security to the said Trustees, and their successors, whether personal, or otherwise, agreeable to such instructions as shall be given by the Common Council of the said Trustees, for maintaining and keeping in repair, during such marriage, the said dwelling-house, garden, and other the premises to which she shall be so intitled in right of her former husband: And if such security shall not be given in manner aforesaid, within the space of twelve months after such marriage, that then, and in such case, the provision hereby made, or intended to be made for the benefit of such widow, shall cease, determine, and be absolutely void, to all intents and purposes; and the said dwelling-house and garden, and all and singular the premisses, shall be and enure to such child or children, or to such other person or persons, who would be intitled to the same, in case the said widow was naturally dead.

"And if tenant in tail male of lands or tenements in the said colony, not having done or suffered any act, matter, or thing, whereby his or her estate therein may be forfeited or determined, shall happen to die, leaving one or more daughter or daughters, and no issue male; then that such lands and tenements, if not exceeding eighty acres, shall be holden in tail male by any one of the daughters of such tenant; and if exceeding eighty acres, by any one or more of the daughters of such tenant in tail male, as such tenant shall by his or her last will and testament in writing, duly executed in the presence of three or more credible witnesses, direct and appoint; and in default of such direction or appointment, then that such lands and tenements shall be holden in tail male by the eldest of such daughters; and in default of issue male and female, either born in the life-time of such tenant in tail male, or within nine months after his decease, then that such lands and tenements, if not exceeding eighty acres, shall be holden in tail male by any one such person; and if exceeding eighty acres, by any one or more such person or persons, as such tenant in tail male by his or her last will and testament in writing, executed as aforesaid, shall direct and appoint; and in default of such direction or appointment, then that such lands and tenements shall be holden in tail male by the heir at law of such tenant; subject nevertheless, in all and every the said cases, to such right of the widow (if any) as aforesaid, provided, that such daughter or daughters, and all and every such person or persons so intitled to hold and enjoy any such lands and tenements, do, within the space of twelve months after the death of such tenant, personally appear, if residing in America, and claim the same in any of the town-courts in Georgia; and if residing out of America, then within the space of eighteen months next after the death of such tenant. And provided also, that no such devise or appointment shall be made by any such tenant of lands exceeding eighty acres, in any lesser or smaller portion or parcel than fifty acres to any one daughter, or other person. And that no daughter, or other person, shall be capable of enjoying any devise, which may thereby increase his or her former possession of lands within the said colony to more than five hundred acres; but such devise to be void, and the lands thereby given, to descend in such manner, as if no such devise had been made. And in default of such appearance and claim, as aforesaid, that all and singular the said lands and tenements shall be and remain to the said Trustees, and their successors for ever. Provided also, that all and every such estates hereby created, or intended to be created, shall be subject and liable to the several rents, reservations, provisoes and conditions, as in the original grants thereof are particularly mentioned and contained; save and except so much thereof as is hereby altered, or intended to be altered, in case of failure of issue male, and the provision hereby made or intended to be made for widows.

"And that in every grant hereafter to be made by the said Trustees or their successors, of any lands or tenements in the said colony, all and every grantee therein named, not doing or suffering any act, matter, or thing whereby his or her estate therein may be forfeited or determined, shall have good right, full power, and lawful authority to give and devise the same by his or her last will and testament in writing, duly executed in the presence of three or more credible witnesses, in manner and form following, that is to say, every grantee of lands not exceeding eighty acres, to any one son or any one daughter in tail male; and every grantee of lands exceeding eighty acres, the whole, or any part thereof, but not in lesser lots or portions than fifty acres to any one devisee, to his or her son or sons, daughter or daughters in tail male; and in default of such devise as aforesaid, then that such lands and tenements shall descend to the eldest son in tail male; and in default of issue male, to the eldest daughter in tail male; and in default of issue male and female, then that such lands and tenements shall be holden in tail male, if not exceeding eighty acres, by any one such person; and if exceeding eighty acres, by any one or more such person or persons, but not in any smaller lot or portion than fifty acres to any one person as such grantee shall by his or her last will and testament in writing, executed as aforesaid, direct and appoint; and in default of such direction or appointment, then that such lands and tenements shall be holden in tail male by the heir at law of such grantee; subject nevertheless to such right of the widow (if any) as aforesaid, provided always, that no son, daughter, or other person shall be capable of enjoying any devise which may thereby increase his or her former possession of land within the said colony, to more than five hundred acres; but such devise to be void, and the lands thereby given, to descend in such manner as if no such devise had been made. Provided also, that such son or sons, daughter or daughters, and all and every such person or persons intitled to hold and enjoy any such lands and tenements, do within the space of twelve months after the death of such grantee, or of those under whom they claim, personally appear, if residing in America, and claim the same in any of the town courts in Georgia; and, if residing out of America, then within the space of eighteen months next after such death; and in default of such appearance and claim as aforesaid, that all and singular the said lands and tenements shall be and remain to the said Trustees, and their successors forever. And provided also, that all and every such estates shall be subject and liable to the like rents, reservations, provisoes, and conditions, as in the former grants of lands heretofore made, save and except so much thereof as is hereby altered, or intended to be altered, upon the failure of issue male.

"And it is hereby required, that publick notice of these resolutions be forthwith given by the magistrates of the respective town courts in Georgia, and also by the Secretary of the said Trustees in London, that all and every the grantees of lands or tenements, within the said colony, may enter their respective claims, either at the Georgia office near Old Palace Yard in Westminster, or in any of the town courts in Georgia, within the space of twelve months from the date hereof, to the end that they may receive the benefit hereby intended, and that proper grants and conveyances in the law may be forthwith prepared and executed for that purpose. And it is hereby expressly declared, that no fee or reward shall be taken for the entering of any such claim, directly or indirectly, by any person or persons whatsoever.

"Signed by order of the said Common Council.

"BENJAMIN MARTYN, *Secretary.*"

We believe this paper will perplex most people, who have not thoroughly studied the law, to make sense of it; and as there were no lawyers in Georgia, it would seem as if it had been sent over with no other end, than that it should not be understood; and, indeed, it rather tended to add to the confusion in the colony, than to promote the benefit of it: We can only assure the reader, that it had no good effect in Georgia,[218] and that it was kept up there as

218. *it rather tended to add to the confusion* etc. It was drawn up by good Lawyers (one of them now a judge) and many of the people thought they understood it for they were pleased with it. Before it was put into form, the substance of it was wrote to Col. Stephens the 2. April 1739 who on the 29 June following, acquainted the Trustees—"I thought it no breach of the Sabbath to declare the welcom[e] news I had received of the honble. Trustees being about preparing an Act to enable the Possessors of land in Georgia, in case of want of issue male[,] to dispose of it by deed or will to their daughters, or for want of such, to their other relations and their issue male etc. Such Tidings soon spread through the Town, nor would it be long unknown in all parts of the Province to the great joy of many people."

Again, on the 26 July following he wrote, "The Publick have reason Sufficient to be sensible of the benefit intended them by a further addition in the Act now framing, of liberty to all such as have no Issue living of their own, to appoint any other person their Successor, under those restrictions named; which surely must put an end to all future pretences of un-easiness about their Tenures: And as for Negroes, I always thought it an impudent attempt to subert [subvert] the original Constitution of the Colony, in all such whom nothing less would please: but there are few now left hardy enough to dwell upon that any longer, and I think under those marks of Indulgence so evidently shewn, we shall at last grow wiser, and quietly Betake our selves to such Industry and labour, as most undoubtedly ought to be the view of such as come to live here."

Again, the 14 August following, he wrote—"The alteration made in the Tenure of lands, by the honble. Trustees in the peoples favour, has already such an influence, that several, even at this time of year, have begun to give a Specimen of what may be expected from them when the planting season returns."

Does this look as if the resolution of the Trustees, was not understood by the people but perplexed them? Or that it added to the confusions of the Colony, and had no good effect in Georgia?

much as possible from the people, only a fictitious abridgment thereof, with the same title and the same way signed, being publickly exhibited in writing; but this was a needless caution; for not one in twenty of them would have understood any one paragraph of it. In October, 1739, the General issues out his proclamation for granting *Letters of Marque and Reprisals;* and the inhabitants being called together in the court house, he there makes them a very elaborate speech, and, amongst other things, tells them, *that he was designed against St. Augustine, and if he did not take it, he would leave his bones before the walls thereof:* But he is now at Frederica,[219] and, as we have too much reason to believe, this castle is

219. *In October 1739, the General* etc. To what purpose this idle observation on the General? did any one ever doubt his courage, or would he not have exposed his person if the Spaniards had engaged him?

still in the hands of the Spaniards. A little after this we had another instance how much our benefactors had our interest and welfare at heart; for at this time it was given out, *that all the cattle, that were unmarked, belonged to the Trustees as lords of the mannor;* and orders were given that they should be marked accordingly,[220] but people strenuously insisting to the contrary,[221] the design was

220. *A little after* etc. Here is a most unjust reflection on Col Oglethorpe and the Trustees: for the unmarked, that is, the wild Cattle do belong to the Trustees, as his Majesties Attorney General in England gave his opinion on the question stated to him.

221. *But the people* etc. Their insisting to the contrary was illegal, and themselves seemed afterwards to be sensible of it (tho the Attorney Generals opinion was not then known: for on the 8 July 1741 The Grand jury of Savannah presented John Goldwyre, "for that he did since the 1. day of May last past, near a place called Bethesda, Kill and bear away one unmarked bull, about the age of 5 years, being the property of persons unknown, contrary to the peace of our Sovereign Lord the King, his Crown & dignity."

dropped for that time. On the 4th of November Mr. Oglethorpe departed from Savannah; and he now seems to have intirely forgot it; and it is certain, that ever since the affair of the Representation; according to his own words, *the very name of the place is become hateful to him, as are all those who he thought were ringleaders in that affair,*[222] some of whom he endeavoured to threaten and bribe to a recantation,[223] but to little purpose; two or three being the

222. *It is certain that ever since the affair of the Representation* etc. Mr. Oglethorpe had good reason to resent the practices and scandals cast on him by the Ring-leaders of that representation, who therein, and in all places have used him in a manner that no gentleman of Spirit can bear, especially one to whom the very being of the Colony was owing, and who exposed his person, fortune and health to settle them.

223. *he endeavoured to threaten and bribe to a recantation.* I am persuaded this is a false and malicious assertion: it is contrary to his character,

and the utmost we can suppose is that he endeavoured to convince them of their Error.

most (to the best of our knowledge) that he could gain, and even those, we believe, never gave anything under their hands. One flagrant instance of the indirect practices he used to draw people into his measures was as follows [There are particular affidavits to prove this whole affair]: In summer, 1739 [224] (when it was thought the Representation would have succeeded, Messrs. Grant, Douglass, Stirling, and Bailie,[225] who had been old settlers in the colony,

224. *In summer 1739* etc. Here is a long narration of a Fact, the truth of which the Trustees can say nothing to, having never heard of it before, nor seen any copies of the affidavits mentioned at the bottom of the leaf whereby to judge how home [?] they were to the case. These writers are so given to calumniate that little credit ought to be given to any thing they say, only that the 4 persons here mentioned were denyed their request, the reason of which will be seen over Leaf, p. 85. note 1.
225. J. Houston and Will Stirling, with Hugh his brother were the only persons who went upon their plantation.

and who had in a manner ruined themselves, as others had done, either by planting or building, wrote to the Trustees for an island, and at the same time applied to Mr. Oglethorpe for it; he appeared mighty glad at their resolution, and told them, that, if they would agree to what he had to propose, the granting of an island should be nothing in respect to what he would do for them: They told him they would do anything that was consistent with their knowledge and conscience: Then they were dismissed, and the next day they were to know his mind; that being come, two of his emissaries were sent separately with proposals; which they afterwards wrote in order to be signed, but refused a copy thereof: These proposals were to the following effect, viz. To acknowledge they were in the wrong for having any hand in the making or signing the Representation; to ask the General's pardon for so doing; and to assert, that they believed the colony might flourish according to the then present constitution: These things complied with, they should have what money they were pleased to ask for, with horses, cattle, and every thing else they wanted, together with the General's perpetual friendship and assistance: If not complied with, they might expect nothing but his highest resentment. They answered, *that they never expected, nor did they think they ever asked for any favours, from the General, and as for his resentment, they believed they had already felt the utmost of it.* In whatever shape the General wrote home of this affair, is not known; but however, from what he wrote, the Trustees thought fit, at first, positively to deny their request,[226] in a letter which came to their hands in July, 1740, of which this is an exact copy.

---

226. *thought fit at first* etc. Tho the Trustees at first denied their request, yet afterwards they granted it and the permission they gave arrived to these men before they quitted the Colony, yet they accepted not the favour. This is artfully concealed.

"To Messrs. Grant, Douglass, and Bailie, at Savannah, in Georgia.

"Georgia-Office, March 25, 1740.

"GENTLEMEN,—The Trustees for establishing the colony of Georgia, have received and read your letter of May 26, 1739, by which they find you have abandoned your settlements upon the Ogeeche river, for the following reasons; because you are not allowed to have black servants to cultivate your lands, and because you disliked the tenure of your grants.

"As to the first, you must have seen by the Trustees' answer to the Representation of some of the people, that they cannot, and will not break into the constitution of the province, by such an introduction of slavery in blacks; and that upon the most mature deliberation, and for the strongest reasons; which indeed are obvious to every considering man, and which they are confirmed in by the danger which has lately threatened South Carolina, by the insurrection of the Negroes, and would be more imminent in Georgia, it being a frontier.

"As to the last, relating to the tenure of lands, the Trustees suppose you may have seen the alteration which they have made since the writing of your letter, and they have no doubt but you are satisfied therewith, as the rest of the colony are.

"The Trustees have likewise received and considered your petition to General Oglethorpe, for a settlement on Wilmington Island; and his answers thereto, which they think are of great force; and therefore they cannot make you a grant there,[227] but hope you

---

227. Col. Oglethorpe wrote to the Trustees that he suspected the reason why these men desired to settle on Wilmington Island was that they might from thence fill the Colony with Rum contrary to law and therefore he refused them leave to remove thither which refusal of his was at first approved of by the Trustees, but afterwards they allowed their request.

will go on improving your settlements on the Ogeeche River, which they perceive by your letter, May 26, that you had made a great progress in.

I am, gentlemen,

Your very humble servant,

BENJ. MARTYN, *Secretary.*"

To this they returned the following answer.

"To the Honourable the Trustees for Establishing the Colony of Georgia in America, at their Office near Old Palace Yard, Westminster.

"Honourable gentlemen, We have received a letter signed by your Secretary, of the 25th March last, owning the receipt of ours to the Trustees for establishing the colony of Georgia, dated the 26th May, 1739, in which we set forth the expence we had been at in prosecuting our settlement on the Ogeeche river, together with the impossibility of carrying on any settlement with success in this colony, according to the present constitution; as an additional confirmation of which, we then presented your Honours with an accompt current, carried on from the commencement of our settlement on the Ogeeche, and continued till we were drove thence by the strongest appearances of destruction, arising from the having expended our ALL in the strenuous prosecution of an impracticable scheme: And here we must beg leave to observe, that it appears to us, you have neither considered our letter or accompt; otherwise you never would have advised us to return to a place on which we have already in vain consumed so much time and money.

"We have seen and seriously considered every paragraph of a printed paper, entitled, *The Answer of the Trustees for establishing the Colony of Georgia in America, to the Representation from the Inhabitants of Savannah;* which, in our humble opinion, is *no answer at all;* but rather an *absolute* refusal of demands to which we are legally entitled,[228] under the specious pretences [229] of

228. *demands to which we are legally entitled* etc. They demanded the use of Negroes to which they were not legally entitled there being a law against them, they also demanded an alteration of the Covenants which they had entered into and of conditions on which they voluntarily took their grants. How they could legally be entitled to demand the reversal of these will be hard to shew.

229. *Specious pretences.* The insolence of these people to the Trustees their governours in this expression must not pass unobserved.

guardianship and fatherly care; without having answered *one* sentence, or confuted, by strength of argument, *any* part of our assertions.[230]

---

230. *without having answered* etc. The reader will judge whether the Trustees answer was no answer at all. But these insolent men put themselves on a level with their Masters and expect they should argue with them on all occasions.

"Because our neighbouring province (of which you are pleased to take notice) has, by an introduction of *too* great numbers, abused the use of Negroes; or, because an undoubted property in our land possessions might prove detrimental or hurtful to idle, profligate, or abandoned people; it does not at all follow that we should be debarred the use of Negroes for the field, or the more laborious parts of culture, under prudent limitations; or that sober and virtuous men should be deprived of just titles to their properties.[231]

---

231. *deprived of just titles* etc. The Reader is lead to imagine (through the whole course of this libel) that the people have no security in their property, whereas their grants are made as strong to them as the law can bind.

"We are surprized that your Honours mention the representations of the people of the Darien, as a confirmation of the unreasonableness of our demands: For did your Honours know the motives by which these people were induced to present you with one or more petitions,[232] contradictory to our Representation, the wel-

---

232. *did your honours know the motives* etc. The Inhabitants of Darien had property to value and take care of as well as the complainants, and this is a hard reflection on them which follows viz. that they presented petitions contrary to the welfare of the Colony and their own consciences. What they petitioned against was the introduction of Negroes on which they thus exprest [expressed] themselves—["]we are informed that our neighbours of Savannah have petitioned for the liberty of Having Slaves. We hope and earnestly desire that before such Proposals are hearkened [?] unto your Excellency will consider our situation and of what dangerous and bad consequence such liberty would be of to us for many reasons[.] 1. The nearness of the Spaniards who have proclaimed freedom to all slaves, who run away from their Masters makes it impossible for us to keep them without more labour to guard them than what we would be at to do their work. 2. We are laborious and know a white man may be, by the year, more usefully employed than a Negro. 3. We are not rich, and becoming debtors for slaves, in case of their dying or running away would inevitably ruin the poor master, and he become a greater slave to the Negro merchant than the slave he bought could be to him. 4. It would oblige us to keep a guard duty at least as severe as when we expected a daily Invasion: and if that was the case, how miserable would it be to us and our wives and families to have one Enemy without, and a more dangerous one in our bosoms!["] They conclude, ["]We therefore for our own sakes our wives and children and our posterity beg your consideration and intreat that instead of introducing slaves you'l put us in the way to get us some of our Countrymen who with their labour in time of peace, and our vigilance if we are invaded with the help of those will render it a difficult thing to hurt us or that part of the Province we possess.["]

New Inverness

3 Jan. 1738–9

---

fare of the colony, and their own consciences; we are persuaded you never would have offered them as reasons for rejecting the Representation from Savannah: They were bought with a number of cattle, and extensive promises of future rewards; [233] a little *present* interest made them forget or neglect their *posterity;* whereas the people of this place,[234] duly sensible of the miseries and calamities

---

233. *They were bought* etc. This is an egregious misrepresentation of the Fact: We see their petition was signd the 3rd. Jany. and it was not till the 5 May following that 200£ was lent to them to purchase cattel the money to be repaid (as part thereof soon after was). This could be no inducement to them to petition against Negroes the allowance of whom they opposed with so strong reasons.

234. *the people of this place.* They were not all the people and this was the only town that did petition for Negroes, divers of whom afterward altered their minds.

---

they have suffered, and do still labour under, *freely* and *voluntarily* put their hands to the Representation of this part of the province: No *artful* means were used to induce them to it; [235] no *artful* man

---

235. *No artfull means were used* etc. This is false. The Ringleaders persuaded the rest that Col. Oglethorpe would himself approve and sign their petition. And Robt. Williams the first promoter promised to help them to Negroes.

---

or men, Negro-merchants or others, persuaded them to it: *Dismal* poverty and the most *absolute* oppression were the *true* fountains from whence our complaints proceeded. But how miserably were these *inconsiderate* deluded wretches rewarded? They were soon after carried against St. Augustine, placed on a dangerous post, where they were all or most of them cut off or taken prisoners by the enemy; which has put a period to the settlement of Darien, of which so many great things have been falsely reported.[236]

---

236. *They were soon after carryd against St. Augustine* etc. False! Col. Oglethorpe would not have taken them, but they forced themselves upon him

declaring if he would not let them go, they would depart the Colony. Neither did Col. Oglethorpe place them there, but Col. Palmer [?] who commanded, contrary to Col. Oglethorpes express orders.

Neither was a period put to that settlement thereby, on the contrary, Capt. Thompson now here (who was last there) says the people exprest [expressed] themselves happier than ever. There were about 35 slayn, and about 16 are now prisoners at Havanah and 2 in Spain who when the Cartel is settled will return to their families. In May 1741 the Inhabitants were 86.

"With regard to our Representation, we shall only beg leave to make one supposition, which it's almost impossible can have happened, viz. that this and all the other representations, letters, suits, or petitions, made to the Trustees by private or a joint number of persons,[237] have been entirely false and groundless: What can

---

237. *Representations, letters* etc. No private Applications have been made for Negroes, but private persons have wrote concerning their particular affairs, which have been considered from time to time and some satisfied others not according to the merit of the requests made.

---

have reduced the colony to the *situation* in which it now is? What can have reduced its inhabitants to one sixth part of the number which we have known to reside here? Or, lastly, to what is the starving and despicable *condition* of the few, that are now left, owing? Is it not, as well as every other matter which we have before urged, owing to and occasioned by the unanswerable reasons at different times given, and laid before your Honours, by honest men (independent of you) who were and are the chief sufferers in this colony; and who could not be *bribed* to conceal, or *terrified* from declaring their sentiments?

"Your Honours may readily and safely join issue with us in our appeal to posterity, who were their best [*Vide* Answer to the Representation.] for it is certain and obvious, that, if the Trustees are resolved to adhere to their *present constitution,* they or their successors are in no great danger of being called to any account by our posterity in Georgia.

"We have likewise seen and read the alterations Mr. Martyn mentions to have been made by your Honours, with regard to the tenure of lands; together with a fictitious abridgement of the same affixed to the most publick places at Savannah.

"Mr. Martyn, in his letter, is pleased to tell us, that your Honours imagine we are satisfied therewith, as the rest of the colony are! Some few, perhaps, may have expressed themselves satisfied; but we will say no worse of such few, than that your Honours will soon be sensible, that even they are deceivers. It is true, such alterations, and the paper, intitled, *An Answer to our Representation*, above mentioned, are artfully penned, and will, doubtless, for a time, amuse even men of the best sense in Europe, or elsewhere, who are strangers to the colony of Georgia; but any man of common understanding, or the least penetration, who, by an *unfortunate* experience, has been well acquainted with *that* colony, can easily demonstrate, that those very papers are further snares to increase our miseries; as it is impossible we can be enabled, by these alterations, to subsist ourselves and families any more than before, far less to put us in a capacity of recovering our already sunk fortunes and loss of time. Some time in the summer, 1739 (whilst we still expected agreeable alterations to have succeeded our Representation) we applied more than once to General Oglethorpe, as on(e) of the Trustees, for the same tract of land which we have since been refused by your Honours: But our petitions and applications were rejected; and for what reason? Because indeed we refused to *contradict* what we had before set forth in our Representation, and so become villains, as (we have too much reason to believe) some others on the same occasion were: We would not accept of *settlements, sums of money, horses, cattle,* and *other valuable considerations at the expense of betraying our country, and contradicting our consciences,*[238] by signing a paper, which

---

238. *We would not accept of settlements* etc. This is a scandalous reflection either on the Trustees or Col. Oglethorpe. The Trustees never made such offers to any, nor could have any interest so to do: On the contrary they long wished these turbulent fellows out of the Colony in which whilst they stayed they were perpetually working mischief. Neither do the Trustees believe Col. Oglethorpe used such means with them as is here related.

---

was prepared and offered to us, purporting a *repentance of the measures* we had taken for our own and the relief of other distressed British subjects; and, consequently, an *approbation* of a scheme which, by all appearance, seems to have been calculated and prepared to form a colony of vassals,[239] whose *properties* and *liberties*

---

239. *A Scheme which by all appearance* etc. Another Scandalous reflection! The Trustees have no interest to form a Colony of vassals, nor does their Plan of Government tend to it. The law against Negroes only obliges free men to labour for their families, and the Plan of Government is formed only to preserve the Colony, by keeping a number of white men in it. They who like it not may leave the Colony as these fellows have done.

were, *at all times,* to have been disposed of at the discretion or option of their superiors.

"Such and many other *methods of corruption* have been *too often* practised in this colony; [240] but we refused and scorned such

---

240. *Such and many other methods of corruption* etc. These are idle generalities flung out to prejudice the Reader against the Trustees. Who ever corrupt others must be supposed to have some interest in doing it.

---

actions, from principles of which every honest man ought to be possessed.

"We are not surprized to find, that we have in vain applied to your Honours, in several affairs, when we see you have been hitherto prepossessed, by a gentleman of superior interest,[241] with in-

---

241. *preposest [prepossed] by a gentleman* etc. Col. Oglethorpe is a Trustee and has no interest in prejudicing the Colony which he went over to settle and protect. Certainly the Trustees will sooner hearken to him than to a set of troublesome malicious fellows who oppose and vilify them. But the Trustees do not blindly follow his advice.

---

formations and assertions full of *resentment,* and which, we well know, cannot stand the test of an *impartial examination;* but we are amazed, and sorry to find, that he has had, for so many years together, the interest of nominating *those,* who have been appointed, from time to time, for the administration of justice,[242] and making an *impartial* inquiry into,[243] and informing your

---

242. *the Interest of nominating* etc. They desire the nomination of Magistrates may be in themselves and to divest the Trustees of that power, hoping thereby to become Magistrates themselves.

243. *making an impartial enquiry* etc. Who so proper to make an impartial enquiry as the Magistrates and Officers whose being depends on the prosperity of the Colony? and who besides their Offices have property in [illegible word] it?

Honours of the *real* situation of the colony of Georgia; we say, such, who have been *implicitely* obedient in carrying on his *arbitrary* schemes of government,[244] and *oppressing* the inhabitants,

---

244. *his arbitrary schemes* etc. Col. Oglethorpe can carry on no arbitrary Schemes of government, but must pursue the Trustees Plan. These fellows call everything that thwarts their turbulent views and practices, by the name of arbitrary scheme.

---

as well as *conniving* at the deceiving your Honours and the nation!

"Gentlemen, as we have no favours to ask, or resentments to fear,[245] we may with the greater freedom observe, that we are in

---

245. *As we have no favours to ask* etc. They may well conclude so, since their

vile behaviour toward the Trustees: and they may well say they have no resentment to fear, being withdrawn into another Province where they are protected.

full hopes, that *all* we can *justly* ask, will be granted us by a British Parliament, who, we doubt not, will soon make an enquiry into the grievances of *oppressed subjects*,[246] which have formerly in-

246. *We are in full hopes* etc. The Trustees themselves laboured for a Parliamentary enquiry but could not obtain it, the Parliament expressing themselves well satisfyed with the Trustees prudence.

habited, or do now inhabit the colony of Georgia; that colony which has cost so great an expense to the nation, and from which so great benefits were promised and expected!

"We are sensible of the freedoms which have been used with our respective characters, in the *misrepresentations* sent your Honours by *partial* men: Nor are we less sensible, that the majority of the Trustees have been kept in the dark, with regard to our *just complaints* and *representations;*[247] or that such *complaints*

247. *that the majority of the Trustees* etc. This is a false and injurious representation of the Trustees as if a few of them imposed upon the rest, whereas when ever there is a meeting of them summons is constantly issued for all to attend the service, and even those who are absent in the country are often wrote to for their oppinion upon matters.

have been communicated to them in lights *distant from truth;* insomuch that, we have reason to believe, two thirds of the Honourable Board are either misinformed of, or are entire strangers to the barbarous and destructive schemes carried on in this miserable colony.[248]

248. It were to be wished they would speak out who they are who give them reason to believe that one third of the Trustees misinform the rest touching the barbarous and destructive schemes carryed on by them. This is another vilanous reflection on the Trust.

"We hope it will e'er long appear to your Honours and the world (whatever has been advanced to the contrary) that we are *honest* men, free from any *base* design, free from any *mutinous* spirit; who have only *stood firm* for the recovery of our *lost privileges,* which have been secretly, and under the most specious pretences, withdrawn from us by some *designing* and *self-interested* men.[249]

249. *that we are honest men* etc. Many falsities are here asserted. The reader will judge by the Spirit of this libel, the many lyes in it and base reflections

whether the authors can be honest men. And their behaviour whilst in the Colony in caballing and distressing the Magistrates is sufficient evidence of their mutinous Spirit. They lost no priviledges that they were justly entitled to, but conditions made with them have been punctually fullfilled. Themselves gave up the privilege of selling their lands when they signed their grants, and they could have no priviledge to use Negroes which his Majesties law forbad. Neither were any Secret or Specious pretences used by designing and self interested men to deprive them of their priviledges. It is they themselves who are the self interested men who insist so much for Negroes to the hazard of the Colony, and who being now out of the Colony labour to defame it and entice a way those who remain, being willing to destroy it if their own interested views are not complyed with. If their behaviour whilst in the Colony was publickly known their honesty and freedom from a mutinous spirit would appear in a frightfull light. Was it honest to persuade the people from labour? or was it no mutinous Spirit to contend with the Magistrates in open Court? to continue doing business in Grand juries after the Court had dissolved them? to harrangue the people into a dislike of the Government, and the Trustees their Masters measures? to misrepresent the Colony to all men in England Scotland the other Colonies and where ever their malice could extend? to assist and encourage persons imprisoned for casting out threats against the Magistrates? etc.

"We should be sorry to write disrespectfully of any *one* of the Trustees; but when *distressed* and *oppressed* people arrive at the last extremities, it must be supposed, they will neither be *ashamed* to publish their misfortunes, or *afraid* of imputing their calamities to the fountain from whence they spring.

"Far be it from us in any shape to reflect in general on the Honourable Board, who we still believe are gentlemen of *honour* and *reputation,* who would not be accessory to any *sinister* or *base* designs; but we can't help thinking, that they are deluded, and brought to pursue measures inconsistent with the welfare and prosperity of the colony, by *some* who of the *whole* corporation are only acquainted with the particular situation of it; and who must therefore, wilfully and from design, form and prepare destructive schemes for the perishing inhabitants of Georgia; [250] and

---

250. *But we cant help thinking* etc. This Scandal on some of the Trustees has been answered before p. 90 note 3. All papers and Accounts received from the Colony are carefully bound up and ly [lie] open for the perusal of all the Trustees, and all are equally acquainted with the situation of it.

---

by *unfair* representations of persons and things, draw the *approbation* of the greater part of the Honourable Board, to such measures for the *oppression* of His Majesty's subjects, which they would, if they were impartially informed, scorn to think of, far less agree to.

"General Oglethorpe, with all his forces has been obliged to raise the siege of St. Augustine, and we have reason to believe the impending ruin of this colony will be thereby determined; [251]

---

251. *General Oglethorpe etc.* These men have hitherto been false prophets the Colony still subsists tho their own fear precipitated their flight.

---

for the Spaniards are reinforced; the General's army harrassed and weakened, and the Indians provoked and discontented; so that every thing *looks* with the *most dismal* aspect. But as his *conduct in*, and the *consequences of* these affairs, will be soon published to the world; and as we doubt not we have already incurred your Honours' displeasure, by reciting thus freely the many *hardships* which we have here and formerly asserted to have been the causes of our ruin; we shall now forbear, and conclude by adding, that the *extremity* of our misfortunes has at last rendered us utterly incapable of staying any longer: [252] And though all the money we

---

252. *The extremity etc.* They should say their folly and extravagancies in spending at taverns that substance which would have engaged new servants when the time of the old ones expired. None who have not desired Negroes make this complaint viz. the Saltsburghers, those of Darien, Frederica, etc.

---

have expended, on improvements in the colony, is now of no *advantage* to us here, nor can be elsewhere; yet poor as we are, we shall think ourselves happy when we are gone from a place where nothing but *poverty* and *oppression* subsists: Therefore we hope, if ever *this* or any *other* paper or letter of ours shall appear in publick; your Honours will impute such publication to have proceeded from no other motives, besides a thorough knowledge of our duty to ourselves, our fellow subjects and sufferers, and to prevent others for the future [253] from being deluded in the same manner as we have been, who are, with the greatest respect,

---

253. *to prevent others etc.* This has indeed been the labour of these men who to make the world believe the Colony cannot subsist without Negroes, and that the Trustees Plan and measures for settling the Colony are destructfull to it endeavour to dispeople it.

"Honorable Gentlemen,
Your most humble servants.
Signed DA. DOUGLASS,
WM. STIRLING,
THO. BAILLIE.

"Georgia, Savannah, 10th August, 1740."

About the latter end of May, 1740, Mr. Oglethorpe set out with his regiment for Florida, and soon after the Carolina forces (consisting of about six hundred men) joined him, with about three hundred Indians, and sixty Highlanders voluntiers from Darien, who were buoyed up by the General with the mighty hopes of reward; [254] besides several stragglers and boatmen from other parts

---

254. *who were buoyed up by the General* etc. This is most Scandalously false. Col. Oglethorpe would have disuaded them from going, but they declared if he did not permit them they would leave the Colony, so eager they were for plunder and action.

---

of the province, and elsewhere; so that, exclusive of seven men of war, there might be about fifteen hundred effective men assisting at the siege (as it was called) of the castle of St. Augustine: But we shall take no further notice of this affair, than as it has affected or may still affect the colony of Georgia: The place being alarmed, the Highlanders, with some others, making in all one hundred and forty-one men, were posted at Musa [255] (this was a small fort about

---

255. They were not posted by Col. Oglethorpe there, but by their Commander Col. Palmer. On the contrary Col. Oglethorpe to prevent their lodging there had taken away the gate of that vilage. His orders were that they should keep the feild and change quarters every day so to distract the Spaniards.

---

a mile distant from the castle, which had been abandoned by the Spaniards, at the General's first approach) where they were soon after attacked by a superior force of the enemy, and a miserable slaughter ensued, scarcely one third of the number escaping, the others being either killed or taken prisoners. Thus these poor people,[256] who, at the expence of their consciences, signed a repre-

---

256. *Thus these poor people* etc. This assertion has been shewn to be false p. 87. note 1. 4.

---

sentation contrary to their own interest and experience, and gave themselves entirely up to the General's service, by their deaths, at once freed his Excellency from his debts and promises, and put an end to the settlement of Darien,[257] for there are now in that place

---

257. *put an end to the Settlement of Darien.* False: see p. 87 note 4. Col. Oglethorpe wrote that he hindered none from going.

not one quarter part of the number who settled there at first, and that is made up chiefly of women and children; and a scout boat is stationed before the town to prevent any of them from going off.

This siege was raised about the beginning of July; the General with the remainder of his regiment returned to Frederica; the Carolina forces were shipped off for that province; the few Georgians that were left repaired, as soon as they were allowed, to their several homes in a miserable condition; and the Indians marched towards their respective countries, very much weakened and discontented; the Cherokees returned (as they came) by Savannah, and of one hundred and ten healthy men, only about twenty got to their nation, the rest either perished by sickness, or were slain; and thus ended the campaign in Florida.

During these transactions, Savannah decayed apace, and, in August and September the same year, people went away by twenties in a vessel,[258] insomuch, that one would have thought the place

258. *During these transactions Savannah decay'd apace* etc. This confirms that it was only fear of the Spaniards after the loss of the seige of Augustine that scared away some of the Inhabitants 7 or 8 of whom afterwards returnd: but the number who went is exagerated: there being but 34 in all who went this year until the 6. October viz. Freeholders of Savannah 9 (of who a good riddanc[e] these Authors being among them) Freeholders of other parts of the province 2, Landholders 6, women children and Inmates 17, in all 34.

must have been intirely forsaken; for, in these two months about one hundred souls out of the county of Savannah left the colony; many others have since left it, and, we believe, more will leave it very soon.

The boats with their hands, which the General employed at that unfortunate expedition, he neither will pay, subsist, or let depart from that place,[259] however, they are stealing away by degrees [We

259. *The boats* etc. The Trustees have received no account of this.

are now informed they are all got away, some of them being paid, and some not]; and at this time, [October, 1740] of about five thousand souls that had, at various embarkations, arrived in the colony of Georgia [260] (exclusive of the regiment) scarce as many hundreds

260. *of about 5000 Souls* etc. This is a strange exagerated Account and can only be delivered at random there may have been about 2500 who at various times came into the Colony, but not to be settlers. The whole number sent from the beginning to this time on the charity account was but 1521, and it were strange if the number of others who voluntarily embarked for the Colony on

their own accounts should amount to 2479 more. Such as were poor had no encouragement to go not being Freeholders or able to pay their passage, and such as had money coveted great lots of land. Of these it has been said before (p. 26 note 1) called Land-holders there never went over but 57 of whom 5 [?] fled the Colony for felony or debt 9 died, and 3 did not take up land but staid a short while. Had these 57 all remained in the Colony and all taken up 500 acre lots, and performed their covenant of carrying over 10 servants each which few of them did they with their servants had been but 627 and with their families not above 800 Souls, which added to 1521 sent on the charity makes but 2351 of whom 300 died before this time.

remain,[261] and these consist of the Saltzburgers at Ebenezer, who are yearly supported from Germany and England,[262] the people of

261. *Scarce as many hundred remain:* By the latest and best Accounts the Trustees could get the Inhabitants were in 1741 near 1400 exclusive of the Regiment and Col. Stephens wrote that in a little time he expected Savannah town would be as full of Inhabitants as ever, for people were daily applying for lotts, and all that were known to be vacant were already filled up.
262. *who are yearly supported from Germany and England.* Their friends may make them presents but they support themselves.

Frederica, who are supported by means of the regiment; the poor remainder of the Darien; a few orphans, and others under that denomination, supported by Mr. Whitefield; together with some Dutch servants maintained for doing nothing by the Trustees,[263]

263. *Dutch Servants maintained for doing nothing* etc. They had been under a corrupt director Mr. Bradley who employed them on his own land and was turnd out for his neglect. The[y] since laboured better.

with thirty or forty necessary tools to keep the others in subjection: And *those* make up the poor remains of the miserable colony of GEORGIA! [It is here to be observed, that we have excluded the settlement of Augusta, it being upon a quite different footing.] [264]

264. *It is here to be observed* etc. I know not what they mean by Augusta being on a different footing, they are governed by the same laws and are under the same Covenants with respect to their grants.

Having now brought down this work to the month of October, 1740, being about the time most of the authors of this NARRATIVE were obliged to leave that *fatal* colony; we shall conclude the whole with a geographical and historical account of its present state.

GEORGIA lies in the 30 and 31 degrees of north latitude: The air generally clear, the rains being much shorter as well as heavier than in England; the dews are very great; thunder and lightning are expected almost every day in May, June, July, and August; they are very terrible, especially to a stranger: During those months, from ten in the morning to four in the afternoon, the sun is extremely scorching; but the sea-breeze sometimes blows from ten till three or four: The winter is nearly the same length as in England; but the mid-day sun is always warm, even when the mornings and evenings are very sharp, and the nights piercing cold.

The land is of four sorts; pine barren, oak land, swamp, and marsh. The pine land is of far the greatest extent, especially near the sea-coasts: The soil of this is a dry whitish sand, producing shrubs of several sorts, and between them a harsh coarse kind of grass, which cattle do not love to feed upon; but here and there is a little of a better kind, especially in the Savannahs, (so they call the low watery meadows which are usually intermixed with pine lands:) It bears naturally two sorts of fruit; hurtle-berries much like those in England, and chinquopin nuts, a dry nut about the size of a small acorn: A laborious man may in one year clear and plant four or five acres of this land; it will produce, the first year, from two to four bushels of Indian corn, and from four to eight of Indian pease, per acre; the second year it usually bears much about the same; the third, less; the fourth, little or nothing: Peaches it bears well; likewise the white mulberry, which serves to feed the silk worms; the black is about the size of a black cherry, and has much the same flavour.

The oak land commonly lies in narrow streaks between pine land and swamps, creeks or rivers: The soil is a blackish sand, producing several kinds of oak, bay, laurel, ash, wallnut, sumach and gum trees, a sort of sycamore, dog trees and hickory: In the choicest part of this land grow parsimon trees, and a few black mulberry and American cherry trees: The common wild grapes are of two sorts, both red; the fox grape grows two or three only on a stalk, is thick-skinned, large stoned, of a harsh taste, and of the size of a small cherry; the cluster grape is of a harsh taste too, and about the size of a white curran[t]. This land requires much labour to clear; but, when it is cleared, it will bear any grain, for three, four, or five years sometimes without laying any manure upon it: An acre of it generally produces ten bushels of Indian corn, besides five of pease, in a year; so that this is justly esteemed the most valuable land in the province, white people being incapable to clear and cultivate the swamps.

A swamp is any low watery place, which is covered with trees or canes: They are here of three sorts, cypress, river, and cane swamps.

Cypress swamps are mostly large ponds, in and round which cypresses grow: Most river swamps are overflown on every side by the river which runs through or near them; if they were drained, they would produce good rice; as would the cane swamps also, which in the meantime are the best feeding for all sorts of cattle.

The marshes are of two sorts; soft wet marsh, which is all a quagmire, and absolutely good for nothing, and hard marsh, which is a firm sand; but however at some seasons is good for feeding cattle: Marshes of both sorts abound on the sea islands, which are very numerous, and contain all sorts of land; and upon these chiefly, near creeks and runs of watar, cedar trees grow.

We shall only add to the above, that considering no land can be sowed (or at least what is sowed preserved) till the same is inclosed, that five acres is the utmost a very able and laborious man can propose to manage; this being the quantity allotted for the task of a Negro in the neighbouring province, which Negro works four hours each day more than a white man can do.

It must next be noticed, that with regard to the above returns (suppose a prosperous season without disappointments; which is not the case in such small improvements as can be expected in an infant colony one year in five) either drought burns, or rain drowns the corn, and makes the pease fall out of the pod; deer (which no fences can exclude) devour those little settlements in a night; rats and squirrels do the same; birds eat the seed out of the ground, and dig up the blade after it is spired; and variety of worms and insects devour the one half of it: But let us suppose none of those evils happened; let us view the amount of the produce valued at the highest rate.

The produce of five acres of pine land raised by one hand, the first year.

	l.	s.	d.
Indian corn, 20 bushels at 10s currency per bushel.	1	5	0 sterling.
Indian pease, 40 bushels at ditto.	2	10	0
Total of first year's produce,	3	15	0

The second year the same; the third less; the fourth little or nothing.

Best oak land, five acres, at 15 bushels of corn [265] and pease per acre, is seventy-five bushels at *ditto* price, is 4l. 13s. 9d. sterling.

---

265. *Best oak land* etc. It yeilds 20 bushells p acre.

Let us next consider the maintenance of every single white serv-ant per annum, at the lowest rate, and then the reader will be able to judge, whether white people can get their livelihood by planting land in this climate without Negroes? And the allowance to the Trustees' Dutch servants being the least at which any white servant could be maintained in Georgia, we shall therefore take our estimation from it, which is eight pence sterling per day, or 12*l*. 3*s*. 4*d*. sterling per annum; so that, at a medium, the expense is three times greater than the produce, besides tools, medicines, and other necessaries.

We must likewise observe, that the proportion of pine barren to either good swamp or oak and hickory land, is at least six to one; that the far greater number of the small lots have none or very little oak land; and if they had swamp that would bear rice, white peo-ple are unable to clear them if they are covered with trees, and though only with canes, which is the easiest to cultivate; it were simply impossible to manufacture the rice by white men; [266] the

---

266. *It were simply impossible,* etc. Tho there are Some in the Colony who sow rice, it must be granted that the labour is only proper for Negroes: but it is not designed [deigned?] that rice should be followed in Georgia for by multiplying the quantity of that commody [commodity] Carolina would be injured and it would become not worth the while to either Colony.

---

exercise being so severe, that no Negro can be employed in any other work or labour comparable to it, and many hundreds of them (notwithstanding all the care of their masters) yearly lose their lives by that necessary work.

SAVANNAH stands on a flat bluff (so they term a high land hanging over a creek or river) which rises about forty feet per-pendicular from the river, and commands it several miles both upwards and downwards, and if it was not for a point of woods which, for about four miles down the river, stretches itself out towards the south-east, one might have a view of the sea, and the island of Tybee: The soil is a white sand for above a mile in breadth south-east and north-west; beyond this, eastward, is a river swamp; westward, a small body of wood-land (in which was the old Indian town) separated by a creek from a large tract of land, which runs upwards along the side of the river, for the space of about five miles; and being, by far, the best near the town, is re-served for the Indians, as General Oglethorpe declares, as are also some of the islands in the river Savannah, and the three most valua-ble islands upon all the coast of that province, viz. Ossiba, St. Katherine, and Sapula.[267] South-west of the town is a pine barren, that

---

267. The Indians reserved these out of the concession they made of their lands to Col. Oglethorpe in behalf of the Trust: but these Defamers conceal this to represent Mr. Oglethorpe as preferring the Indians to the white Inhabitants.

---

extends about fourteen miles to Vernon river.

On the east side of the own is situated the publick garden, (being ten acres inclosed) on a barren piece of land, where it is hardly possible for what is planted to live, but impossible to thrive; and from this garden were all the planters to have been furnished with mulberry trees, &c.[268]

---

268. *where it is hardly possible for what is planted to live,* etc. The more barren the ground the better for trees that are to be transplanted such as the Mulberry, etc. as Hugh Anderson himself wrote over to the Trustees in his Account of this garden. Many and many thousands have been so transplanted. On the 16 Jan. 1734–5 Joseph Fitzwalter at that time Publick gardiner wrote as follows: "The garden I have made great Improvements in, most of the trees stumps I have rooted up: planted the front walk with trees of oranges 6 foot high which will bear fruit some this year, and all in general thrive; some orange trees shot this last year in the nursery 4 foot and the rest shot 2 foot. I have a 1000 of them. Of Mulberry plants I have 8000, some of them this last season shot fairly 15 foot and this season will be capable of feeding abundance of the worms. The Olive trees like the soil and situation, for I have some of them shot 6 foot this season; I have met with some cotton Seeds from Guinea from which I have raised 1000 plants and the Second Season will come to their bringing forth fruits in abundance, so that I shall be able to send a large quantity of Cotton to the Trustees uses. As for the kitchin garden every thing thrives as well as any thing in Europe, and as for wheat, Rye, oats, Tares [?], beans, pease, Rye grass, Clover, Trefoyl, Cinquefoil, and Lucern Seeds, I have never seen finer than this Country produces. Hemp and flax have as well as in any part of Europe. Rice I have very good; Indian corn and pease in great plenty."

The plan of the town was beautifully laid out in wards, tythings, and publick squares left at proper distances for markets and publick buildings; the whole making an agreeable uniformity.

The publick works in this town are, 1st, a court house, being one handsome room, with a piache on three sides: This likewise serves for a church for divine service, none having been ever built, notwithstanding the Trustees, in their publick acts, acknowledge the receipt of about seven hundred pounds sterling, from charitable persons for that express purpose.[269]

---

269. *none having been ever built* etc. This is a malicious reflection on the Trustees. The money given for building a Church came in at different years, and when it amounted to a Sufficient sum orders were sent to build a Church, and this was done some years ago, but the unsettled times with respect to the Spaniards and the death of Capt. Thomas the Ingenier who had the plan and was to erect it delayed the work, for which preparations are now making. Will the world think the Trustees had no intention to build a Church or that they have sunk the money or misemployed it?

2dly, Opposite to the *court house* stands the *log house* or prison (which is the only one remaining of five or six that have been successively built in Savannah) that place of terror, and support of *absolute* power in Georgia.[270]

270. If prisons want repair or rebuilding must it not be done? a prison is necessary, and only disorderly persons can object to one. To restrain such is here set forth as an act of absolute power. The malicious revilers give an ill turn to every thing that is done.

3dly, Nigh thereto is a house built of logs, at a very great charge, as was said, for the Trustees' Steward; the foundation below ground is already rotten [In August, 1740, a new foundation was begun], as the whole fabrick must be in a short time; for, the roof being flat, the rain comes in at all parts of it.[271]

271. The Trustees have no Steward, but this house was build contrary to their knowledge by a rogue who had care of the Trustees servants, and built this house for his own use. But if he built ill, what injury was that to these men who paid nothing towards it neither did any of the Inhabitants.

4thly, The *store-house,* which has been many times altered and amended at a very great charge; and it now serves as a store for the private benefit of one or two, as before mentioned.[272]

272. If publick works require repairing or ammendment or enlarging must it not be done? When the Trustees put down their publick store private persons took it up, and by the use of the house were enabled to furnish the Inhabitants cheaper than other private Storekeepers would do which was a general benefit.

5thly, The *guard-house,* which was first built on the bluff, soon decayed; as did a second through improper management; this, now standing, being the third.[273] Several flagg-staffs were likewise

273. The Guard house etc. What injury was this to the Authors? or to what purpose is this said but to cast reflections some where. The Guard house if faulty must be repaired, but the Trustees know nothing of 3 being built. Were it true it occasioned a circulation of money by employing workmen.

erected, the last of which, according to common report, cost 50*l.* sterling.[274]

---

274. *cost fifty pound:* The Trustees have not found this in their accompts [accounts] nor is it credible, themselves relate it only as a report.

6thly, A *publick mill* for grinding corn, was first erected at a considerable expence, in one square of the own; but in about three years time (without doing the least service) it fell to the ground: In another square of the town, a second was set up, at a far greater expence, but never finished; and is now erased, and converted into a house for entertaining the Indians, and other such like uses.[275]

---

275. *a publick mill* etc. Things at first thought usefull may afterwards be found otherwise and if a mill fell down on whom is the reflection to fall but upon the builders, or perhapps the wind blew it down. If the 2nd. mill was before finished converted into a house for the Indians, we may suppose the Magistrates did it on good reason.

7thly, Wells and pumps were made at a great charge; but they were immediately choaked up, and never rendered useful, though this grievance was frequently represented both to the General and magistrates; the want of wells obliging the inhabitants to use the river water,[276] which all the summer over is polluted with putrid

---

276. *but they were immediately* etc. They were neglected because the place abounded with springs of fine fresh water as Mr. Christie has printed and all the Accounts from thence inform the Trustees, so that they have no occasion to drink the river water.

---

marshes, and the numberless insects that deposit their ova there, together with putrefied carcasses of animals and corrupted vegetables; and this, no doubt, occasioned much of the sickness that swept off many.

Several of the houses which were built by freeholders, for want of heirs male, are fallen to the Trustees (even to the prejudice of the lawful creditors of the deceased) and are disposed of as the General thinks proper.[277]

---

277. *Several of the houses* etc. The Trustees never received any complaint from Creditors, that they were thus prejudiced.

At least two hundred lots were taken up in Savannah, about one hundred and seventy of which were built upon [Several of these had more than one house upon them]; a great many of these are now ruinous, and many more shut up and abandoned; so that

the town appears very desolate, scarce one quarter part of its inhabitants being left, [278] and most of those in a miserable condition,

---

278. *The Town appears very desolate* etc. By Mr. Christies Account so late
as 9 April 1741 there were about 130 houses besides ware houses and hutts
which were as many more, and in Aug 1741 there were 140 Free holders of
the town who did guard duty or paid for doing it, so that it cannot be so
reduced as here represented. Later than this Col. Stephens wrote that all
the [known?] vacant lotts were filled up and if those who were gone could
be prevaild on to quit theirs, there were others who would take them, and
he believed in a little time the town would be as full as ever.

---

for want of the proper necessaries of life.

St. Simon's Island, having on the east of the gulf of Florida, on
the other sides branches of the Alatamaha, is about one hundred
miles south of Savannah, and extends in length about twenty, in
breadth from two to five miles: On the west side of it, on a low
bluff, stands FREDERICA, having woods to the north and south,
to the east partly woods, partly savannahs, and partly marsh.

The soil is mostly blackish sand; the fortications are augmented
since the retreat from Augustine, and here lie most of the remains
of General Oglethorpe's regiment: Frederica was laid out in form
of a cresent, divided into one hundred and forty-four lots, whereof
about fifty were built upon; the number of the inhabitants, notwithstanding of the circulation of the rigiment's money, are not
above one hundred and twenty, men, women, and children,[279] and
these are daily stealing away by all possible ways.[280] On the sea

---

279. *the number of the Inhabitants* etc. The Inhabitants when at the highest
in October 1738 but 139 heads ⅓ [probably meaning one third were heads
of families]. The Authors acknowledge there are now 120 Inhabitants. Tis
no wonder that some of idle or unsettled tempers should since 1738 be gone,
or that others who were in debt or had made new schemes of living should
go. The miscarriage of the Seige of Augustine also frightened some away
there being several who left the Colony from more distant parts on that
account. By the latest account there were 6 Aug. 1741 42 freeholders (there
never were more than 54) and the number of Inhabitants were 161. Thus do
these Lyars take all occasions to diminish the number of the people.

280. *these are daily stealing away* etc. On the contrary there are some daily
taking up lots, and we know of none gone since August 1741.

---

point, about five miles south-east of the town, were three companies
of the soldiers stationed before the attemt upon St. Augustine;
several pretty houses were built by the officers,[281] and many lots

---

281. *several pretty houses* etc. but 2 or 3 at most

set off to the soldiers, and entered upon by them; most, if not all, now desolate.[282] Several of the officers of the regiment brought over

282. *most if not all now desolate* Capt. Thompson who was last there says otherwise

servants to cultivate land; Col. Cochran, twenty servants; Lieut. Horton, at Jekyl, sixteen servants; Capt. Gascoign, at least as many; all gone;[283] and according to the best of our information, about two hundred of the regiment are diminished.[284]

283. *Col Cochran etc.* No wonder his and Capt. Gascognes [Gascoigne?] servants are gone when their Masters are: but as to Capt. Horton he says it is a lye he having all his servants.
284. *about 200 of the Regiment are diminished.* Can this be subject of complaint that in time of war soldiers should be slain or that any should die or desert?

About twenty miles north-west from St. Simons, is DARIEN, the settlement of the Scots Highlanders; the town is situate on the main land, close to a branch of the Alatamaha river, on a bluff twenty feet high; the town is surrounded on all sides with woods; the soil is a blackish sand: Here were upwards of two hundred and fifty persons settled,[285] who in Spring, 1736, built a large fort for their own protection; and the poor remains of these are now no more than fifty-three [286] (above two thirds of which are women and children) besides eleven of the Trustees' servants inlisted as soldiers,[287] and stationed there under the command of an officer, in

285. *Two hundred and fifty persons settled:* They were but 177 making 45 families.
286. *fifty three:* They were in May 1741 86 Souls and by Capt. Thompsons account well contented. We have the names and ages of all.
287. *eleven of the Trustees Servants etc.* False again; they were 30. But placed at Fort St. Andrews, to saw timber. Col. Oglethorpe wrote that the profit of their labour exceeded their charge.

order to keep the others from going away, who are nevertheless making their escape daily.

The southernmost settlement in Georgia, is FORT ST. ANDREWS, fifty miles south from Frederica, on the south-west side of Cumberland island, upon a high neck of land which commands the river both ways; the walls are of wood, filled up with earth, round which are a ditch and pallisade; two companies of General Oglethorpe's regiment were formerly stationed there, but are now mostly drawn to Frederica.

Opposite to Frederica, on the main, were settled Messrs. Carr and Carteret, with above twenty servants,[288] where they cleared a

---

288. *Messrs. Carr and Carteret* etc. Mr. Carteret returned to England in hopes of preferment, no wonder then his plantation is quitted and his servants dispersed and Mr. Carr was obliged to withdraw by a Sudden attack of the Spanish Indians. As this passage is artfully worded, the Reader is left to think that Mr. Carr quitted his plantation before this accident.

---

considerable tract of land; but that plantation is now quitted, and their servants either dead or dispersed. We have lately heard from Frederica, that, the General having stationed ten or twelve men upon this place, they were attacked by Spaniards or Spanish Indians, four were killed, four carried on and two left wounded.

NEW EBENEZER, to which the Saltzburgers removed from their former habitation at Old Ebenezer, consists of about one hundred persons,[289] under the government of Mr. Boltzius, their

---

289. *about 100 persons* etc. These writers every where diminish the number of the Inhabitants contrary to fact in 1741 the Saltsburghers were 194 and the same year 63 more were sent to them.

---

pastor; they live and labour in a kind of community, and never commix or associate with strangers; they have been hitherto liberally supported both from Germany and England, and their rights and privileges have been much more extensive than any others in the colony: [290] This town lies six miles eastward from the old,

---

290. *their rights and priviledges* etc. This is absolutely false. They have no other priviledges than the rest of the Colony.

---

on a high bluff upon the side of Savannah river, and forty miles from Savannah. Near to this place, on a creek of the same river, was built a saw mill,[291] which cost of the publick money about

---

291. *a Saw mill* etc. The mill was blown up by the floods, and the Trustees had not money to restore it. The Sarcasm *like most other publick work ruinous* is added to make the reader believe the Trustees neglect their affairs. The expence is much exagerated.

1500*l.* sterling but, like most other publick works, is now intirely ruinous.

About ten miles east of Ebenezer, on a creek, three miles from the river, was the village of ABERCORN: In the year 1733 there

were ten families settled there, and several afterwards:[292] In the year 1737, Mr. John Brodie, with twelve servants, settled there: But all those are gone, and it is now a heap of ruins.[293]

---

292. It is here represented that more lots than for 10 families were taken up here but the new families only settled on the deserted lots.

293. *it is now a heap of ruins* etc. 3 owners died, 2 changed but are still in the Colony and 5 deserted. Mr. Dobel says when he was there in Jany. 1740/1 there were 2 families, and since that time the Saltsburgers have spread thither.

Four miles below Abercorn, upon the river-side is Joseph's Town, which was the settlement of some Scots gentlemen with thirty servants; but they have now left it, most of their servants having died there.[294]

---

294. *They have now left it* etc. 5 or 6 Scotsmen went to settle there but soon grew out of humour that they might not be erected into a Corporate town, and have provisions given them contrary to agreement. Some died, one entered his Majesties Service and removed to a new Grant to the Southward, and one continues on the Spot and thrives.

A mile below, on the river side, is the settlement where Sir Francis Bathurst, with twelve in family and servants, was placed, now in ruins, without an inhabitant.[295]

---

295. *now in ruins* etc. Sr. Francis Bathurst never had 12 in family he and his wife died, and his idle son being indebted ran to Carolina where the Negroes in an insurrection killed him. None claimed the Succession so of course the plantation went to ruin. It may be observed that through the whole events of this pamphlet truth is not set forth in its full and fair right.

A quarter of a mile below was the settlement of Walter Augustine, with six in family: Within this settlement was another mill erected,[296] at the charge of above 800l. sterling, all now in ruins

---

296. *was another mill erected* etc. Not at the Trustees charge

---

without an inhabitant.

A mile below is Landiloe, the settlement of Mr. Robert Williams, with forty servants,[297] who made large improvements there, and

---

297. *Robert Williams with 40 Servants* etc. Not all his own for he was in partnership with others. He built two houses and clear'd about 30 acres of land.

---

continued for the space of four years, planting each season with great industry in various shapes, still expecting (with the other settlers) an alteration in the constitution; but at last, having sunk a great deal of money, he was obliged to leave it, with the loss of above two thousand pounds sterling; [298] and it is now uninhabited,[299] and very much decayed. Next below that is the five

---

298. *with the Loss of above 2000£ etc.* What ever loss he sustained it was not all his own: neither did he declare his loss to be more than 1500£ if all his own. But there is reason to believe his loss was little or nothing for he exported several freights of lumber, and when he left off to cultivate[,] hired his servants to the publick works by which he got 3 times what their keeping cost him. He was paid by the Trustees Storekeeper over 500£ for making a road, besides he made good profit by furnishing provisions to the Colony, and to the Trustees store. All this these Libellers conceal.

299. *it is now uninhabited:* Not true, when Mr. Williams was last there he put Servants upon it.

---

hundred acre tract belonging to Dr. Patrick Tailfer; which was settled, but found impracticable to proceed upon, by reason of the hardships and restrictions in the colony. Next to that is Mr. Jacob Mathews's plantation (formerly Mr. Musgrove's) called the Cowpen, who lived there some time with ten servants; but has now left it,[300] and keeps only two or three to look after his cattle. Adjoining to this was Mr. Cooksey's settlement, with five in family; now entirely abandoned.[301] Next to this was Captain Watson's plantation, with a good house,[302] now in ruins. All these lie upon the side of the river. And upon the east and southward, were the settlements of Young, Emery, Polhill [303] and Warwick; all forsaken.

---

300. *but has now left it.* So far from this, that he has wrote to the Trustees for a confirmation of his Land. He was called Southward to erect an Indian store on the Alatahama [Altamaha], but frequently returns to his plantation which is the great rendevouse of the malecontents.

301. *Mr. Cooksey's Settlement etc.* He Settled at Carolina to turn Merchant no wonder therefore if he abandoned his plantation.

302. *with a good house:* Never more than the case of a house, nor did he ever take out a grant.

303. Emery turned to keep a passage boat and Pothill died: Young took to his trade of making Bricks: when men cease to be planters their plantations must be forsaken. Warwick also became Patroon of the Trustees scout boat.

Next upon the river side is the Indian land before mentioned, separated from the foregoing settlements by a creek, and running all along to the town: A little below this creek is a place called Irene, where Mr. John Wesley built a pretty good house for an Indian school; but he soon wearied of that undertaking, and left it. A little below is the Indian town called New-Yamacraw, where the remainder of Tomo Chachi's Indians reside.

Five miles south-west of Savannah, on a small rise, stands the village of Highgate: Twelve families were settled here in 1733, mostly French, now reduced to two. A mile eastward of this is Hampstead, where several German families were settled in 1733, and some others since, now reduced to none.[304]

---

304. When this pamphlet was wrote there were 2 families, and most of the others are still in the Colony.

Five miles south-east of Savannah, is THUNDERBOLT, where there was a good timber fort, and three families with twenty servants were settled; but it is now all in ruins and abandoned.[305]

---

305. all in ruins and abandoned; Of these 3 families one Master died and 2 ran away the one for debt the other for felony.

Four miles south of this, is the island of Skiddoway, on the north-east point whereof ten families were settled in 1733; now reduced to none.

A creek divides Skiddoway from Tybee Island, on the south-east part of which, fronting the inlet, the light-house is built: Twelve families were settled here in 1734, who have now forsaken it.[306]

---

306. twelve families etc. But they have not forsaken the Colony. The Pilot lives there, some died, the others found it very inconvenient to remain there because of the muskettoes. These Lybellers would have the reader believe that when a place is forsaken, the Inhabitants left the Colony and this because of ill usage and oppression which is false.

Twelve miles southward by land from Savannah, is Mr. Huston's plantation, kept with one servant. And,

About thirty miles from that, up the river Ogeeche, was the settlements of Messrs. Stirlings, &c., with twenty-five servants: This place, when they went there, was the southernmost settlement in the colony, and very remote [This was the only spot allowed them to settle upon, any other place being refused]; so that they were obliged to build, at their own expense and at a considerable charge, a strong wooden fort for their defence. And the said Messers. Stirlings have resided there about three years with the servants, they were obliged to leave it, after having exhausted their fortunes to no purpose in the experiment.[307]

---

307. These Scotch were the plague of the Colony their vanity and extravagance was of pernicious example. All the Colony confest [confessed] it was

their extravagant living that reduced them, they had no reason to complain of the goodness of their land which was some of the best. One of the years that they remained upon it proved remarkable bad for crops all over America and this discouraged them from going on, they brought their Servants to Savannah and by letting them out to hire got more than treble the expence of maintaining them, but spending the gain they made of them at nightly Clubs found themselves unable when their Servants time was out to engage new ones.

Twenty miles above this, on a high bluff on the same river, stands Fort Argyle [This is the place where a body of horse called the Southern Rangers under the command of Captain James Macpherson, were stationed for several years. They were paid by the government of Carolina; but have been discharged for some time past]: Tis a small square wooden fort, musquet-proof: Ten families were settled here and about it; now all gone; and the fort itself garrisoned by one officer, one Dutch servant, and one woman, who were lately surprized [308] in the officer's absence, by two prisoners

---

308. The Garison of Fort Arguile [sic] is put in a ridiculous light. General Oglethorpe abandoned it after the frontier was better strengthened to the Southward. Yet afterwards on Account of the murther here mentioned replaced a garison of 10 men with an Officer, not soldiers but Inhabitants and invited others to Settle there.

---

that broke out of the log-house in Savannah, and both murdered.

Near the mouth of Vernon river, upon a kind of an island (which is called Hope Isle) are the settlements of Messrs. John Fallowfield, Henry Parker, and Noble Jones: They have made some improvements there, but chiefly Mr. Fallowfield, who has a pretty little convenient house and garden, with a considerable stock of hogs, and some cattle, &c., and where he generally resides with his family. Near adjoining to this, upon a piece of land, which commands the Narrows [This is a narrow passage, through which boats are obliged to pass and repass in going to and from the southward], is a timber building, called Jones's Fort; which serves for two uses, namely, to support Mr. Noble Jones, who is commander of it, [and] to prevent the poor people of Frederica from getting to any other place, where they might be able to support themselves.[309]

---

309. is a timber building etc. This which they call Jones' fort has cannon and is of great use for hindering the Spaniards to creep with their boats within land and so surprise the Inhabitants of Savannah and the boats can pass with out bringing to. Mr. Jones resides there but has no Sallary from the

Trustees as Governour of it and tis a scandalous reflection to say that one of the uses to which it is applyed is to hinder the people of Frederica from getting to any other place where they might be able to support themselves, for those people are not hindered from going away, nor is any one in the Colony but such as run from their Creditors.

About three miles south-east of Savannah, upon Augustine Creek, lies Oxstead, the settlement of Mr. Thomas Causton, improven by many hands and at a great charge, where he now resides with a few servants. Between Oxstead and the town of Savannah lie; 1st, Hermitage, the settlement of Mr. Hugh Anderson, who had seventeen in family and servants; but he was obliged both to leave that and retire from the colony about two years ago, upon account of the general hardships.[310] 2dly, the settlements of Mr. Thomas Christie, and six others, belonging to the township of Savannah; all now forsaken.[311] 3dly, the settlements of the Germans of Count Zinzendorff,[312] who were twenty families; which are likewise now entirely abandoned, they having all gone to other colonies.

---

310. *Hermitage the Settlement of Mr. Hugh Anderson* etc. This Man the penner of this libel built his house on the most unwholsom [unwholesome] side of a bog which occasioned a general Sickness of his family under which himself lingered [?] long. He over built himself and at length went to Caroline where he was invited to keep a School and read Philosophical Lectures he underwent no hardships but had particular favours shewn him as he acknowledged by his letters, nor did he complain of any to the Trustees.
311. *Thomas Christee* etc. He came to England to obtain a new grant of land and is returning.
312. *The Settlements of the Germans* etc. Count Zinzendorfs people were Moravians, Enthusiasts, and went to Pensilvanea [sic] liking the Quaker principles better than those of the Church of England, and declaring they would not take arms in defense of the Colony.

Upon the west side of Savannah, lie the township lots of the Jews, now deserted (they having all gone to other colonies, except three or four) as are all others on that quarter, excepting one or two.[313]

About three miles from Savannah, on the south, the settlement of Mr. William Williamson is in the same condition: And also,[314]

---

313. *the Jews* etc. The jews went away under apprehension of the Spaniards after the miscarriage of the seige of Augustine but not all, and [illegible word] returned.
314. *Mr. Williamsons* etc. No wonder when neglected by him who is Provost Marshal of Carolina.

the settlement belonging to the Trustees adjoining to Mr. Williamson's; which was committed by them to the care of Mr. William Bradley, their Steward, to be cultivated and improved by him at their charge, as an example to others, and to satisfy themselves what improvements in land were practicable by *white servants:* The event might have opened the eyes of any that would see: Upwards of twenty, sometimes thirty servants, were employed; above two thousand pounds sterling expended in the experiment; and never so much of any kind of grain raised from it, as would have maintained the numbers employed about it six months: It now lies on a par with the most ruinous plantation in Georgia.[315] Part

---

315. The cause of the ill success of this farm is unfairly conceald [sic]. Will Bradley (not Steward to the Trustees but sent over to instruct the people in agriculture) had Servants appointed for that purpose and land, but having obtained a grant of land for his Son abused his trust and made use of the Trust Servants to cultivate his private lot. He also usurped an authority to employ them on works not ordered by the Trustees and thus the farm was neglected. In the end he fled the Colony to avoid accounting with the Trustees. Who acquainted these writers that above 2000£ was expended in the experiment I know not, but the Servants whilst under Indenture must have been kept wherever else employed and if the cost of the farm was too great it was owing to the ill conduct or roguery of this vile man who was a Rioter in open Court, and convicted of Stealing cattle which he confest [confessed], and afterwards put his own mark on the Trustees cattle, killing others [imp---edly?]. At the time this pamphlet was wrote the Authors might have known that the farm was better taken care of.

---

of their Dutch servants have been employed last year by Mr. Thomas Jones, upon a new plantation about a mile to the southward of Savannah; they were twenty-five in number, and maintained at the expence of eight-pence sterling each per diem; and we have lately been credibly informed, the whole produce did not exceed one hundred bushels of corn.[316]

---

316. *a new plantation* etc. This last mentioned farm is in a very hopefull way as Mr. Jones informed the Trustees, tho the last year proved a remarkable bad season, and the Servants were often called away to labour on bridges, and publick roads, at the crane and publick garden etc. how they came to determine the fixt number of bushels of corn raised there on to be 100 bushels were curious to know since on the 1 July 1741 the only grain planted thereon was rice, the produce thereof was not then known.

The Orphan-house is situated about fourteen miles south-east of Savannah: This famous work was begun in March, 1740; and, during the space of six months, there were about one hundred people, men, women, and children, maintained and employed about it; and according to their own calculation, they have expended near four thousand pounds sterling: But ever since Mr. Whitefield left Georgia the latter end of August, in the same year, it has decayed apace; for besides those he then carried to the northward with him, a great many have since left them; and their money growing short, they were soon obliged to discharge most of the workmen; besides of late, many divisions have arisen amongst them: In short, the design seems to be drawing near a period, although at this time the house itself is scarcely half finished.[317] It is built upon a low

---

317. *But ever since etc.* All that is here said of the Orphan house is false: for it is in a flourishing condition and almost finished and Mr. Whitfield having read this Account remarks that if this pamphlet is not more true in other particulars than in this, there is no credit to be given to it.

---

pine barren, surrounded on one side with a large tract of salt marsh, extending to Vernon River, to which they have a passage by water, when the tides are up, for small craft; on the other side it is surrounded with woods; they have cleared about ten acres of ground,[318]

---

318. *They have cleared about 10 acres of ground etc.* These fellows on all occasions lessen the cultivation of such as remain in the Colony. 1 Sept. 1741 Mr. Habersham wrote that they had planted 20 acres and cleared 20 more.

---

and have built several houses and huts. The frame of the Orphan-house is up, the roof shingled, and the sides weather boarded: It is sixty feet in length, forty feet wide: It has two stories, besides cellars and garrets; the cellars are built of brick, which likewise serves for a foundation to the whole building: It would certainly be a fine piece of work, if finished; but if it were finished, where is the fund for its support? and what service can an Orphan-house be in a desart and a forsaken colony.

About three or four miles from the Orphan-house, on the side of Vernon River, William Stephens, Esq; (formerly mentioned) has a plantation with five or six servants, who have cleared about seven or eight acres;[319] however if he reaps no benefit from them,

---

319. *Who have cleared about 7 or 8 acres:* Mr. Stephens wrote to the Trustees that he had 19 acres under crop and one acre produced him 20 bushels of corn: besides his 5 acre lot well filled with mulberry plants and vines.

---

he is at as little charge to maintain them. [The trustees allow him so many servants and their maintenance.]

As it would be too tedious to mention particularly the township or five and forty-five acre lots, being in all about one hundred that were settled; we need only therefore in general say, that there are few or none of them but what are in the same condition with those before specified, viz. ruinous and desolate.

The last place we shall mention is AUGUSTA, distant from Savannah two hundred miles up the river, on the same side: It was founded in 1737, at a considerable charge, under the direction of one Mr. Roger Lacy, being at that time agent to the Cherokee nation: It is principally, if not altogether, inhabited by Indian traders and store-keepers, the number of whom may now be about thirty or upwards; [320] and a considerable quantity of corn has been

---

320. *about 30 or upwards:* If there are 30 Traders or storekeepers there settled Inhabitants they with their families and Servants cant be less than 120 Souls.

---

raised there: To account for this singular circumstance, we shall only assign two reasons; the first is the goodness of the land, which at so great a distance from the sea is richer than in the maritime parts; the second and chief one is, that the settlers there are indulged in and connived at the use of Negroes, by whom they execute all the laborious part of culture; and the fact is undoubted and certain, that upwards of eighty Negroes are now in the settlements belonging to that place: [321] We do not observe this as if it gives

---

321. *They are indulged and connived at etc.* Neither the Trustees or Magistrates indulge them in the use of Negroes, but they take that liberty lying so remote from the Seat of Government as not to be discovered. Col. Stephens account of this affair (who certainly is to be believed before these fellows who to serve their cause boldly advance what ever they please) is this with a N. B. "Some of the people of Augusta having plantations on the Carolina Side of the river as well as in Georgia where they find it more advantageous to settle and carry on the trade with the Indians together with making great improvement on their lands, by such means they have an opportunity of sliding two or three Negroes now and then at a pinch into their plantations, where during their Skulking awhile (which is not hard to conceive considering the great extent of the Township of Augusta by reason of large tracts of land) they are not presently discovered." vid. Journal Oct. 24, 1741. The Reader will judge whether, if this Account be true, the people are indulged in the use of Negroes, and whether there can be 80 Negroes now on the Settlements which are here represented as permanently Settled on the place.

---

us any uneasiness, that our fellow planters are indulged in what is so necessary for their well-being; but we may be allowed to regret, that we and so many British subjects, who stood much more in need of them, should have been ruined for want of such assistances.

Having now taken a survey of the colony of Georgia, we shall conclude this treatise by taking notice of two or three of the most remarkable transactions in it since October last.

On the tenth day of November a court was called at Savannah, where Col. Stephens read a paragraph of a letter, which he said was from the Trustees, desiring the inhabitants to set forth their miseries, hardships, and difficulties in writing, in order to have the seal of the colony annexed thereto, and so transmitted to the Trustees: [322] Whereupon Mr. Stephens gave the Recorder a paper

---

322. *In order to have the Seal* etc. They purposly omitt that it was also to be Sworn to to give it the greater weight and credit, whereby they hope the Reader will consider it as a partial interested Account The Trustees designed to lay it before the Parliament but it came too late. Their directions were not to have an account of the miseries hardships and difficulties of the Inhabitants, for they did not believe they were under any but to have a fair relation made to them.

1. Of the State of the Colony and progress of cultivation with the peoples ability to support themselves.
2. The Climate, Soil, and proportion of different Soils
3. The Produces that might be raised.
4. Whether White men might not raise them.
5. The nature and goodness of the Ports and Harbours and Coast. The defensible State of the Colony, and benefit to be expected to England from its produces.

There was no intention or direction given to send over the complaints of particular persons, the Same being unfit to trouble the Parliament with.

---

to read, in which the colony was respresented in a most flourishing condition, (in the town of Augusta alone, there were represented to be 600 white people, and 3,000 pack-horses belonging thereto, who were employed in the Indian trade) enumerating the many useful, fine, and curious productions of it, such as hedges with pomegranates growing upon them, wine, silk, oil, wheat, &c. with many other hyperboles: This paper Mr. Stephens said he had been at great care and pains about, and which he took to be a just answer to the Trustees' letter, with the true state of the colony: But the poor people, seeing the absurdity and falseness of it,[323] soon dis-

---

323. *The poor people.* They Should Say the Malecontents. It is hard to accuse an Authentick Account Supported by the Town Seal and the Oathes of 25 persons, of being absurd and false.

---

covered their dislike thereof by their leaving the court house; and only eighteen persons signed the same,[324] every one of whom were supported in one shape or other by the publick:[325] Mr. Fallowfield,[326] then on the bench, used what arguments he could to persuade him, that it was reasonable every person should represent his own case to the Trustees,[327] and he apprehended the design of

324. *only eighteen signed the same.* False: the number were 25.
325. *Every one of whom were Supported etc.* Suppose this true[,] does that invalidate their oathes? This is only thrown in to make the Reader believe that the Trustees influenced them to give a false account of the Colony. The persons in Office who swore to it were such as the Trustees esteemed the best fitted for their places and being of Superior character may be supposed the best informed of the State of the Colony and the best inclined to the Support of it, and therefore would not knowingly deceive the Trustees. But it is not true that all who signed and swore were supported in some shape or other by the publick. Otherwise than they partook of the publick encouragements given to all the Inhabitants for cultivation and raising Silk and wine.
326. *Mr. Fallowfeild:* he was a Ring leader of the Malecontents and frequently opposed the other Magistrates in the just execution of their Offices, having a personal pique against one of them.
327. *That it was reasonable every person etc.* It has been already shewn that this was not the Intention of the Trustees. It had been an idle thing to have laid before the Parliament the quarels and noisie complaints of private persons.

the Trustees was such; but Stephens in a passion said, *except they would sign this, they should have the publick seal to no other paper;*[328] so it was to no purpose what either he or the Recorder Mr.

328. *Except they would sign this etc.* It had been absurd in him and contrary to order to suffer the Seal to be put to another paper not authorized upon Oath and full of private differences.

John Py could urge, who very soon left the court, declaring their dislike and abhorrence of such proceedings; but immediately they, with the rest of the inhabitants, to the number of above sixty, drew up a remonstrance to the Trustees,[329] in which they fully set forth

329. *A Remonstrance etc.* A very insolent scurrilous paper full of lyes as Col. Stephens wrote.

the *true* state of the colony, with their own miserable condition in it: This paper, and soon after a petition to the King and Council,[330] &c., were lately transmitted to the authors hereof, who im-

330. *a petition to the king & council etc.* An insolent procedure in a few Malecontents to accuse the Trustees their Masters to his Majesty.

mediately forwarded them for London; but as the issue thereof is now depending, we do not think it proper to expose them to the publick.

On the 2d of April last, a fire broke out by accident in a smith's forge in Savannah, which consumed almost one whole square; and in the highest rage of the devouring flames, Mr. Thomas Jones stood an idle spectator with his hands in his bosom, and with the utmost unconcernedness,[331] insomuch that when he was applied to

331. *Mr. Jones Stood an idle Spectator* etc. This is not to be believed: but by the Spirit with which this pamphlet is wrote it appears the Authors (who were then out of the Colony[)] were ready to catch at any malicious information given to them by Mr. Jones Enemies.

by several of the miserable people for a small quantity of gunpowder to blow up an adjoining house, in order to prevent the fire from spreading, his answer was, *I can do nothing in it, I have no orders concerning such matters.*

We have lately been informed from Frederica, that the General having stationed twelve men upon the place which was the settlement of Messrs. Ker and Carteret, before mentioned, they were attacked by Spaniards or Spanish Indians, and four were killed, four carried off, and two wounded.[332]

332. *We have lately been informed* etc. To what purpose is this related? Must Such accidents as daily happen in time of war be charged upon Col. Oglethorpe?

A good many of the people have come away from Frederica lately, and, in order to get off, were obliged to make use of stratagems, such as going a hunting upon the islands, &c.[333] We are

333. *A good many of the people* etc. The false account of the number of persons who have left Frederica and of those who remain has been shown p. 100 note 4. None needed to make use of Stratagems to go away except such as ran away to defraud their creditors for all others had permission to go when they pleased as Col. Oglethorpe wrote to the Trustees. If to the words *lately come away* the 7 months from Dec. 1740 to June 1741 (when this pamphlet was wrote) be allowed there were but 7 freeholders who departed, and 2 who died, and since June 1741 we know of none to be gone away. But the Reader is left to suppose a great number.

informed, that some differences have happened betwixt the General and some of the magistrates there, and that, in the place of one of them, he has appointed one of his waiting-boys.[334] Several of the

334. *One of his own waiting boys* etc. This waiting boy as they abraid-

ingly[?] call him is as well born as any of these defamers being the son of Capt. Mariot. He wrote an excellent hand and on that account. Col. Oglethorpe probably employed him to copy for him. He has a sober virtuous character and behaves well in his Office. He is of age tho called here a boy.

poor remainder of the Darien people have likewise escaped, notwithstanding the body of forces stationed there to prevent them.[335]

335. *have likewise escaped notwithstanding* etc. Observe again that who ever leave a place are represented as making their escape all to cast a reflection upon Col. Oglethorpe as a Tyrant that would in an arbitrary manner detain them.

Having thus brought this Historical NARRATIVE within the compass proposed, and endeavoured to dispose the materials in as distinct a method and series as the necessary conciseness would allow: We readily admit that the design is far from being complete. To have acquainted the world with all the hardships and oppressions which have been exercised in the colony of Georgia must have required both a larger volume than we were capable of publishing, and more time than we could bestow: [336] We therefore satisfy ourselves, that we have, with care and sincerity,[337] exe-

336. *We readily allow* etc. Here is more dirt cast upon the Magistrates of Savannah which under pretence of conciseness and want of time they pass over, but by the Spirit with which this libel is wrote tis most likely their invention was at an end.
337. *with care and Sincerity* etc. The Reader will judge of their care and Sincerity by the notes.

cuted so much of the design, as may pave the way to any others who can descend more minutely to particulars; and those, who are best acquainted with the affairs of that colony, will be most capable of judging how tenderly we have touched both persons and things.[338]

338. *how tenderly* etc. intollerable insolence!

It only remains, that we in a few paragraphs endeavour to exhibit to the view of the reader, the REAL causes of the ruin and desolation of the colony; and those briefly are the following.

1. The representing the climate, soil, &c. of Georgia in false and too flattering colours; [339] at least, the not contradicting those

339. It is the Inhabitants themselves and Passengers who have been in the Colony who constantly represent the Climate Soil etc. in the best manner and

the Trustees have reason to depend on their Accounts. Experience has shown how healthy the Country is and how Superiour to Carolina and as to the Soil the notes in this book and Several affidavits sufficiently Shew the goodness of it.

---

accounts when publickly printed and dispersed, and satisfying the world in a true and genuine discription thereof.

2. The restricting the tenure of lands, from a fee simple to tail-male, cutting off daughters and all other relations.[340]

3. The restraining the proprietor from selling, disposing of, or leasing any possession.[341]

---

340. *The restricting the tenure* etc. The Tenures have been gradually extended as the Safety of the Colony allowed thereof and now Females do succeed: but it must be observed that for several years the Inhabitants exprest [expressed] themselves well satisfyed with these restrictions until the few factious members fixt their thoughts upon Negroes.

341. *The restraining the proprietor from selling* etc. They must always be restrained from selling otherwise a few would engross the possessions of many but they may lease for 21 years, and give away at their death.

---

4. The restricting too much the extent of possessions; it being impossible that fifty acres of good land, much less pine barren, could maintain a white family.[342]

---

342. *The restriction too much* etc. The Authors of this pamphlet have no reason to make this complaint being all Landholders of more land than 50 acres. As to 50 acre lotts the Industrious part of the Colony do not complain they are too small and they find it sufficient to support their families.

---

5. The laying the planter under a variety of restraints in clearing, fencing, planting, &c. which was impossible to be complied with.[343]

6. The exacting a much higher quit-rent than the richest grounds in North America can bear.[344]

---

343. *The laying the Planter* etc. When this was found uneasie to them, the Restraints were eased to their satisfaction, and this by consulting with some of themselves.

344. *The exacting a much higher Quitrent* etc. This only affects the large lotts of Landholders, for the 50 acre lotts (which are infinitly the grater number) pay no more than the other Provinces.

---

7. But chiefly the denying the use of Negroes, and persisting in such denial after, by repeated applications, we had humbly remon-

strated the impossibility of making improvements to any advantage with white servants.[345]

---

345. *But chiefly the denying the use of Negroes* etc. This indeed is the great grievance of idle people who want to see their work done by others: and it will be long before the Trustees consent to remove it, For of themselves they cannot do it but the king must also concur therein yet these defamers charge it solely on the Trustees that the law is not repealed. They pretend they have demonstrated it impossible to cultivate the land without Negroes, but Fact is a stronger demonstration than figures, and the Germans are an evidence against their assertion.

---

8. The denying us the privilege of being judged by the laws of our mother country; and subjecting the lives and fortunes of all people in the colony, to one person or set of men, who assumed the privilege, under the name of a Court of Chancery, of acting according to their own will and fancy.[346]

---

346. *The denying us the priviledge* etc. This is the most impudent assertion of any. They are governed by the laws of England and by 3 laws[?] his Majesty thought fit to pass. The Trustees are at a loss to know what they mean by being denied the laws of England. By the law of England his Majesty may erect Colonies under such municipal restrictions as he judges convenient for the support and defence of such Colonies and if his Subjects Settle there under the Settled Government it is at their choice but by the behaviour of these malecontents and their friends it appears they do not know what the law of England is, as in the instance of the Grand Jurys taking on them to continue to Set and do business after dismist [dismissed] by the Court: their presenting persons for refusing to be examined to general questions whereby they might accuse themselves, their riotous behaviour in open Court, their disobedience to lawfull authority etc.

---

9. General Oglethorpe's taking upon him to nominate magistrates, appoint justices of the peace, and to do many other such things, without ever exhibiting to the people any legal commission or authority for so doing.[347]

10. The neglecting the proper means for encouraging the silk and wine manufactures,[348] and disposing of the liberal sums con-

---

347. General Oglethorpe only nominated Magistrates provisionally for the Trustees approbation and confirmation. It was necessary some body should do this in case of vaccancy at such a distance that Government might not fall and no man more proper to be trusted with that power than he who is a Trustee.

348. *The neglecting* etc. This is false. There is bounty granted on the Silk of 4 Shill per pound on Silk balls, and if the prospect of raising wine continues

there will be further encouragement given. It is but lately the people are taken into it and DeLyon the jew was advanced 200£ to introduce wine. Nothing will want encouragement if the Parliament grants money for it. They must [torn manuscript] not prove that the Trustees have employed the publick money in ways of no service to the Colony.

tributed by the publick, and by private persons, in such ways and channels as have been of little or no service to the colony.

11. The misapplying or keeping up sums of money which have been appointed for particular uses, such as building a church, &c. several hundreds of pounds sterling (as we are informed) having been lodged in Mr. Oglethorpe's hands for some years by past, for that purpose, and not one stone of it yet laid.[349]

349. *The misapplying or keeping up Sums,* etc. This is another outrage upon Col. Oglethorpes character. The money for building a Church at Savannah is all in the Magistrates hands there, and the Chapel at Frederica is actually built by Col. Oglethorpe in the Fort.

12. The assigning certain fixed tracts of land to those who came to settle in the colony, without any regard to the quality of the ground, occupation, judgment, ability, or inclination of the settler, &c. &c. &c.[350]

350. *The Assigning certain fixt Tracts of land,* etc. When the Town of Savannah was laid out the people cast lots for their parts as being the most equal method of settling them and what would best content them as they worked in common in clearing the land: which is a false[?] answer to this complaint. If these defamers had given particular instances of what they have complain[ed] against, a fuller answer might be given. If they mean the Settling of the Sterlings where they set down, their land is very good, and Col. Oglethorpe judged it convenient to place them there for a defence to the Colony it being a Pass.

By these and many other such hardships, the poor inhabitants of Georgia are scattered over the face of the earth;[351] her plantations

351. *By these and many other such hardships* etc. Here is a pathetical and Rhetorical winding up of all the Scandals and falsities contained in this most Defaming Libel designed to work upon the passions of the ignorant Reader. The face of the Earth is very broad, but the most of the Runaways went only to Carolina where they were kindly received, and where these Authors were encouraged by a subscription to publish this Libel in order when it should make its appearance in England to persuade all men that the Colony cannot succeed under the Trustees management and that tis fruitless for the Parliament to give more money to support it, being in effect already aban-

doned. From hence they hope the Trustees will be obliged to resign their Trust and that his Majesty will then re-anex the Colony to Carolina, after which those who were formerly possesst [possessed] of antiquated Grants (made void by his Majesty) will renew their claim to them. But it is certain Carolina will not be able to keep Georgia without a greater expence to England than has been laid out upon it hitherto, which if not furnished, it must fall into the hands of the Spaniards or French, and all the Indians in the English Interest must go over to them to the loss of Carolina herself.

---

a wild; her towns a desart; her villages in rubbish; her improvements a by-word; and her liberties a jest: An object of pity to friends, and of insult, contempt and ridicule to enemies.

THE END.

Appendix

Egmont's List of Notes

[The following "list," written by the Earl of Egmont, constitutes, in most respects, a topical index to his commentary. In the manuscript, this list appears after the concluding page of the *Narrative*.

Although the references are faithfully reproduced from the original, the editor has placed in brackets the number of the reference as it appears in this publication. In this way Egmont's "index" will be useful when referring either to the original document or to this publication. For example, under the "Falsities in this Pamphlet Confuted," Egmont lists his first topic, entitled "That the land is bad and the Inhabitants cannot maintain themselves," and one of his citations is given as p. 60, note 1, indicating, of course, the location of his comment in the original. After this citation, in brackets, appears the note number 175, which designates the location of his comment in this publication.—Editor's Note.]

Design of this Pamphlet P. 2. 3. Note 5.

Falsities in This Pamphlet confuted.

1. That the land is bad and the Inhabitants cannot maintain themselves Pref. 9. 10. 11. 12. Note 1. [2, 3, 4] Narrative p. 31 Note 2. [58] 3. [59] 4. [60] p. 32. Note 1. [64] P. 38 Note 2. [98] P. 54 Note 2. [160] p. 60 Note 1. [175].
2. That no measures have been taken to Encourage the Silk Manufacture. Preface P. 15. Note 1. [8] Narrative p. 111 Note 9. [348]
3. That the Inhabitants are deprived of their Birth rights, liberties, and Properties Preface p. 15. 16. Note 2. [9] Narrative p. 66 Note 6. [196]
4. That they are harrast by the Magistrates. Narrative p. 2. Note 3. [14]
5. That they were refused to quantity of land they desired. Nar. p. 27. Note 1. 2. [25, 26]
6. That they are not free Subjects and governed by the laws of England. Nar. p. 28. Note 5. [38] p. 111. N. 7. [346]
7. That they are confined. Narrative p. 2. Note 4. [15]
8. That the Water at Savannah is bad. Narrative p. 29 Note 5. [48]
9. That Building houses ruined the Inhabitants. Nar. p. 31. Note 2. [58]
10. That the Inhabitants had only water to drink. Nar. p. 31. Note 7. [63]
11. That they had only Salt meat to eat. Nar. p. 31. Note 7. [63]
12. That the Trustees were Angry with Capt. Thomson Nar. p. 32 Note 3. [66]
13. That people were terrified from coming to the Colony Nar. p. 33 Note 5. [73]

14. That the publick money has been cast away. Nar. p. 33. No. 6 [74] p. 111. Note 9. [348]
15. That Carolina in 1734 persuaded every body from Settling in the Colony. Nar. p. 33 No. 6. [74]
16. That Mr. Gordon was refused provisions from the Store. Nar. p. 34 Note 2. [76]
17. That Mr. Gordon made no Representation to the Trustees. Nar. p. 34 Note 2. [76]
18. That Mr. Parker was a Sawyer. Narrative p. 34 Note 4. [77, 78]
19. That Forts and Publick Buildings were Erected with no design to serve the Publick. Nar. p. 37 No. 2. [93]
20. The the Indian trade has suffered since Col. Oglethorpe intermeddled therein. Nar. p. 39 No. 3. [103]
21. That there is no Battery at Savannah Narrative p. 41. Note 1. [108]
22. That Suspected Roman Catholicks are favoured as Saints. Nar. p. 42. Note 2. [115]
23. That there are no Deists in the Colony Narrative p. 49. Note 2. [136]
24. That there was a design to enslave the people. Nar. page 43. Note 2. [117]
25. That many died of Hunger. Narrative p. 51. Note 3. [148]
26. That the Trustees have not kept their promises with the people. Nar. p. 67. No. 1. [197]
27. That men are forced to discharge their Servants for want of provisions. Nar. p. 67. No. 3. [199]
28. That no care is taken of the peoples Children. Nar. p. 67. Note 4. [200]
29. That the People are hindred of their Labour. Narrative p. 70. Note 1. [205]
30. That they have no personal Resentment against Mr. Causton. Nar. p. 48. No. 4. [134]
31. That Persons from Selfish Views impose on the Trustees. Nar. p. 64. No. 3. [185]
32. That the Town of Darien is ruined. Nar. p. 93. Note 2. [257]
33. That the Inhabitants are hinderd from going away. Nar. p. 93. N. 2. [257]
34. That Jacob Mathews has deserted his plantation. Nar. p. 103. Note 5. [300]
35. That Watson had built a good house on his plantation. Nar. p. 103. Note 7. [302]
36. That the Village of Hampstead is quite abandoned. Nar. p. 104. Note 1. [304]
37. That Mr. Christie has abandoned his plantation. Narrative p. 105. Note 3. [311]

Calumnies

1. They Calumniate the Trustees for their Care of the Indians. Nar. p. 28. Note A. [43] p. 29. N. 1. [44]

2. They Calumniate Mr. Causton. Nar. p. 32 Note 4 [67] p. 33 Note 1. 2. 3. 4. [69, 70, 71, 72] p. 36 Note 1. [88] p. 40. Note 1. 2. [104, 105]
3. They Calumniate Col. Oglethorpe. Nar. p. 32. Note 5. [68] p. 40. Note 2. [105] p. 50 No. 1. [141] p. 52 Note 3. [154] p. 75. Note 3. [213] p. 83 Note 1. 2. 3. [222, 223, 224] p. 86. Note 1. [228] p. 87 Note 3. 4. [235, 236] p. 89. Note 6. 7. 8. [242, 243, 244] p. 98. Note 2. [267] p. 112. Note 1. [349]
4. Calumniate Mr. Jones. Nar. p. 34 Note 6. [80] p. 75 Note 2. [212] p. 109. Note 8 [331]
5. Calumniate Col. Stephens p. 50. Note 5 [145]
6. Calumniate Mr. Parker. Nar. p. 75 Note 4 [214] his Character vindicated p. 34. Note 4. [78]
7. Calumniate the Trustees of being preposest [prepossessed] by Col. Oglethorpe p. 89. No. 5 [241] and that a few keep the rest in the dark p. 90 Note 3. 4. [247, 248] p. 91 Note 1. [250] and of Secretly depriving the people of their privileges. p. 90. Note 5. [249] Other Calumnies cast on the Trustees p. 82. Note 3. 4. [220, 221] p. 86. Note 1. 2. 3. 4. [228, 229, 230, 231] p. 89. Note 2. 3. 4. [239, 240, 241] and for not having built a Church p. 99. Note 1. [269] and for not encouraging the Silk p. 111. Note 9. [348] and of misemploying the publick money p. 111. Note 9. [348]
8. Calumniate Mr. Boltzius the Saltsburg Minister because against Negroes p. 60. Note 2. [176]
9. Calumniate Capt. Dunbar because against Negroes. p. 61. Note 1. [177]
10. Calumniate Mr. Moore Mackintosh because against Negroes. p. 61. Note 4. [180]
11. Calumniate the Darien people because they Petitioned against Negroes. p. 61. Note 5. [181]
12. Calumniate the Magistrates for building Prisons p. 99. Note 2. [270]
13. Calumniate persons who swore to the State of the Colony. p. 109. Note 2. [325]

Exaggerations

1. They exaggerate the Number of landholders. Narrative p. 26. Note 1 [22]
2. And their wealth. p. 26. Note 2. [23]
3. And the Indiscretions of Mr. Westley [Wesley] insinuating talk and wicked Conclusions from them. p. 41. Note 3. 4. [110, 111] p. 42 Note A. [113]
4. And the Number of Georgians deceased in Carolina p. 72. Note 3. [209]
5. And the Number of persons who in 1739 left the Colony p. 72. Note 2. [208]

Unjust Complaints

1. They Complain of things they never felt. Nar. p. 28. Note 1. [34]
2. Of want of Negroes tho not necessary. p. 28. Note 2. [35] p. 31. Note. 4. 5. 6. [59, 60, 61]

3. That the Trustees give Ear to the Accounts Sent them by their proper Officers and Magistrates p. 28. Note 8. [38]
4. Of hardships laid on them p. 30. Note 3. [51]
5. Of the Admission of certain Jews. p. 30. Note 7. [53]
6. Of Mr. Oglethorpes purchasing transport Servants. p. 30. Note 8. [54]
7. That tar did not quit Cost. p. 31. Note 1. [57]
8. That Building Houses ruined the Inhabitants. p. 31. Note 2. [58]
9. That the Trustees refused them Negroes. p. 32 Note 2. [65]
10. That the Magistrates erected Prisons. p. 36. Note 4. [91]
11. That the Trustees Claim the Property of unmarked Cattle. p. 82. N. 3. [220]
12. That the Storekeepers opprest [oppressed] the People p. 45. Note 3. [123] p. 46. No. 1. [124]
13. Complain unjustly of Mr. Causton. p. 41. Note 1. [108] p. 46. No. 3. [126] p. 47. No. 1. 2. [127, 128]
14. Of want of Roads. p. 47. Note 3. [129]
15. That the Light House was on the decay and neglected. p. 48. Note 2. [132]
16. Complain unjustly of their Tenures. p. 57. Note 1. [171]

Deceits cast on the Reader

1. That they are ruined by Cultivation, which is owing to their own extravagance. Nar. p. 26. Note 3. [24] p. 44. Note 1 [120] p. 54. Note 1. [159]
2. They make Supposition of a thing they know to be true p. 49. Note 5. [139]
3. They conceal and give a false Reason why Mr. Christie and Mr. Williamson were not allowed to enter on their Offices. p. 75 Note 3. [213]
4. They conceal that private Storekeepers of their own Clan were in fault and opprest [oppressed] the people. p. 46. Note 1. [124]
5. They conceal the disposition the Town of Frederica was in to petition against Negroes p. 61. Note 5. [181]
6. They conceal that the State of the Colony was given upon Oath p. 108. Note 2. [322]
7. They deceive the Reader in making him believe that all who leave the Colony do it by making their Escape. p. 110. Note 1. 3. [333, 335]
8. And that 50 Acre lots pay more Quit Rent than what is due to the King by Charter p. 111. Note 5. [344]
9. They conceal that the Trustees granted their desire to Settle on Wilmington Island. p. 85. Note 1. [227]
10. They belye the Saltsburgers as to their Inclination for Negroes and Change of their Tenures, and conceal that they petitioned against Negroes p. 60. Note 1. [175]

Their Insolency

1. They Insolently censure the Laws of the Province past by his Majesty. Narrative p. 25. Note 3. 4. [19, 20] p. 29. Note 4. [47]

2. They Insolently ridicule the Treaty made with the Indians. p. 28. Note 6 [40] and abuse the Indians p. 28. Note 7. 9. [41, 42] p. 29. Note 2. [45]

3. They send over a Scandalous and lying Remonstrance to the Trustees in Opposition to the State of the Colony, given upon Oath. p. 109. Note 2 [325]

4. They insolently send over a Petition to his Majesty against the Trustees. p. 109. Note 7. [330]

5. They avow their Resolution to dispeople the Colony as far as they are able. p. 92. Note 1. [253]

6. They discourage people from remaining in the Colony or returning to it. p. 56. Note 2. [169]

7. They impose on the Trustees in a Representation for Negroes. p. 59. Note 1. 2. [173, 174]

8. They endeavour to intimidate Mr. Bolzius to bring him into their measures for obtaining Negroes. p. 60. Note 2. [176]

Sober Inhabitants

1. Desired not Negroes, only white Servants to be furnished them. p. 47. Note 4. [130]

2. The Conditions in their Grants reasonable. p. 27. Note 5. 6. [29, 30]

Carolina

1. Great Cause to Suspect they have in View to destroy the Colony, and get it re-anext to their Government. Narrative p. 4. 5. 6. [16]

Darien and Saltsburgers

1. The Inhabitants thoroughly contented. p. 3. [16]

Savannah

1. No Malecontents but of that Town. p. 3. [16]

Trustees

1. Their Plan of Government conformable to the Charter. p. 25. Note 1. [17]

2. Justified in the Laws and Restrictions made. p. 25. Note 2. [18]

3. Their Caution not to allow of Lots being sold Justified. p. 27. Note 8. [32] p. 55. Note 3, [165]

4. They remitt all Forfeitures. p. 27. Note 9. [33]

5. And take off Restrictions p. 28. Note 3. [36]

6. Never denyed the people when applyed to, to Settel their lands on Daughters p. 28. Note 4. [37]

7. Their Answer to an Objection that Carolina can undersell Georgia p. 55. Note 1. [163]

8. Their Alteration of Tenures fully Satisfactory to all the People but the Malecontents, and why not to them. p. 57. Note 1. [171]

Misrepresentations

1. They Misrepresent the Soap Ash Patent Narrative p. 27. Note 7. [31]
2. They misrepresent the time of Mr. Dairnes death. Narrative. p. 35. Note 1. [81]
3. And Mr. Watsons Case. Narrative p. 35. Note 3. [83] p. 36. Note 1. [88]
4. And the Trustees Plan for Settling the Colony as impracticable. Preface p. 9. Note 1. [2] p. 10. 11. [4] Narrative p. 3. [16] 36. Note 2. [89]
5. They misrepresent the Quitrent acquired by the Trustees. Nar. p. 27 Note 3. [27] p. 111. Note 5. [344]
6. And the Publick Garden. Narrative. p. 37. Note 3. 4. [94, 95] p. 98. Note 3. [268]
7. And the Case of the Silk Sent over in the Late Queens time Nar. p. 38. Note 1. [97]
8. And the Case of abandoning Fort St. George Nar. p. 39 Note 1. [101]
9. And the Case of Mr. Caustons stopping the Carolina Boats. Nar. p. 39. Note 2. [102]
10. And the Case of Stopping the Erecting a fort at Savannah. Nar. p. 41. Note 1. [108]
11. And the Number of People who have left the Province, as also the Causes thereof. Nar. p. 41. Note 2. [109] p. 51. Note 3. [148] p. 55. N. 5. [167] p. 56. N. 2. [169] p. 93. N. 1. [256] p. 66. N. 5. [195]
12. And the Case of Mr. Jones and Col. Stephens keeping a Private Store Nar. 51. Note 5. 6. [150, 151] p. 52. Note 5. [156]
13. And the Condition of the Town of Frederica. Narrative p. 52. Note 5. 6. [156, 157]
14. And the Reason why Servants fly the Colony. Nar. p. 65. Note 5. [190]
15. And the difference between the Labour of Negroes and White Men. Nar. p. 66. Note 1. [191]
16. And the State of the Plantations. Narrative p. 69. Note 2. [203]
17. And the Case of Bountys promised. Narrative p. 72. Note 1. [207]
18. And the State of the Publick Stores. Narrative p. 75. Note 1. [211]
19. And the good effect of the Trustees Resolution to enlarge the peoples Tenures p. 82. Note 1. [218]
20. And the Trustees refusal to let them Settle on Wilmington Island. Narrative p. 84. Note 1. [227]
21. And the Case of the Darien People Petitioning against Negroes. Nar. p. 86. Note 5. [232] p. 87. Note 1. 2. 3. [233, 234, 235] p. 93. Note 1. [256
22. And the Case of the Darien people going against Augustine Nar. p. 87. Note 4. [236] p. 92. Note 2. 3. [254, 255] p. 93 Note 1. [256]
23. And the Number of Inhabitants there Nar. p. 94. Note 1. 2. [260, 261]
24. And the Case of lands reserved to the Indians. Nar. p. 98. Note 2. [267]
25. And the Number of Inhabitants at Savannah. Nar. p. 100. Note 3. [278]
25. And the Number of Inhabitants at Frederica. Nar. p. 100. Note 4. [279] p. 110. Note 1. [333]

25. And the Number of Inhabitants at Darien Nar. p. 101. Note 6. 7. 8. [285, 286, 287]
26. And the number of Inhabitants at Ebenezer. Nar. p. 102. Note 2. [289]
27. And the Privileges of the Saltsburghers Nar. p. 102 Note 3. [290]
28. And the Expence of the Trustees Saw mill Nar. p. 102. Note 4. [291]
29. And the Reason why some plantations are deserted. Nar. p. 102. Note 5. 6. 7. 8. [292, 293, 294, 295] p. 103. Note 6. 8. [301, 303] p. 104. Note 2. 3. 4. [305, 306, 307] p. 105 Note 2. 4. [310, 312] p. 106. Note 1. [314]
30. And the losses of Robert Williams. Nar. p. 103. Note 2. 3. [297, 298]
31. They misrepresent the Case of the Trustees farm. Narrative p. 106. Note 2. [315]
32. They misrepresent the New Plantation. Nar. p. 106. Note 3. [316]
33. They misrepresent the Orphan house. Nar. p. 106. Note 4. [317]
34. They misrepresent the number of Acres Cultivated by those who remain in the Colony. Nar. p. 107. Note 1. 2. [318, 319]
35. They misrepresent the Case of Negroes employed at Augusta Nar. p. 108. Note 1. [321]
36. They misrepresent the Number of those who signed to the State of the Colony upon Oath. Narrative p. 108. Note 2. [322]

Extract of Col. Stephens journal

24 June 1741. Among other things sent me from Mr. Hopton by Penrose, I received the famous (or rather I should say infamous) Narrative of the State of Georgia, that had been so long expected, and advertised to be ready for publication, written by some of our acquaintance the Remnant of the Scotch Club; and which I had bespoke Mr. Hopton to get for me, as soon as it came abroad: and I hope he will also take care to send the same for the perusal of the Honble Trustees. Such a heap of mali— cious calumny and vile falshoods, perhapps no instance can be found of, put together in the like compass. Jwould be vain and silly in me to pretend here taking it to pieces, or to offer at answering any particulars, when I find almost as many lies as pages — pos— sibly I may foul a little paper in making some attempt to expose a few of those falshoods in a true light. which with such unparalel'd impudence they have dared to assert as Facts, without any foundation.

If the honble Trustees are contented to sit tame under such audacious Ribaldry as they will find in this Libel void of all shame and truth, then it may become me to be passive too, whom the world owes little or no re— gard to in comparison of those I serve: but I neither think they'l acquiesce patiently under such insults, nor leave me unprotected to the mercy of a wicked Crew, employ'd to worry my good name, which I must set at a very low value, if I did not esteem it a little more durable than the little remains of life yet left me.

Some passages will be found now in this journal, wch I conceive will appear sufficient to draw conclusions what farther may be expected from a Band, whose rage and madness plainly means bringing all into confusion:
my